AS SIMPLE AS THAT

AS SIMPLE AS THAT

collected essays

EDIE CLARK

BENJAMIN MASON BOOKS
DUBLIN, NEW HAMPSHIRE

Photographs on page 20, courtesy Historic Harrisville, Inc.;
on page 142, courtesy Andrew Maneval and Mary Lou DiPietro.
Cover photographs (*Bottles* and *Ice Flowers*) by Edie Clark
Book design by Jill Shaffer, Powersbridge Press,
    PO Box 332, Peterborough NH 03458

With the exception of "Pelicans, Herons, and All That," "Winter's
Surprise," "Child of *Dune*," and "On Fire," all the essays in this
book originally appeared in *Yankee* magazine.

First edition

Printed in the United States of America

10 9 8 7 6 5 4 3 2 1 paperback

Publisher's Cataloging in Publication Data
    Edie Clark, 1948–
        As simple as that / Edie Clark
        p.   cm.

ISBN 978-0-9719934-9-5
Essays — nonfiction — memoir
Title
Library of Congress Control Number: 2015948525

Benjamin Mason Books
PO Box 112
Dublin NH 03444
Ordering information: www.edieclark.com

CONTENTS

Preface

WHENEVER I RECEIVE the current issue of *Yankee* magazine, hot off the press, the first thing I turn to is "Mary's Farm" by Edie Clark. Of course, during my thirty years as *Yankee*'s Editor I would have already read it, as well as everything else in the issue, over and over. But now that I'm semi-retired (although still at the office for part of every day) the issue comes to my desk brand new. And for me what Edie has to say that month comes first. Always. How I wish that my uncle, Robb Sagendorph (1900-1970) founder of *Yankee* magazine in 1935, could read them, too. He'd be so pleased.

Back in that first issue of *Yankee* magazine he wrote that *Yankee*'s "destiny" was "the expression and perhaps, indirectly, the preservation of that great culture in which every Yank was born." Later, in quoting him, I would alter "that great culture" to simply "the New England culture," and then, month after month, year after year, we'd attempt to have the contents of each issue somehow define and express that mysterious culture. I never wanted to attempt an actual written-out definition. That would, I felt, build a fence around it, restricting it, maybe even trivializing it. No, the New England culture had to be something recognized within one's inner being. So, sure, we'd sometimes celebrate Maine's brand of understated humor of the "you can't get there from here" variety, or New Hampshire's frugality and independent spirit or the New England conscience and work ethic of the Massachusetts Puritans or Rhode Island's historical tolerance (first civilized nation in the world to allow freedom of religion) or Connecticut's "Yankee Ingenuity" (more things invented in Connecticut per capita than anywhere else — in the world!). Yes, with all that taken together — while adding in the ethnic influences of the French, Portuguese, Irish, Italians, Poles and Armenians — one can come close to a vague definition of our New England culture. But only close — and perhaps some of that sort of thing echoes more of New England's past. Edie's essays in this book, on the other hand, especially when absorbed one after another, reflect New England's timeless culture forever and ever. To me they beautifully, gently, lovingly represent what Robb Sagendorph had in mind when he wrote about *Yankee's* "destiny" so many years ago.

So now, temporarily cast aside any pre-conceived notions about New England, open your heart and soul and read on. If you're like me, you'll find it to be like listening to beautiful music.

Judson D. Hale, Sr.
Editor-in-Chief, *Yankee* magazine
and *The Old Farmer's Almanac*

Introduction

TWENTY-FIVE YEARS AGO, my friend and then-colleague, Mel Allen, suggested I write a column for *Yankee* about my garden. I had been writing for *Yankee* since 1978, and in those first dozen years, I wrote profiles of fascinating and quirky New Englanders who ranged from Melvin Longley, a farmer who was such an expert on grass that he was celebrated by the Smithsonian to the well-known photographer Berenice Abbott. I wrote profiles of distinctive New England towns like Cutler, Maine, a town that had not quite emerged from the 1950s, and Bethlehem, New Hampshire, where Hassidic Jews came to spend summers. I had written a five-part series about the Connecticut River, and then a four-part series on water pollution and the crimes of W.R. Grace and another series on land development in northern New England. And a disturbing piece about Karen Wood, who was shot and killed by a hunter in Maine, not so far from Augusta. (She was hanging clothes on her clothesline. Her crime? She was wearing white mittens. The shooter was never prosecuted.) The list of articles is long. I traveled frequently into areas of New England rarely visited where I found unique people living in remote places. I sometimes remarked that I spent more time behind the wheel of a car than I did in front of my typewriter (in those days, that is what I worked on).

Then Mel suggested that I write a column. It was 1990 and my husband Paul had passed away the year before, at the age of 39. I was living at the house that Paul and I had bought just months before he died. Paul had been in remission from his cancer, for which he had been in long treatment. Our purchase was somewhat impulsive but we were in the mood to celebrate and seize the moment. The place we bought was an old chicken farm in the village of Chesham (a section of the greater town of Harrisville, pop. 961), New Hampshire, where we had been living for some years, in a tiny cottage concealed in the woods. The new place, with all its rooms and outbuildings, was just a short distance from our little cottage, known locally as Bide-a-wee. Driving by, we had often admired the house, and wondered if it could ever be ours.

The new place was everything we wanted — built in the nineteenth century and never updated, there was lots of space and more acreage and fields for sheep. What the new house did not have were gardens. We found that puzzling. But we had plenty of plantings at our old house, much of it transplanted from the gardens of friends and family, including the exotic iris and lilies of an 80-year-old neighbor who had to give up her garden because her knees were shot and the one-hundred-year-old peonies from my grandmother's gardens in New Jersey. Before winter, we tilled up the gardens and transplanted it all once again to the new house. By the time spring came, Paul had passed away and the new gardens and I languished.

And so when Mel asked me to write this column, I was inspired, although I was also a bit abashed as I didn't think of myself as a great gardener, just someone who loves to have flowers growing and fresh vegetables to harvest. Weeds sometimes flourish, depending on what is going on in my life, but I've found that my plantings, over the years, have been kind to me, perhaps kinder than I deserve. Many plantings have survived when they shouldn't have, many of these beautiful flowers have brought back to me the lives of others who are now gone but who contributed greatly to my pleasure in the earth.

But the idea was appealing. For one thing, it was the right time in my life as I was looking to fill up a huge vacancy. I didn't want to pass myself off as an expert gardener so I hoped my readers would accept me simply as a lover of the miracles of the earth and a teller of stories.

We decided to call the column The Garden at Chesham Depot because the old railroad station was right around the corner. For a few years, when living in our toy-sized house in the woods, we had rented the depot. It had space for Paul's carpentry shop (the freight room) and a writing studio for me (the waiting room, which still had the ticket window with its iron bars, a two-holer "rest room," and the benches where passengers waited for the train to Nashua — I once was told by one of the town's elders that Mark Twain had waited in this station on his way to Dublin, a bit of historical gossip that, whether or not it was true, I enjoyed repeating). We plugged our woodstoves into the old chimney and set up shop. Even though by the time we bought the new farm, we no longer rented the station, it felt much a part of us and very much a part of our neighborhood so The Garden at Chesham Depot felt appropriate.

I found that one of the bigger hurdles of writing a monthly column was that the magazine comes out six months after it is put together. So I was always writing about winter when the garden was in full bloom and conversely, I was always writing about summer when ice and snow surrounded my vistas. In defense of that, I jotted down ideas throughout the month so that when it was time to write the January column in June, I had only to turn to my notebook to find my wintry material. Also, many of those Chesham Depot columns provided me with a subtle place to grieve. With words.

At first, I remember wondering where I would get my ideas for the column. But I soon learned that my life provided many more ideas than there were months to fill. I never ran out of ideas and, even today, I find that writing the next essay is my best day. *Yankee* has changed a great deal since then and so have I.

After eight years at the Chesham house, I bought part of Mary's farm, a story that has been told in my earlier collection, *The View from Mary's Farm*, and again, from a different perspective in this book. Looking back now, I realize that a column such as this one is a live organism, an evolution, which grew with me as the months and years passed. What is offered in this book is something of a chronology of those years, the things that have happened, the events large and small that have taken place in these two places which are, in fact, one place — all located in the town of Harrisville, New Hampshire, where I have been privileged to live for more than thirty years. Living in one place for so long makes for a wonderful experience of community, where folks come and go and many stay. The landscape changes somewhat but, since the center of Harrisville is a National Historic District, it also resists change, as do I.

The view here at Mary's farm, the direct outlook on the powerful Mount Monadnock, the broad fields, stone walls, and the sylvan edging, all this is what drew me and I have often said that if the house had been in better shape, I likely would not have had the opportunity to buy it, which was true but it did mean more than ten years of work to update and restore the house to comfortable living conditions. I did one room at a time, as much as I could afford. If the column started out to be about a garden, once I moved to Mary's farm, the focus shifted to be about a difficult renovation of a nearly 250-year-old house by a woman over fifty. Not exactly a parallel to Fine Homebuilding or Martha Stewart Living. It was never supposed to be a how-to column or about houses, or even about what it takes to gut a room or take down a barn. But, as it happened, the column became what was happening.

Once I moved, in 1998, the column had to change its name, which was not difficult to find: The Garden at Chesham Depot became The View from Mary's Farm, which precipitated the predictable questions: Who is Mary? And what kind of farm is it? (A hay farm, the only animal I keep is a dog.) Also, quite often, people call me Mary. That's a compliment. Mary's farm is what everyone in town called this place. Since she and her family had lived here since the 1940s, I expect it will be some time before that changes.

As opposed to the barren chicken farm in Chesham, Mary's farm had more gardens than I could keep up with. I always wonder how she could have kept up with all those gardens herself — she was elderly and I understand that she had very bad arthritis. Maybe the gardens helped her. I don't know. I know that feeling. And then, once the house was done, other issues came forward, in many cases, my dogs who have been my companions throughout it all

Each essay is an individual story, about a snapping turtle using my garden as a place to hatch her eggs; about neighbors I admire like Vallie Wells, who spread her love of daffodils from Chesham to the rest of New England; about the mystical connection between us and our animals; about two unforgettable ice storms; about the hard cider my father made; about the perils of mud season; about snow bunnies and Santas and wedding cakes and bats and bulls, about the longing for spring, about the small things of life on a hilltop in New Hampshire but now that I see these stories all together, I see that it is quite simply an homage to a place, a place where I feel privileged to have lived and to have had the opportunity to write in its surroundings. Chesham Depot was once but now Mary's farm is my Motif # 1, my lily pond at Giverny, my Walden Pond, my sanctuary from a world that sometimes changes too fast for me. I was just past forty when I started writing the column, in my late forties when I moved to Mary's Farm and now I'm getting toward my late sixties. The passage of those twenty-five years has changed my energy, my focus, and my physical abilities but it does not diminish my love for not only this startlingly beautiful place, with its sunsets and sunrises, its bright stars and big skies, its stout and wonderful trees, its peepers in the ponds and birds in the rushes, but for other places like it, where we can find a stillpoint, a place of quiet refuge, nor does it reduce in any way my fervor for saving these simple places — which is what brought me here to begin with.

I owe a substantial debt to *Yankee* magazine and its editors, Jud Hale and Tim Clark and Mel Allen, as well as to Jane Williams, who suggested the title, and Cynthia Schlosser who has been helpful in all ways. May we always be able to keep the beautiful places in our lives, come hell or high water.

HARRISVILLE, NEW HAMPSHIRE, 2015

As Simple As That

MANY YEARS AGO, my first husband and I moved up here from the city. We built a little house, paying cash as we went and doing all the work ourselves, including the building of the four-flue center chimney. This was in the early 1970s. While most of the rest of America was going forward, we were going backward, chopping wood, carrying water, leaving behind the frantic pace of the city and finding peace in the bosky woods of New Hampshire.

At that time, we bought a beautiful cast iron wood cookstove, smooth as polished stone with nickel trim hinting at its worth. After much trial and error, I learned to cook on that stove and I still cook on it today, three houses later, with a great deal more finesse than in those days. It's hard to believe that forty years have gone by and in that time, I've experienced divorce, the death of my second husband, and the rebirth of the farmstead where I currently live. Through it all, the stove has come with me and I find that as time passes, fewer and fewer people understand or even trust what this stove can do. It makes me wonder: Have I held on too long to this anachronism? Have I myself become an anachronism?

We had come up here with the idea of simplifying our lives. For a number of years, this dream came blissfully true. The place we had chosen was our Paris, where we could live cheaply, allowing time to pursue our dreams, which, for me, was to become a writer. But then it began to unravel. I suppose that this is life and who alive has not experienced the extinction of a dream, the disappointment of a broken promise? Change is a constant. We make adjustments; we move on.

After my husband died, I made the conscious decision to continue on alone. Many urged me to move back to the city and be among people, maybe meet someone new. I guess I'm a contrarian but I wanted to stay where there are no houses within sight of my own and I wanted to be able to hear the birds at first light and see the stars glow through dark skies. What is here could never be duplicated. Storms are fiercer up here and sometimes peel the shingles right off my roof but the closing in of winter and the opening of the spring remain thrilling to me, no matter how much time passes.

Television reception on this hill is spotty and cable services unavailable. I read newspapers and magazines to stay in touch. Everyone seems to have a GPS and a smartphone. Though these devices seem to have been invented with the goal of simplifying our lives, they seem to me to be complications in a world that I already sometimes find bewildering. I am left wondering, what is simple? What really simplifies our lives?

In the winter, my porch serves as a woodshed, handy to the woodboxes in the kitchen and living room. In the spring, we move whatever's left of the woodpile back into the shed, sweep away the wood chips, roll out the old rug, put the screens back in and carry the porch furniture up from the horse barn. My summer porch. At dawn on a clear May morning, I settle into one of the old familiar summer chairs and sip my tea, listening to the joyful notes of the bobolinks, building their nests in the fields all around me.

Unless the power has gone out, I don't carry water anymore but I still chop wood. My lovely black beauty still provides the ease of a spreading warmth on an early summer morning. There is a continuity in that. I guess it is just as simple as that.

MAY 2014

The house in Chesham. One of the previous owners, the widow Fidelia White, stands in front, circa 1920.

Chesham Depot was one of three train stations in the town of Harrisville. In 1870 the controversy over the railroad caused the manufacturing section of Dublin to secede and name itself Harrisville for the Harris family who owned the mills. After much ado, the railroad was built in 1878 and four trains ran daily, carrying freight and passengers between Keene and Nashua until the 1930s. There were numerous train stations like this one along the way.

PART ON∃

The Garden at Chesham Depot

Chesham Village grew up around the train station. My former house is at the far right of the photo, the train, coming into the station is at the far left. The tracks were removed in the 1970s.

🌀 Foliage Futures

M Y MOTHER was born in the month of October, a fiery month. According to astrologists, she was a Scorpio: passionate, strong-willed, secretive and with a tendency to enslave. The stock market crashed in the month of October. It happened on my mother's 13th birthday, an unlucky day. She says it was the quietest birthday she ever had. She remembers the silence at the dinner table and the ticking of the hallway clock. The stock market has fallen again and again in October. Financial analysts wonder why. What is there about October that brings the markets down?

All I can think of is our world of green, green leaves turning and falling, not a crash but a gentle emptying of the pockets of summer.

October is my favorite month. It is the apocalypse of our year, the crescendo of all the heat and creativity of the summer months. The frost has come and brought rest to the weary gardener but there is still the pageant ahead, the great color show we wait for all year, a show that requires no work. I am trying to think of a natural event so celebrated as the foliage and I can't think of one. Here in New England, it becomes the focus of our days. We talk about "peak" and the television weathermen give us percentages: when the color in the forests comes into its absolute fullness, it is "100%" but it is the approach we anticipate: In Burlington the foliage can be assessed at 75% while we remain at 35%, which means we have a lot more in store for us. And it is a moveable feast: when our foliage deserts us, we can journey south and find more. Like starry-eyed lovers, we seem to forget the good times that have come before. We love the one we're with: "I don't remember a year when it was this good, do you?"

But, of course, like the market, there are risks. Heavy rain can bring the leaves off the trees before their time. High winds can do that too. And all the folks who have traveled so far to see this annual show return home from their day trips to report that this business of the foliage is not all it's cracked up to be.

Oh, but it is! The thing is that you have to be here for the entire performance. Coming here for one day is like leaving the play in mid-act. A quote out of context. Living here, inside the drama, we watch the spectrum turn, a wide prism of the natural world that revolves at the pace of the turning of the earth. That tree that was tinted red yesterday is more intense today and then, gradually, like the flame turned up on a lamp, it's sizzling, roaring, lipstick red.

If we speculate in foliage futures, we will lose. Our role is to stand back and observe. If the show disappoints, there is always next year. And, in the meantime, a small corner of foliage paradise can always be found, in a particular tree that outdoes all the rest or a small canvas of bittersweet and woodbine where the color outranks the disappointing browns that surround it.

It was predictable that my mother loved the fall. She looked on it as an opera performed just for her and her exclamations of pleasure over a particularly fiery tree very nearly caused accidents. "Oh!" she would gasp as we drove along a back road and my startled father would hastily apply his brakes, thinking she was trying to alert him to our imminent demise. But, no, it was only an oncoming tree in stunning hue.

As for my mother and the stock market and the shades of autumn, I think that all three were born under the sign of Scorpio: passionate, strong-willed, secretive and with a tendency to enslave. Pretty dicey characteristics. Just the same, I'll put my money on October, any day.

OCTOBER 2007

Fall's Last Flower

THERE ARE a lot of things that can persuade you to buy a house — location, price, number of bathrooms, view from the kitchen window — but when we bought our house, there was something less tangible, maybe even a little silly to those who are not easily persuaded by such things. For us it was the hydrangeas, two of them, tall and broad-branched. At the time of the sale their heavy blooms pushed against the screens of the porch, and from the bedroom window they waved just beyond the glass, hinting of previous lives in the empty house.

A neighbor once showed me her hydrangea tree, which, like ours, reached up even with the second-story windows. I liked driving by, seeing her tree in bloom. It seemed to mimic a giant bouquet, rooted in the lawn. One day I stopped and admired it. She told me it was a bit over 80 years old. She had planted it when she was very young, with the help of her father. And had watched it grow. Hydrangeas, she told me, are the last trees to leaf out in the spring, and in the fall they are the last of our flowers to die.

She taught me to pick the blooms after the frost, when the petals are tinted pink. A good, stern frost brings out their color. Cold nights turn their creamy petals that soft, almost tropical pink, surely the most delicate of all our autumn colors.

When that pink comes, I go out with my shears. The branches are long and surprisingly fragile, the blooms so heavy they'll snap the stem if I don't handle them gingerly. I gather all the stems I can reach.

Inside, I trim off most of the leaves and arrange the branches into my biggest vases. These are earnest, full bouquets. As my friend taught me, I put no water in the vases and place them around the house on windowsills and tabletops.

The hydrangeas defy all laws of nature and stay just as they were when I picked them in the fall. The leaves wither, but the blush stained from those first cold nights holds fast on the petals through the dark of winter and into spring.

When I gather the hydrangea blooms each fall, it reminds me of why we're here.

OCTOBER 1991

The Green of Green Tomatoes

I F WE HAVEN'T had a frost by October, I listen carefully to the weather forecast every morning and every night. I'm always especially concerned about the tomatoes. It seems that no matter how many ripe tomatoes I've harvested by then, there are still just as many, sometimes a great many more, that are green.

In themselves, green tomatoes can be considered a crop, a vegetable as different from its riper version as an apple is from a plum. Over the years I've made some interesting things with these supposedly unripe fruits. I've cut them in thick slices, dusted them in flour and fried them in oil. This was how my mother made use of them, and it's true that my sister and I did not really love the meals that included this seemingly desperate use of a throwaway food. But I've matured in my tastes and have gone even further in the art of green tomato cookery. I've slivered them and mixed them with sugar and cinnamon and apples to make an interesting autumn pie. I've seeded them and ground the hard outer meat for relish. I've cut them into wedges and made pickles from them. I've used them in chutney.

The green of green tomatoes is almost an indescribable green, a whole spectrum of greens — the green of a summer pond, the green of a new lawn, the green of my sister's eyes. Over the years I've come to look more closely at these colors as I put the hard fruits away on cold nights that threaten frost. Because I cannot bear to let them go when there are frost warnings, I bring them in. Even though I love their greens, they are better ripe. Red. I've learned that even if they have not ripened by the time the night of the first frost comes, they can still come of age indoors, under cover. I cannot explain this. For a vegetable that so dearly needs sunlight to ripen, why it is able to continue on its course to ripeness in the dark escapes me. Completely. Though there are other ways — one friend of mine dunks his green tomatoes into a bucket of wood ash — I choose to shroud mine in newspaper.

On the evening before the first frost, I go out to the garden with my basket. By now the vines are old and hard. They lie across the dying landscape of my garden, stringing the greens like baubles, round, erratic, stunning in the vanishing evening light. I pick the tomatoes that are the lightest green, ones that show hints of pink or crowns of red. If they resist, I use pruning shears to cut through vines as tough as hemp. Though I love darkest greens perhaps the most, I leave most of them behind — still too young to ripen.

Inside, beside the warming stove, I wrap these shiny hopefuls in sheets of *The Keene Sentinel,* and as if they were bone china destined for a rough journey, I pack them carefully in boxes and tape the covers shut. In order to ripen fully, these tomatoes need the darkest dark I can create, like the darkness of night, of a womb. The packed boxes are not heavy, but I carry them with care into the basement, stack them on shelves in the root cellar, and turn out the light.

These don't last all winter. Not even half the winter. But every night, for a few weeks past the frost, I bring up a ball of newspaper, smelling damp and musty, from the cellar. It looks as if I've retrieved some treasure from my hope chest. On the kitchen counter I unfold the paper and bring forth a ripe red tomato, a treasure indeed, and, as is, perhaps the most fragile mystery of the garden.

OCTOBER 1993

❈ Cracking the Code

I T GOES BY so quickly, this summer that we long for. Here it is, once more, at the end. I wonder if the frost is greeted elsewhere with quite the same sense of stealth as it is here, where it can come as early as September. Once I remember it coming at the end of August, a horrid surprise that abruptly ended work three months in the making.

I say a sense of stealth and I mean it as in a secret government code that we ordinary folk have no hope of cracking. It doesn't matter how many men (and now women) we send up into orbit, we still can't say just when the first frost will strike. Or exactly where. Still we try, prying clues from the earth and from the sky.

Out here in the boonies, we listen to the Boston television stations. They are 80 miles east and a whole climate away, but still we tune in at six and hear that it will be mild and in the sixties today, knowing that out here it may rain — fifties, if we are lucky. And so the meteorologists sometimes put out the frost warnings. But here we have to look harder. I sense it on those clear-blue-sky days, a certain stillness in the trees, and the promise of a full moon. That's when I get a little nervous — and watch.

I take cues from my neighbors. Dot puts a gauzy cover on her garden on chilly afternoons, putting me on alert. Alan also seems to know. When I see his blue tarp laid lightly over his marigolds, I go home and prepare. In the shed I have a painter's tarp, a length of orange cotton fabric from a rummage sale, and my father's old army blanket. Thus armed, I head out to the garden. Before I cover,

I harvest. I fill the wheelbarrow with tomatoes, peppers, squash, all my delicate vegetables and wheel them inside. I leave the carrots, the beets, the potatoes, the parsley, and the leeks. The frost is a blessing to them and will sweeten them. I bring in the phlox, the asters, lilies by the armload and place them, the last hoorah, in vases around the house. From the porch I carry the pots of geraniums inside the shed, the safe house.

Then I cover. The tomatoes get top priority, then peppers, and then squash, if I can fit the blankets around their voluminous vines. Some years, when the garden is particularly good, I bring out a few extra sheets from the linen closet and continue on my big garden quilt. I weight their corners with stones and chunks of cordwood. In the night I sometimes wake and peer out at the garden under its patchwork, a ghostly bed in the faint moonlight.

This doesn't always happen. Last year when the first frost struck, I was 200 miles away on the coast of Maine, and I called home to hear the news that there had been frost that night. In my faraway place I felt trapped and helpless, a poor mother, and I grieved a little and came home to find the bright abundance I'd left turned to a black pall. But if I get the garden well covered and we can pass through the first frost, some years we are set for a whole other month of warm weather and somewhat lazy gardening. I suppose we call this Indian summer, though I don't know why. I've always liked that phrase. It brings to mind warm days, and I can almost feel the sun on my bare skin when I think of it. Indian summer is a lucky turn, and if I keep the garden protected, it's something like finding money in the street. We go on from that cold spell back into heat, And in the garden the tomatoes keep on ripening while the crickets telegraph the news of the coming cold. Years like that, our summer no longer seems so short. There's a peace to it, like the gentle rest at the end of a long and happy life.

OCTOBER 1996

Pine Cones

MY FATHER USED to keep a wooden bucket of pine cones next to the fireplace in our house when I was growing up. These were big and sturdy, perfect in shape, like small brown pine trees. He gathered them in bags from under the big pine trees in Georgia, where he and my mother made an annual pilgrimage to find warm weather. In their travels south, they would stop by the side of the road for a picnic, rolling up their sleeves and reveling in the warm air they had driven into. As much as the warm air, Dad loved the big pine cones and always left space for them in the corner of the station wagon for the trip home. Mostly he set them beside the hearth at home for decoration. When he was short of kindling, he would use these to start his fire. Every once in a while, for a special treat, he would press one of the big, prickly fruits in beneath the burning logs. My sister and I would sit in close, as close as the heat would allow, and watch it burst into a rainbow of colors, as sudden and exciting a display as any fireworks.

In Chesham, there were tall pines next to our house. They hung in close by the house, carpeting the lawn with needles and darkening the windows. Down they came. We cut them to let in the light. We kept three, to shade us in the summer and to soften the wind in the winter.

In the fall the pine cones drop. These aren't like the ones my father used to buy. They are long and slender and not much bigger than cigars. Yet they are full of sticky sap. The first fall I raked up the pine cones from the lawn and dumped them at the edge of the field. Grumpy from work, I wondered if we shouldn't have taken all the trees down at once and been done with it.

Maybe. But during that next winter, I ran short of kindling. I remembered my father's pine cone bucket. By then, the pine cones I'd dumped at the edge of the field were covered by a foot or so of snow. So I bought scraps of pine from a sawmill to get me through the winter.

The next fall I went out and gathered the pine cones in brown paper bags, lining up the bags in the woodshed by the back door. We don't have a fireplace, only woodstoves. I found that when the fire died to embers, I could easily revive it by throwing two or three pine cones on the coals. Our stoves offer heat, but they hide the fire. I toss them in and close the door. I hear them sizzle like hot oil and love to imagine the colors, the blues and yellows and reds and the odd, brilliant turquoise, bursting like a Roman candle behind the door.

NOVEMBER 1991

🌀 Cider Pride

N THE FALL, my father would take us to the orchard and we would select a basket of apples, probably MacIntosh, and a gallon of cider. The cider came in glass jugs, with a single, ear-like handle. My father kept the apples and the jug of cider in the autumn coolness of the screened porch. In the evening, he would bring in the jug from the porch, shutting the door to the dark of the evening, and he would pour glasses of the cold cider and carry them in on a tray to the living room where we watched "*Leave It To Beaver*" or "*The Andy Griffith Show.*" The cider was a rich, coppery color with a rim of froth around the edge of the glass. The drink had a tang, almost like beer, and my sister and I looked forward to the treat. Somehow it seemed grown up, to drink the foaming cider and discover the slight giddiness it gave us.

My father made little of his technique for making hard cider. In fact, he didn't even think of it as a technique. Hard cider was really the only cider, so far as he was concerned. We drank it sweet, sometimes, when we couldn't wait. But for my father, fresh cider was nothing more than fruit juice. If kept in that steady dark coolness, the cider would stay fresh for a remarkably long time. It was the slow aging of the cider that gave it its edge. Time, and the kind of refrigeration that cannot be rendered from anywhere but the slow cooling down of the earth.

By Thanksgiving, my father had a cider to serve that he was proud of. From the silver pitcher, he poured it like fine wine and stood back for the praise. It always came.

When cider began to come in plastic jugs, it didn't take my father long to figure out that the plastic turned the cider to vinegar much faster. He slowed the hands of progress by keeping his own supply of gallon glass jugs on a shelf in the garage. When we got home from the orchard, he transferred the cider right away. My sister and I would watch as he poured the sweet golden liquid out of the filmy gray plastic into the clean glass jar. It was like watching the sky clear.

Recently, there have been rumblings about cider. It is not a sanitary thing, this business of pressing cider, the food gurus tell us. The apples come into contact with the hands of the pickers and the hands of the sorters and then these apples are crushed by a press that cannot always be kept perfectly clean. Bacteria, they hiss, though no one, as yet, has fallen ill or died from nasty cider. The solution is perilously close to becoming a reality: homogenization. That is, that the cider has to be heated and cleared before it can be bottled. When that is done, we will not have apple cider but apple juice such as we now get from cans and bottles in the grocery store. Cider as we have known it, as my father knew it, will be no more.

My father weathered the introduction of the plastic jug but how would he have gotten around this new entanglement of the cider house rules? Apple juice cannot be hardened off like cider. It cannot concoct a foamy head. It cannot make little girls feel grown-up. And you cannot pour homogenized cider through a funnel and have it revive to the ember-red colors that grew richer and deeper every day that it sat on the floor of my father's November porch.

NOVEMBER 1998

✿ The Flock

I HAVE A FLOCK of sheep in my field. Sometimes. I don't own these sheep. I don't have to care for them or help them birth their lambs. I don't really even have to feed them. But when they are here, they are mine to watch, to hear the gentle ringing of the bells they wear around their necks. I think of it as the best of both worlds.

These sheep belong to my friend David. He keeps them in various fields in town, moving them about by truck and sometimes herding them down the road with the help of his sheepdog, Gwendolyn. In fact, the whole business is a little competitive. When my field has been empty for a while, I call David and casually mention that I miss the sheep. He usually says something like, well, Ellen wanted them up in her field, and then there is a pause while I imagine he is trying to work out a fair distribution of the sheep.

Of course, the sheep keep my fields open. That's meant to be the primary benefit. But they bring something else, a kind of presence that's hard to describe. There is the undeniable feeling of importance that washes over me when I drive in and 40, 50, 60 sheep stampede to the fence, baaing and mawing their unconcealed excitement that I have arrived. That's pretty nice. And the peaceful scene they offer every time I look out the east window, a kind of living watercolor through the glass. But the thing I like most are the bells. The sheep may be out of sight, but I can hear their bells, and it's soothing, the nicest kind of company.

For the most part, the sheep are summer visitors. David brings them, he takes them away. It's always a guessing game how long the sheep will stay. Once he left the sheep in the pasture well into cold weather — six big burly rams. It was an open winter, not much snow, and there was still grass to be had. But they needed more to eat, so mornings we would wheel a bale of hay to the fence and break it apart as they shoved and butted each other. Dessert was a can of corn. Their noses steaming in the cold, they'd nuzzle under the thin layer of snow and matted grass to get down to it. Every day I thought would be the last one, that I'd come home one night and they'd be gone. We counted off the days of December. "Maybe," I said to my husband, Paul, "We'll still have the sheep for Christmas."

Christmas Eve came and the sheep were still here, a tacit gift from our shepherd friend. In the darkness, we loaded the wheel-barrow with two bales of hay and two cans of corn and rolled it cautiously to the fence by the light of our flashlight. The rams blat-ted their appreciation, their yellow eyes reflecting brightly up at us. The stars were brilliant, but there was a cold dampness, like a storm coming. We stood listening to the sharp crunch of their teeth against the hard kernels. The bells danced lightly against their necks, giv-ing clear, singular notes that rose in to the cold air like hope. We went inside and turned out the lights, leaving only the star on top of the Christmas tree lit. In bed, even with the windows closed, we could hear their bells ring as the rams worked away on the hay and the corn. On that particular night it was a magical sound, one that might make the unbelieving listen one more time to the Christmas story.

DECEMBER 1993

Kennebecs

I N FEBRUARY, with a lot else cleared out of the root cellar, I start thinking of potatoes. In the cellar, on a middle shelf, I have a hundred pounds, in heavy, brown-paper bags.

I love the potato, with its thin, gingery skin and lumpy shape. I store potatoes without cleaning them. They keep longer that way. But, better than that, when I go down cellar to fill the kitchen bin, I reach into the bags and bring out these cool, hard tubers, the garden dirt still clinging. It's almost like a second harvest. In the middle of winter, I somehow need that.

Last winter I did a lot of reading about potatoes. Catalogs offer staggering new varieties. One place, in Idaho, boasts 188 choices — Black Russian, Huckleberry, Mrs. Moherle's, Yellow Snowflake, Nosebag, Pink Pearl. The names alone made me want to write a novel. They also made me want to grow potatoes, differently — better. Branch out! Be bold! I told myself. To date, I had grown potatoes in the most lackluster manner, carting the old Kennebecs up out of the cellar in the early summer, cutting them up and hilling them at the shady end of the garden. No big fuss. I've even made a decent harvest by heaving them into the compost pile and coming back in the fall to claim the buried treasure. Effortless, like the potato itself. No gem with a fancy name, but a loyal, stalwart part of our lives here.

Well, it was time to change that. Feeling like a prospector, I sent off my order for a pound of Yukon gold seed potatoes. I won't say how much I paid for them, but it seemed like a lot then and seems like a lot more now.

My Yukon Golds arrived in a mini burlap bag, cute, with a drawstring and lengthy planting instructions. Inside, the little potatoes seemed almost unreal. They were perfect, dollhouse potatoes. I took them out to the damp spring soil and carefully set them in, following all the steps. I even fussed over the patch, weeding it, preening almost. This was not going to be any ordinary potato patch. Every morning I checked, anxious for that first press of green through the dark, hilled-up loam. A week passed and then two. I rechecked the instructions, poked timidly into the hills. Three weeks passed. At last, one single straggly potato plant reached forth. It was clear, what I had was a crop failure.

The summer was cresting. I didn't have time to feel humiliated or even disheartened. I had to think about getting some potatoes into the ground. I went to the cellar and hauled up the tired bag, a quarter filled with soft, sprout-ridden Kennebecs. With the blade of a hoe, I opened up the hills wherein I'd so recently laid the regal Yukon Golds. There was no sign of them. No matter, I spaced out my tired cellar spuds and pulled the earth back over them. In a week, they were up, green, leafy, rugged. I left them then, like I always do, a kind of benign neglect. I knew they would be fine.

In the fall I went down. It is my favorite part of growing potatoes, my favorite harvest of all, in fact. Like a magician reaching into a hat, I pushed my hand under the soil and came out with (drum roll) a potato! Cool, hard, gingery. All around, under there, I felt the nubs of more. A good crop. I was already thinking about that second harvest, the February harvest from the cellar, and a meal of potatoes on a long winter's night. Kennebecs at that.

FEBRUARY 1994

Heading South

MY HUSBAND'S FAMILY calls a spring snowstorm "poor man's fertilizer." They say that's because it falls, new and white, on the dark rich soil of freshly plowed fields and then sinks in as the day warms — something like an optical illusion. The moisture, like the first rain, does the thawed earth some good and it doesn't cost anything. For myself, I favor spring snows because they're usually beautiful, cover up the drab landscape, and the snow melts before it needs to be shoveled. What could be better?

One year I went away at this time of year. To be truthful, I drove south. I say that sheepishly because for a lot of years I have held that the "snowbirds" are missing the best part of New England, the slow drama of the passage of seasons, especially the dramatic and lengthy unfolding of spring. Well, the wait finally got to me. We'd had an unusual amount of snow, which made the winter seem as if it would drag on.

So, in mid-March, I packed up. A snowstorm was forecast the day I was to leave. My strategy seemed shrewd enough: If I got going early, by the time I reached the Mason Dixon line, our snow would be their rain.

This wasn't how it happened. This "snowstorm" is now a well-recorded part of our history known as the Blizzard of '93, surely the only time in modern history when it was snowing in Maine at the same time it was snowing in Georgia. I got as far as Maryland before giving up and getting a room, where I remained for three long days. There was nowhere to go. If the roads were not closed, they hadn't been plowed. Families sought refuge at motels such as the one where I was staying, since power failures had robbed their houses of heat and running water. I sat amid the bleak motel décor, watching the storm rage outside the window.

At last, crews opened the roads and I started back on my way south, past the devastation left by the storm. Stranded cars littered the roadside. Their tires weren't up to the job or the drivers simply lacked the equipment we in the North wouldn't go anywhere without. I stopped to help one elderly couple whose windshield was so shrouded with ice and snow that they couldn't see anything. When I emerged from my car bearing my long-necked ice scraper, their eyes grew large. "Where did you get *that*?" they asked. "I'm from New Hampshire," I explained. Farther along, a truck driver was trying to dig himself out of a snowdrift, using the broken end of a tree branch. The folding shovel my father gave me long ago for just such emergencies provoked a similar reaction from him and he got busy liberating himself like a beaver on a dam. I felt like a crusader from the North.

But when I finally reached my destination in Georgia, the snow, which had set records there, had already melted, and except for downed limbs and cockeyed billboards, it was hard to discern that such a fierce storm had passed through. I called home. Incredible, they said. I felt pangs of regret, like a traitor, being where I was, away during a time of need. In three weeks' time, I returned home. I heard all the stories, but to my eyes, the storm could have been a bad dream or a tall tale. An illusion. The snow had all sunk in, the grass was greening, the earth in the garden was dark and ready for pea seeds. No matter what, it had been a big storm. Rich man's fertilizer.

MARCH 1994

✿ Setting the Table

WHEN I WAS growing up, one of my chores was to set the table, which I did rather reluctantly. *Knives and spoons on the right, forks on the left,* I'd recite to myself as I spun around the table, completing the task as fast as I could. Now, when I set the table for holiday meals, I take my time. I savor it. What happened is that over the years, a few things have come down to me that I keep in drawers and cupboards, treasures I don't use every day. Maybe more than decorating the Christmas tree, I look forward to setting the Christmas table.

I start with the tablecloth. I have one that belonged to my grandmother, and this is the only time I use it. I get it out from the drawer. It smells of the old wood and of the polished chest and of the dark. I wash it and iron it. The letters ESC are embroidered in the corner, and I pass the warm iron carefully over them. I have the same initials as my grandmother, though our names were not the same. There is a slight yellowing in certain places, and the edges are frayed. I tuck these under and press tight. I think of her table. I think of her house and wonder how old this cloth could be. It could be 90 years old, easily. I think of how she used to sit at the head of the table after my grandfather died, her head tilted just so, regarding her grandchildren with a special smile. I slide it across the table, also hers, and smooth the edges.

Everything I use to put together the table is like this cloth. Nothing magnificent, just special, laden with memories. There is the silverware that my godmother gave me when I was born, a gesture of faith, I would say. I get it from its box. I am not even sure of the purpose of some of the spoons, but I set them all out. There is the silver bowl that my aunt June gave us for our wedding. There are the glass candlesticks that were a wedding present to my parents, passed now to me. There are long-stemmed wine glasses that came to me from my grandmother's best friend, a woman with an infectious laugh and the interesting name of Iloe. There are napkins to match the tablecloth. I've ironed them into thick triangles, folding them cleverly to hide the marks of age. There is the ornate silver ladle that belonged to my great-grandmother. I set it aside to polish and remember how, in our house, it was my father who polished the silver. He'd sit at the kitchen table with newspaper spread in front of him, and I could tell by the way he worked that he enjoyed what he was doing.

I carefully arrange the table. My family lives far away. On holidays I like to invite as many people as need company at these times, which I know can be hard and lonely for those who are alone. It is usually a lively, eclectic gathering. The table is set. Steaming dishes crowd on top of it. My friends gather around. I know now why my father enjoyed polishing the silver. These treasures bring with them something else: family.

DECEMBER 1992

🐚 Down Under

M Y HOUSE HERE in Chesham was built in the 1858. My friends might love their basements for the game room or the laundry center, but I love mine for its dirt floor and the strength of the big stones that hold up the house. Because I heat the house with woodstoves, the temperature down there holds steady between 35 and 40 degrees, just right for keeping vegetables over the winter. This is not a basement; it's a cellar.

In sacks on pine shelves I keep potatoes and onions and carrots. Along the next row of shelves, I line up the creamy-colored butternut squash, each one separate — if they touch they share their bruises. I keep beets in boxes of sand, and if I grow cabbage, I uproot the heads and hang them by the root from nails in the floor joists. Long ago I bought some old wooden boxes at an auction. These I fill with apples — Macs and Cortlands and in the smallest box I keep Northern Spys for pies. These are not from my trees. In the late fall I drive to Vermont and pick them by the bushel from incredibly fruited trees of a big hillside orchard and drive home, the warm car filling with their scent.

Meal planning is dictated by the vegetables' frailty. When I switch on the light over the shelves and find one of my squash crowned with a bushy forest of light blue mold, I feel neglectful. And so the winter goes by in layers. The carrots and squash are first. By December they will have gone soft. And the beets and cabbage need to be eaten by the first of the year. But the apples and potatoes and onions, I have found, will keep right up until spring. And so I let them stay there. There is always more than I can eat, which is OK because, come spring, it all goes out to the compost.

In June I take the wheelbarrow down cellar. The cellar is still cool, but the potatoes by now are spongy and have sprouted great green tails that reach out toward the light coming in through the opening of the bag. The onions are growing up green, too, like winter hyacinth, emerging from the tired brown bulb. The apples are the ones that don't grow. They turn in on themselves and die, becoming tight little brown faces.

I load up, potatoes first. In the garden I furrow down deep into the ground and set the tubers in where they will grow next year's crop. Onions next. I heave them into the compost, a green flag. From the boxes I take each apple, wizened but surprisingly firm, and place it in the wheelbarrow, chastising myself for not making applesauce before they went by.

The last trip is for the boxes. I know from years past that if I leave them down there, when the fall comes, they won't be ready to receive the new apples. The boxes are light but unwieldy. By placing them one on top of the other, I can balance them, three high, and wheel them out into the driveway. In the light, on the darkened wood, I can see the mold and growth from the winter's decay. With the garden hose and a scrub brush I hose the boxes down and then leave them, upended, to dry in the good, warming June sun.

JUNE 1992

The Immensity of Sacrifice

WE USED TO HAVE parades in this town, back when we had a band. There are stories of that band and its leader, who was stone-deaf and not a veteran of any war but life itself. With the band, a couple of fire engines, and a string of kids on decorated bicycles, the parade would proceed the short walk into town, an old mill town dotted with ponds and a canal. Young and old stood beside the road and waved little flags and cheered on their neighbors as they marched purposely forward. The proud little battalion strutted around the circular town center, paused to toss a commemorative wreath into the canal, and then continued on to the town cemetery, which is on an island in our pond. But with the old deaf band leader gone, it got harder and harder to create a parade, so the tradition ended. For a number of years we had no observance of Memorial Day in this town. This stirred one of our number, a veteran of the Vietnam War, into action.

He is not a young man, but he is not old. His uniform is worn and a bit faded. He is my neighbor, Rodger Martin. I know him as a teacher and as a keeper of horses. I hardly recognize him, dressed as he is, brimmed hat set square on his head, ribbons on his chest. He stands on the bridge that crosses the canal, and he speaks to us, reminding us first that this bridge, which we cross thoughtlessly many times in a day, was built in the significant year of 1918; and second, that the Bible from which he intends to read was presented to our town's church in May of 1861, just three weeks after the first shots were fired in the Civil War.

We gather around. Beside him are members of a local VFW post, their uniforms taut against their soft bellies. They carry the flags and the rifles. Also there are two high school students, in their band uniforms. They are both girls and tucked under their arms are their trumpets. Off to the side, Elaina, who runs the restaurant in the next town, stands with her fiddle. Steve, who tends bar for her, has his guitar. And Diane, who lived next door to me for several years, also has her guitar, by which she makes her living. A quotient of townspeople are here. We stand together. This is not a parade. This is a Memorial Day service, a quiet moment in the life of our town's 981 residents.

Rodger begins: "It is my hope that in these next few minutes, we once again recognize the immensity of the sacrifice of these soldiers who but for the grace of God could be you or I. . . ."

And then come the names. We are a small town, and even inside of our long history there is time today to read the names of all the men who have died in the wars we have fought. Rodger begins with the name Micah Morse, who he tells us died in the service of the Continental Army, shortly after the Battle of Bennington, August 16, 1777. And he continues down the list of the men from the Revolutionary War and then to the Civil War. I recognize some names, for their descendants still live among us. I hear the name Pvt. Levi Willard, who, we are told, was killed in the Second Battle of Bull Run, August 29, 1862. There is a stained-glass window in our church inscribed in his memory, and I have often stared at that name during long sermons. It was his son, perhaps, who built my barn. I had not known how the man with that righteous name had died.

The service leads us through the wars, all the way to the most recent sacrifice of our town, a young staff sergeant named Richard Robinson, who was killed in action over Iraq, in April of 1994. At certain names, Rodger chokes up and he stops, unable, for a long moment, to continue. At once, I place Rodger on a field of battle.

The losses he may have endured come into focus, losses I might otherwise never have supposed, seeing him move about town as we all do, in the business of our unhurried and unthreatened lives.

In between the centuries, Elaina and Steve and Diane lift their fiddle and guitars and give us sad songs. Beribboned black laurel wreaths, which were made for this service by our town clerk and her daughter, are dedicated and prayers are offered, and the men from the VFW Post 799 stand outside the church and fire the blanks in their guns into the air of our quiet, peaceful Sunday morning. The two high school girls (one is the daughter of my physician) bring their trumpets to their young lips and play "Taps," each note drawn out into the sadness of the end of a day that these girls have yet only to imagine.

MAY 1996

🌀 Stealth Gardening

There is something so contrary about the fact that as soon as the weather gets nice here, the blackflies come out, as if to remind us that life is not all beauty and dreams. In June we do not need to be reminded. For me June is the month for the garden, but like the KGB, I need to be stealthy about it or else the blackflies will keep me from my work. It is almost like a game, how we can coexist and never meet.

For anyone who doesn't know, blackflies are tiny bugs with the bite of a lobster claw. I have had welts on my forehead the size of marbles, compliments of these nearly invisible pests. To avoid this kind of treatment, I have found that timing is everything.

When I first began gardening in New England, some 25 years ago, my husband and I were astonished to acquire these horrid red bites during our first tilling of the soil. We worked and swatted and waved our hands about in that wild and desperate gesture that is now so fondly known as the New Hampshire Salute. We went first to buy bug dope, as it is known (though I'm not sure why). We found some in the fetching scent of wood smoke (which the bugs apparently find offensive), came home, lathered ourselves in it, and went back out to the garden. I found the odor so nauseating I didn't care if the bugs were there or not. And apparently they did not find it nauseating enough because I got bitten anyway. We needed more ammunition to fight this war.

"Ha!" we thought when, at the local store, we discovered hats that included attached nets. It was vaguely stylish, like a Victorian hat with a veil that tied at the chin. We bought one for each of us and went back home to garden. Suitably attired in long pants, long-sleeved shirts, and our exotic headdresses, we went forth into the sudden heat of the June afternoon. We worked. We sweated. We laughed at each other in our ridiculous anti-bug armor. Blackflies swarmed around our nets. And we got bitten anyway.

The misery and tears (yes, there were tears) continued for some long while as we fought our way into our gardens every spring. It seemed so unfair. But it must have been true love. If not, we would have given up gardening long ago.

Somewhere along the line, probably quite by accident, I discovered that blackflies are late sleepers. Or perhaps you could say they enjoy the warmth of the sun. Whichever the case, they aren't out in the early hours of the morning. And so, in the first light of a good day, I emerge, feeling an odd sense of freedom. I wear shorts and a short-sleeved shirt, sometimes even bare feet. It is cool, but the earth is warm underfoot. I start the rows with my hoe, scoring a line in the newly tilled black earth, deep and frothy from the tiller. And then I go back, seeds in hand, planting the rows, one vegetable at a time. At last I cover, using my feet and my hands to mound the earth over the miraculously small seeds. At that hour the birds are working, too, especially the swallows that swoop and trill around me. I work quickly, hilling and planting, making the plan for the garden out of my head as perhaps an artist might, while working on a large canvas. If too much time passes, the first flies start in, a quick blur in front of my eyes. Was that a — *blackfly?* I retreat.

It sometimes takes two days to get the garden in. But then it is done. And I wait out the month of June from behind the glass, watching the new plants emerge into the warm air, abuzz with the insects of spring. I let them have their time, in the heat of the noonday sun. Mine is the cool of the mornings and I am glad of it.

JUNE 1998

Little Marvel

A LOT OF PEOPLE celebrate the Fourth of July with a meal of salmon and peas. I don't know where the custom came from, but around here, where salmon is an expensive, imported treat, peas are what represent the celebration for us.

I plant peas even before the rest of the garden, sometimes by late April if the weather is favorable. I choose an early variety, Little Marvel or Daybreak or Knight, any variety that matures in less than 60 days, which will give us peas by the Fourth of July.

It doesn't always work. Sometimes the weather is too cool and rainy. But one year, everything seemed to fall into place just right. The seeds sprouted well and the plants came up so willingly that we could almost stand there and watch them grow.

The rows bushed out and bloomed, the small subtle white flowers almost hidden under the flourish of green leaves. By July there were pods, long and plump, the peas distinct beneath the bright green skin, a little arsenal of good eating swelling out from inside.

I called our neighbors, Betty and Arthur, gardeners who also appreciate these tiny gardening milestones, and invited them for dinner on the Fourth. "We've got peas," I said.

We didn't serve salmon. We bought chicken instead and barbecued it over an open wood fire. While the fire heated up, we picked the peas, my husband, Paul, at one end of the row and I at the other, picking toward each other until we met in the middle. Seated in lawn chairs with a bowl between us, we opened the plump pods, pushing the little marvels into the bowl with our thumbs. Every once in a while, we could hear the exuberant whack and pop of distant cherry bombs and firecrackers.

Our neighbors arrived, bearing flowers. From her garden Betty had cut blue delphiniums, white daisies, and dark red bee balm: the bouquet of a patriot.

They sat with us and helped with the new harvest. We sampled the peas, popping them into our mouths like peanuts as we worked. They were tender and sweet. Unbelievably good. When the last pod was opened, the bowl was practically filled, a great bounty. Inside, I put a quick burst of water into the bottom of a saucepan and dumped in the Little Marvels, setting the pot over the hot burner just long enough for the water to steam. When the chicken was done, we brought our plates around, heaping them with the darkened chicken and the brilliant green of the new peas. We raised our glasses in salute. We were back to the garden once again, a different kind of freedom, but one worth celebrating just the same.

JULY 1992

🦢 The White Nights of Chesham

NORTHERN GARDENERS crave light. It is part of why our garden inventory is shorter than that of our friends in the South. Even when our weather is hot, our days are not long enough. To prepare, we scan the garden catalogs, looking at the bottom line, which in this case tells us how many days it takes for the plant to mature, to bear fruit, which is the whole point.

In Chesham we aren't that far north, really, but there is a strong feeling about the summer solstice. It is often an occasion for celebration, for some of us a better reason to gather together than the more familiar holidays that appear on our calendar. At our house, friends come and we sit out on the porch and talk softly as the evening cools. We tip our watches up — nine o'clock! — and marvel at the light that still fills the sky. I have been in places where they have white nights — nights when there is no darkness — and I can almost capture that feeling on this, our more restrained white night of the solstice. It is a feeling of elation, that the sun will never set on us, a fantasy that seems to say that we would keep going, if the sun would let us.

Being here, in this less-than-forgiving gardening climate, is like being the underdog, and it has its advantages. I think it makes us take chances. For the most part, we accept our lot, and in our gardens we tend toward rhubarb and potatoes and rutabagas, earth vegetables that we can depend on, vegetables that can do very well without the light. But there is still that edge. Few gardeners I know can resist taking just one chance in the garden — melons or hot peppers or really big beefsteak tomatoes, the kind that do so well in New Jersey. Instead of turning us into cautious, conservative garden-ers, the cool brevity of our season seems to have the opposite effect. A friend of mine has grown artichokes in northern Vermont (no, not Jerusalem artichokes and, yes, outdoors), and another man I know likes to boast of his persimmons in northern New Hampshire. I've read about another man in New Hampshire who has succeeded in producing kiwi fruit, and a man in Maine who raises figs.

There's no real need of this. We can, quite a bit more easily, get all this and more down at the grocery store. But the rewards are so sweet when these schemes pay off that they turn us into gamblers, hedging our bets, hiding our losses in dreams of the perfect harvest.

Every year I plant eggplant because once, years ago, during an unusual summer filled with long, hot nights, I had a good harvest. But every year since then, the tiny, midnight fruits, still as small as teardrops and far from ripeness, have been snuffed by the frost. And yet, when the new season comes around, I think it over carefully and decide, in spite of this terrible record, to put in "an eggplant or two," just in case.

I like to think that I learn from my mistakes, but there is something else going on here. Like the modest white nights of Chesham, it has to do, I think, not with stubbornness or, God for-bid, stupidity — but with hope. We do it because sometimes, just sometimes, we win.

JUNE 1993

🐚 Sunflower Worship

THERE SEEMS NEVER to have been a year that I have not planted sunflowers. In my mother's album is a snapshot of myself and my sister standing beneath the protective arch of two giant sunflowers, one for each of us. We are both clutching our favorite dolls. The sunflowers tower above us. We are perhaps four and five. The sunflowers are no more than five months. With the help of our father, my sister and I had planted the big, zebra-striped seeds in the warm earth of an April morning and then watched them grow, first a twin-leafed shoot, like small propellers coming up out of the earth, ready to soar.

Every day they were bigger, the stalks alone like small tree trunks. The head of the flower feathered out with bright yellow petals and then the seeds expanded inside the wide head, a lesson in good packaging. My father planned that we would dry the seeds in the fall and feed the birds in the winter. I liked the idea of the flower's purpose advancing through the seasons.

Another photograph in another album, this after I first married. My husband stood in our garden, naked, beneath our prizewinning mammoth sunflower, the biggest one, taking a mock shower from the big blossom, which bent reverently above his head. In that garden we grew the food that we ate all year round. It was a task we set for ourselves, a challenge to be able to spend as little time and money as possible inside a grocery store. It worked, pretty much. But the sunflowers were just for fun. The hugeness of them was comical, parodies of everything else we had grown, a measure of success if there ever was one. That year our biggest sunflower turned out to be more than 11 feet tall. The seed head was as big around as a soccer ball. We left it on its stalk in the garden, and in winter the chickadees and nuthatches came to it as if it were a bird feeder, pulling the seeds out one at a time, their feet locked onto the seed ball while they gobbled. After the birds had eaten it clean, the dried stalk and its heavy head stayed bowed throughout the winter, snow piling up on its crown. My winter druid, praying for an early spring.

I have read that the Hopi Indians carved wooden sunflowers and held them as sacred objects. This was more than 1,000 years ago. They believed the carvings could help them enrich their harvest. Vincent Van Gogh painted a brilliant likeness of the flowers and died a poor man. In 1987 a Japanese investor bought this sun-rich painting for $39.9 million. And now we see sunflowers everywhere, on our curtains, on hairpins, on lampshades. There are hundreds of other flowers that might take their place, but it is the sunflower that shines back at us, from our coffee mugs, from our wallpaper, from our doormat. Why? What is it about the sunflower? Even our sports heroes chomp on the seeds and spit out the hulls, as if they were getting to the heart of things.

Perhaps it is that they *are* like suns, the ring of fire around the seed-rich core, their heads held high above the others. Van Gogh painted the sunflowers most likely because they inspired him, not because he thought they would net him a fortune. The Hopis believed that sunflowers warmed the earth and brought important rains, two things that mattered very much to that spiritual culture. They paid homage by carving the flower's likeness and worshiping the image. They stacked them in a cave, a way of remembering the flower's importance. We plant them in our gardens in similar homage, a way of reassuring ourselves that it is possible to grow things bigger and better than we might imagine. And then we take pictures of them and put them in our albums, so that we won't forget.

SEPTEMBER 1998

Raspberries for Christmas

SOMETIMES, when you buy an old house, you don't see everything that's good about it. We thought we did, of course, but it was fall by the time we moved in, and so it wasn't until the following summer that we found the raspberries. Rugged canes bent low with the weight of these extraordinary berries, deep red, solid, and as big as my thumb. They were behind the chicken house in a patch big enough to feed the neighborhood.

The first year I did invite the neighbors to pick. Why not? Standing in one place I could pick a quart in ten minutes. There was no way we could eat all of them ourselves. I thought about making jam, but I never seemed to have time for that. Sated from the initial treat of the first-of-the-season berries, I felt the diminishing desire that comes with abundance. There was so *much*. The spoils could go to the birds. It was after the berries had gone by that I began to long for them.

The next summer, late in the season, I visited my cousin down in Massachusetts. She had just been out to pick raspberries at her local pick-your-own stand. She had paid such a fearsome price for those berries, I don't dare put it in print. But she had cardboard pints, handsomely heaped on the counters next to the fridge. With a great deal of care, she was lining the berries up, one by one, on cookie sheets. She was treating those berries, which truly were not as big or as sweet as mine, with the respect due an item that cost so dearly. This, she was explaining, was the only way to freeze raspberries. She ferried sheet after sheet to the freezer, balancing trays on top of the frozen goods, then sealing them inside the frost. Several hours later, she went back and removed the trays. The berries were as hard as candies and made clicking sounds as she gently transferred them into plastic containers and returned them to the freezer. This way, she said, they don't turn to mush when they thaw. The berries stay — berries. "I save these for Christmas," she said. "Everyone's amazed. They come out looking whole and fresh."

I went home in a rush and took the buckets down from their nails. I felt the end of the season looming and wanted my freezer filled with this hot-night harvest. As the sun lowered, I picked. Thorns pierced my knees as I pushed deeper into the patch, looking for more. Juice stained my hands, my elbows, my T-shirt. When the light faded, I carried the buckets inside. I unearthed my cookie sheets. I readied my plastic containers.

By the next day, one whole shelf in my freezer held the lightweight packets of summer. It was several days before the stain left my hands.

I liked my cousin's idea about Christmas and brought some out then, showing off their perfection by studding the top and sides of a chocolate cake with them. But as years passed, I kept them longer and longer. You might say I hoarded them. Now I save the raspberries for March. Out back, the canes are just coming out from under the snowload. But inside, we have berries — berries on our cereal, berries over ice cream, just plain berries in a dish, deep red, solid, and as big as my thumb.

MARCH 1993

🐚 Snapper

ONE DAY LAST JUNE I went out to the compost, which is at the sandy edge of my garden. As I shook my canister of orange peels and onion skins onto the pile, I heard a rustling in the ferns beside the stone wall and turned to see who hid there. I saw nothing. But the sound of movement through the underbrush came again, this time louder. Whoever made the noise was surely bigger than a chipmunk or squirrel.

Just the night before, I had read in the local paper about a man who had been chased down the main street of a neighboring town by a rabid woodchuck. Rabid coons are now commonplace. We all take this seriously and have learned how to defend ourselves. If there were such intruders here, in my garden, I wanted them out. I stamped my foot. The rustling came again, slow, lazy, one twig snapping at a time. I stood still, staring into the thicket of ferns and berry bushes. Suddenly, from within this shimmering green veil emerged, gray and scaly, the unmistakable head of a snapping turtle. My heart pounded. This was the biggest turtle I had ever seen. Every time I tell this story it gets bigger, but believe me, with a shell the size of a knight's shield and a neck as long as my forearm, it was *some* turtle. And it was slowly rising up out of the ferns, the enormous claws gripping the earth with slow but sure authority. Like a powerful leg, the long tail trailed behind. Jurassic Park, right here in Chesham.

My eyes shifted to the ground under my feet. I saw a disturbance in the sand and knew instantly what the turtle had been about: She had laid her eggs in my garden. I had seen this often near the lake up my road. At this time of year, turtles come out from under the muck, find dry sand, dig down deep, deposit their golf-ball-sized eggs, cover them, and lumber off, leaving the eggs to hatch in the fall when the tiny hatchlings fend for themselves. A friend of mine, who has devoted his life to preserving turtles, calls these hatchlings "trail mix," since they are small and defenseless, snack food for foxes or skunks. If they make it through their first year, though, they're golden, destined to a long life. Lord knows how old this momma was as she scraped her way up over the stone wall and away from her tender nest. I'd read that once turtles lay their eggs in one place, they return to that same place every year for another round.

Now I'm all for saving turtles, but I confess I lay awake that night. I wanted to grow corn there, not snapping turtles. And to think, a crop *every year*. A brief calculation revealed hundreds of snappers by the year 2020. I feared I'd be over-run, feared — feared! An impulse almost brought me out of bed to go out into the garden with my shovel, dig up the eggs, and shatter them — end the invasion.

But something tempered my murderous instincts. Instead, every time I went out to the compost, I eyed the ground beside it, watching for signs of the hatching. All summer long I watched. But the sand stayed as the turtle had left it, and little ones never emerged. I have no way to explain that, but I confess I was relieved. I've often heard the farmers around here say that one way or another Nature takes care of everything, and I would like to say that in this case Nature took care, but that's a selfish view. I lucked out, that's all. And the turtles lost. This June, though, I'll be watching.

JUNE 1994

❀ *Classé!*

'VE BEEN READING lately, in expensive gardening magazines, that annuals are making a comeback. *"Declassé* no longer!" one article trumpeted. I hadn't known they had left. Annuals are flowers that germinate, bloom, set seed, and die in a single season. There was a time when I thought that this was the only way flowers came and went.

Then I discovered perennials, which have flourished here and there in my flower gardens ever since. But still, I can't imagine a summer without snapdragons, cosmos, zinnias, and oh, the much-maligned marigold.

So I read this news carefully and considered the report that the reason these venerable flowers had withered from view in the gardens that count was that they showed up so routinely in window boxes of not-very-classy cottages and, even worse, in triangles and in spelled-out messages at gas stations and fast-food restaurants.

I pondered that a while. Seeing a neatly tended bed of orange and rust marigolds at the edge of a service station has always somehow touched my heart in ways that few other gardens have. That man who emerges from the station, his hands masked in gloves of grease, his heart heavy with the news of yet another deceased carburetor, has time, somehow, to brighten our roadside with his display. It is gratuitous, this merry garden beside the shop of metal and fumes, a message that seems to tell us that we should all take heart, that even out of grease and pavement can come color, can come beauty.

Besides, I've never linked the fact that these flowers show up in such places with what I decide to show in my own rectangle of blooms. That was probably the other piece of news in all this — that there is a fashion in the garden, trends, like in foods or designer clothing.

I suppose I am prone to this. I hear about new plantings and try them out. Or I see a pretty face in the catalog and succumb. Over the years I've planted in waves, my favor coming and going with certain flowers, but never has a year gone by without the marigold. Partly that is because I use marigolds to encircle my vegetable garden. I read once long ago that the scent of the marigold is repellent to pests. I have no idea if it's true, but I've rarely been bothered by pests of any sort, so, as a kind of talisman, I plant the bright African orange and yellow double blooms. I like these for their brilliance. On moonlit nights I swear they glow.

I recall, some years ago, that one of the big seed companies had a contest in search of a pure white marigold. I think that they succeeded, but it seemed then and still seems today to be an oxymoron — a *white* marigold. Why? It is tantamount to bleeding the color out of our faces or working on a project to turn the leaves in the trees white instead of green. Some things just should be as they are, always. Not everything needs improvement.

As for the return of the annual, if that is so, welcome back. We hadn't really missed you, those loyalists among us. And if any service-station owners are reading out there, please do continue to plant those beautiful gardens. We need that message, that telegram of color from out of the pavement: *Classé!*

JULY 1995

🌀 Heaven on Earth

QUITE A NUMBER of years ago, I clipped a recipe from *The Mother Earth News*. Actually, I don't think I clipped it. It was so simple that I remembered it, probably the only recipe I've ever committed to memory. Steam up and mash together equal parts potato, turnip, and apple, then fry up some bacon and sprinkle it over the top. Voila! The dish was entitled *Himmel und Erde* or, translated from German, Heaven and Earth. For us this concoction was a natural. With the exception of bacon, which sometimes came to us from our generous neighbors, we grew all the ingredients and in November had a porch loaded with bushels of each. I served it first for a family Thanksgiving to rave reviews, most frequently veiled in the declaration, "I never thought I liked turnips before." So I continued to bring it out for Thanksgiving gatherings year after year, until it became a tradition. Even I have to remind myself that I once took this recipe from a magazine. Everyone thinks of this as mine.

"What is it that you call this?" an uncle would ask.

"Himmel und Erde," I would reply. "That's heaven and earth in German."

"Oh, yes, that's right," he would say and go back to his steaming plate.

But no one ever seemed to remember the name for long. My mother, whose own father was of German descent, called it "hummel and erdee." Always in September, when we were planning for the holidays, she'd urge me to serve it. "It's heavenly!" she'd say.

Myself, I love the way the three ingredients blend into one delicious flavor, like the sweetest turnip or the sweetest potato I ever had; I can never quite figure out which. I play around with the proportions sometimes, but it doesn't seem to make a whole lot of difference. From the beginning I've added butter and sour cream to the mix, which lifts it a little closer to heaven. After a few years, several among us became vegetarians, so I dropped the bacon and no one seemed to love it less. Himmel und Erde became one of those resilient culinary faithfuls: No matter what I did to it, it still seemed to come out fine, a characteristic beloved of any cook.

Still, it was the name I loved the most. I don't know much about German cooking, so I don't know if Germans name all of their recipes in this way, but with the possible exception of Devil's Food Cake, I can't think of any American recipes with a poetic title. We tend to state the obvious in naming our dishes: macaroni and cheese, chicken and dumplings, carrot cake. Every time one of my relatives asks me what my turnip dish is called, I want to launch into a hymn of praise: "Himmel und Erde! Heaven and Earth — you see, the turnips and potatoes grow in the earth, the apples grow in the sky! But they did not name it Earth and Sky, no, they went for heaven, a benediction! It's truly a mix of all that is blessed to us, roots and inspirations, truly a concoction of heaven and earth!"

But I don't. I keep it to myself. Every year the name becomes more appropriate, like some great symphony for which you gain greater and greater appreciation as time passes. Truly, Himmel und Erde is everything. The way it uses the autumn overflow from my garden? Heaven on earth. The way it turns ordinary vegetables into something much greater? Heaven on earth. The way it tastes? Heaven on earth. The way it's so easy to fix? Heaven on earth. The way it makes my relatives think I am a creative cook? Heaven on earth.

NOVEMBER 1994

🐚 Nights of the Solstice

F OR A BRIEF PERIOD of time, I lived in Iceland, island in the Arctic, country of extremes. I was young and I was so far from home, it felt as if I were on another planet. I worked on a dairy farm there and learned the rhythm of their days, entirely different from ours. In the summer, the sun literally never set. It would drop down to the horizon, sit there a while and then, sometime after midnight, it would rise again, as if it had changed its mind.

In such light, the farming day has no limits. There were nights when we mended fences at one in the morning and times when we stayed up all night shearing sheep. In the summer, there are many meals during the endless days. I slept, during that long bright summer, but by doing so I missed a major mealtime, served sometime around 3 a.m. I think they called it breakfast. I was told that some people never went to bed at all in the summer. I can imagine why it might be. Their calendar year is like a single day, divided into one long day and one very long night.

On the evening of the summer solstice, I think of my friends in Iceland, always. It is their national holiday, a time of celebration and joy. That is the balance of their scale, so terribly black and white. And that is why some Icelanders choose never to shut their eyes in sleep when the sun is up. More than in summer, I think of my Icelandic family on the evening of the winter solstice. I tell people that in Iceland it is dark all the time in the winter and they do not believe me. "No. That can't be," they say, flatly. Oh, but it is, a long darkness that provokes sadness and, at the extreme, suicide.

Our winter solstice gives us just a hint of this. Few of us are farmers and our working days are spent in cars and in buildings. In the early morning hours in December, headlights guide our way as we travel through darkness to our workplace. There is midday light, but we are inside, working. Darkness falls before we leave work to drive home, aided once again by those guiding lights. We could as well be in Iceland for all the daylight we see. Recently, doctors identified a new disease they call SAD, which stands for Seasonal Affective Disorder. These experts must have worked hard to find a combination of words whose first letters would spell out the apparent consequence of being deprived of sunlight. For a cure, patients, like frail plants, sit beneath special lights, created to imitate sunlight. An alternative is to travel toward the equator, where the sun stays out longer. Apparently the effect of more light is immediate and satisfying. But so hard to acquire, so unnatural.

My friends in Iceland have never left their shores. They stay on their farm and have no idea what it would be like to walk on a tropical beach in bright sunlight in the middle of their accustomed darkness, their endless night. They do not mind the winters. They use those nights to spin wool, to knit beautiful sweaters. And to sleep.

December 20th was my husband's birthday, the almost solstice, we called it. That evening always seemed so cozy to us, so special. It was an evening to stay in by the stove and read stories out loud. If we were lucky, there was a snowstorm, and we would bundle up and go outside and walk into the storm. It was an incomparable sensation, the snow falling through darkness onto our warm faces.

But, more often, we celebrated the solstice in the midst of a still and velvet darkness. There is a reason, they say, why Christmas comes so near to the solstice. On that longest and darkest of nights, it is easier to sense the angels, near the earth, and the light from the stars shines much more brightly. From these celestial signs, we can find our way home.

DECEMBER 1998

❦ My December Vegetable

ELSEWHERE, Brussels sprouts may be one of our more maligned vegetables, but in our house, Brussels sprouts were exalted. They were my father's favorite, and my mother would search for them on those special occasions. I'm not sure where she found them. This was before you could find just about anything either on the produce shelves or in the frozen-food department. Nevertheless, I remember them sitting in the gold-rimmed blue bowls, pale and soggy and not the least bit appetizing.

Long after, I read in a gardening magazine about the virtues of Brussels sprouts in northern gardens. Thinking more of extending my garden season than anything else, I ordered a packet of Jade Cross, and early in July I planted a brief row of the tiny round seeds. They came up, looking a lot like broccoli at first. But the plants kept spiraling up, growing gawkier and gawkier, a long sinewy stalk with thick, platterlike leaves jutting out all around it. All around this rather grotesque stalk the sprouts grew, for all the world like warts on a neck, possibly the ugliest garden vegetable I've ever seen. I nearly pulled them up. They offered nothing aesthetic to my garden plot and tempted me not at all with the possibilities of their fruits. Aren't these two things we want most from our gardens? The beauty as it grows, and the taste of its harvest. Brussels sprouts appeared to offer me neither.

Out of apathy, I let them languish, giving them a wide berth as I went about my weeding. In the late fall, after the first hard frost, the Brussels sprouts came into their own. The rest of the garden had broken down and blackened from the cold nights, but the Brussels sprouts stood up proud, impervious to the change in season. I'd taken several harvests from them, snapping the sprouts, which look like miniature cabbages, off the stem with my thumb. I was surprised by the flavor, which was rich and, after the first frost, sweet.

But their true virtue didn't appear until December. The snow came and I forgot about the garden for the most part. The Brussels sprouts were out there, sticking up out of the snow, very ugly by then, the leaves slumped down against the stalk. My parents were coming for Christmas dinner. I remembered how much my father liked Brussels sprouts. Christmas morning, I pulled on my boots and went out across the snow into the garden and knelt beside the plants, which looked hopelessly decayed. The article I'd read said they liked cold weather, but surely they didn't mean this cold. I lifted one of the dead leaves and snapped off a sprout. It seemed impossible, but it looked — good. I went back into the kitchen for a bowl and brought it back out to the garden and filled it.

At dinner, as I had hoped, my father looked up in astonishment and asked, "*Where* did you find the Brussels sprouts?"

"Picked them this morning," I told him, somewhat smugly. They were bright green and unusually sweet. I plant them every year now, my December vegetable.

DECEMBER 1991

🌀 The Silent Flock

THIS USED TO BE a chicken farm long ago. It was called Valley Vue Farm, and the slant-roofed chicken barns huddled in twos and threes across the fields. The farm belonged to Ralph Bemis, a man who kept his chickens in apparent splendor. In the main barn behind the house he insulated the walls with sawdust and ran hot-water pipes under the nests. He wanted to keep his hens warm during those long Chesham winters. The winters are still with us, but the hens are long gone. All that's left are the buildings, some of them too dilapidated for me to keep up. But that one, the one with the ingenious heated-nest system, I've tried to bolster.

This big, empty building had space enough to house probably a thousand hens at one time. Though I love them and hope someday for a flock of at least a half dozen cooing broodies, at the moment I have no chickens here, no vestiges of farm life but this building and its scattering of feeder trays and watering pans, still dusted with a patina of laying mash. The barn instead has taken on another purpose. In the winter, I store cars for my neighbors.

These are not ordinary cars. They are wonderful, shiny creations that their owners use only on Sundays or days when there is a leisurely feel and a bright sun in the sky. Summer cars. Never-tasted-salt cars. Beloved, fussed over, polished, smooth-running *dream* cars.

I know it's November when they come. I don't need a calendar or a date. I wake up. The last lingering warm days of autumn are gone. The sky is rugged gray, like a forbidding sea. Wind is passing through the pines, a cautionary hiss, and the maples at the edge of the field are colorless, naked sticks against the cold sky. Flecks of snow pass by the window. Just as a farmer knows the day to mow the hay, I know this is the day the beauties will roll into my driveway. Like some kind of bird with a migratory instinct, they all come on the same day. They ease into the yard, one and then another as the day passes, a slow-motion parade of black curving fenders, bright spoked wheels, scrolling red pinstripes, flaming hoods.

They congregate, as if I were hosting an engine meet, waiting for Rusty to come. Rusty is the local mechanic and thus the shepherd who gathers most of these cars here. It is up to him to arrange them, in order, in the long, wide space beneath the old nesting room. The first one in will be the last one out. Rusty drives them, one by one, into the dark coldness. Standing inside, I use hand signals to guide Rusty through the narrow door. The sounds of the engines, muscular and vibrant in the open air, are amplified by the ceiling and the closeness of the cement walls. For an instant, while Rusty maneuvers them into place, it's a booming, mooing, stomping herd.

He tucks them in close, nudging the bumpers almost to a touch. When he shuts off the last engine, there is a dead silence, a shush that seems to magnify the cold wind just outside the door. Batteries and essentials are removed. Soft, chamois-colored cloths are fitted over each. With his hands, Rusty smooths the covers over the exotic, rounded shapes. We talk briefly, softly, about the coming winter, and then we part until spring. It is a ghostly barnyard that I keep. I lock the shrouded beasts in, a silent flock, to begin the long winter's sleep.

NOVEMBER 1993

❧ Pot-bound

On a recent Sunday the minister, in his sermon, spoke about being pot-bound. He was using the word as a way of describing how some people grow in their faith. He was talking about religious groups that are very restrictive. Some people, he said, need to be pot-bound, need those strong boundaries in order to contain their faith, to keep it from getting away from them, just as some plants like to be cramped, the roots pressed tight against the sides of the pot. He was heading somewhere with that, he always is, but I left him there. Snow was piled deep outside the church, and the word, pot-bound, led me, somewhat circuitously, back to the garden.

I know enough about indoor gardening to know that there are some plants that need to be cramped in order to grow, in order to flower. I learned this the hard way. Years ago, I was given a little geranium that looked in good proportion, plant to pot. On my sunny windowsill it seemed to grow and grow and grow inside its small flowerpot. One day I set about to transplant it to a bigger pot, a task I figured was long overdue. I spread newspapers on my kitchen counter and upended the ever-strengthening plant. It came out whole. There was almost no earth at all, just a tight confusion of roots, pressed together like so much spaghetti in a bowl. It was almost painful to see it in such a state, and I quickly set to liberating it into roomier quarters, pressing potting soil in to fill the void. I sprinkled a bit of fertilizer, gave it a long drink of water, and set it back in the sun, feeling I'd given it a great gift.

Instead, my geranium went into a decline. It ceased to bloom and its big green leaves became edged in brown. Later, I found out there are plants that like being pot-bound. Geraniums, African violets, fibrous begonias are among these. The giant, showy amaryllis that bursts forth into our winter living rooms appears to flourish on practically nothing. It defies logic to me. If you really want your geranium to flower profusely, starve it — keep it bound up in a little pot and keep the soil poor and pretty close to bone-dry. This somehow didn't appeal to me. I felt more comfortable growing things outdoors, where plants made and kept their own rules.

I still keep a few geraniums on the windowsill in the winter. I like the flag of red in the black and white of winter. But in general, I plant outdoors, where I never think about where the roots are off to. Though my mind wandered so during that sermon, I feel sure that's what the minister was talking about — how if we give our faith a little extra space, it grows on its own. Out in the great expanse of the garden, the plants can find their own balance, down under the soil. They always seem to find what they need. But I think his other point was one of tolerance — that just like indoor gardening, pot-bound is OK. It's just not for those of us who like a little freedom, those of us who need a bit of legroom.

JANUARY 1993

❀ New Year's Bonfire

AROUND HERE, in recent years, we have had fireworks to enjoy on New Year's Eve. In Keene, which is not too far away, they celebrate "First Night," and at the stroke of midnight the town's firemen launch multicolored rockets, little bombs that pop and boom and explode brilliantly into the cold air of the new year. A crowd is gathered in Central Square. We are suitably attired in heavy coats and big boots and thick socks, mittens and scarves and hats, so that mostly just our eyes show. The cheers go up, just the same, for the fiery bomb blasts that shower us, and with mittened hands we give a muted applause.

I am accustomed to fireworks on hot summer nights, a celebration to remind us of war and victory, to remind us most of all of freedom. But this new tradition thrills me. It is better than champagne — to welcome a new year, a new hope, with light and color and noise.

Even more than fireworks, I like a bonfire on New Year's Eve. Fire consumes, cleanses, redeems. A few years back, we had a bonfire for New Year's. We had it planned since fall, when we swept up the crackled, tired remnants of the garden foliage. The soggy tomato vines and the pepper plants we layered into the compost, but the corn stalks were so dry that year and so were the pumpkins, the thick, bristly vines like dried tubes. We raked them to the center of the garden and stacked them, a high haystack. We added wood scraps from the repairs to the shed, stacking them crosswise, Boy Scout style, in a high pyre.

We left it there, through the fall and early winter, a poetic mound that spoke to us as winter took hold. By New Year's Eve some snow had fallen, edging the pile in a frail lace of snow and ice. We invited the neighbors to join us, and as the evening grew late, we sat beside the warming stove, sipped hot toddies from steaming mugs, and thought back on the year. Not a bad one, we assessed. Next year will be better, we promised.

As the magic moment approached, we bundled up. We laced our boots and set off down the garden path. The stars were bright overhead, the moon a dim crescent. Paul had in his pocket a rag and a vial of kerosene. He soaked the rag and stuffed it into the lattice of corn husk and lath. We stood in a semicircle in the dark crystalline midnight and watched as he lit the long wooden match and extended it to the pile. The flame leapt, and in greedy bursts it ate up the stack. In measures of light and heat, the first flames consumed the garden chaff, a beast of flame and energy, snapping and roaring, sending up a shower of sparks high above us, orange flares in the dark canyon of the first night.

The fire grew. We basked in the heat of its life. From his other pocket, Paul drew out strings of little Chinese firecrackers. He threw them into the burning stack and, rat-a-tat, they shot back in rapid blasts. "To the garden!" he said. "To the garden!" we answered as the quick fire died to a small hill of glowing embers. In the spring, we tilled the sodden circle of ash into the eager earth and started fresh.

JANUARY 1995

Prayer Ice

I N February it's the ice that saves us. When I step out onto it the first time, every time, it's so strange, to be walking on our water, where not so long ago, we touched the sandy bottom with our toes. At this time the lake is transformed into a place where men drill holes in the ice and sit on stools in the cold and wait for the tip-up to flip the flag up. The more serious fishermen drag small houses out onto the lake and take up a kind of winter residence. Inside they might have stoves or gear or lanterns behind gingham curtains. The fish shacks are colorful: yellow and red and blue against the flat white field of the lake. They are set here and there on the wide expanse of the lake, and all around them snowmobiles whine, skiers glide, skaters twirl.

From the boat landing, trucks and cars test the ice. Those first few brave ones give the signal, and then there is traffic on the lake. Cars come and go as if it were a road. Trucks park next to the little houses, making it seem like a neighborhood, everyone home for the afternoon. Smoke puffs from the chimneys. Music plays from small radios. Old men chew tobacco. Children run in circles around their winter huts. The little village has a merry feeling, like a makeshift carnival, no admission necessary.

Near the lake we have a neighbor named Hans. He came here from Germany and put out his shingle as a tailor. Beautiful, flawless vests and suit coats came forth from his needle. Hans is a talented man and perhaps a bit restless. Soon he was making kites — huge, colorful, complicated, fantastic kites that rose aloft like airplanes. I think of kites flying through summer skies, but Hans thinks of them going up anytime. In winter he takes his kites out to the middle of the lake and makes them fly, the frozen lake the perfect showroom for his creations. One year a few years ago, he put an ad in the local paper. Valentine's Day Kite Festival. People came, with their kites. The day was warm and the kites were interesting, none so spectacular as Hans's. The fishing families came out from their huts to watch the aeronautical wonders floating above them. Cars going by on the road past the lake slowed to a stop, dazzled by the winter sky crowded with pink and turquoise and yellow and red nylon birds, bobbing, plunging, dancing. Every year since, Hans has made the call, and the kite people come and walk out onto the lake and urge their creations up into the thin, cold air.

The limit to the season of the ice is fairly elastic. Some years we can walk and ski and drive on the frozen field all the way into April. Other years, a warm spell takes the rug out from under us before the end of February. There's a scramble then. At night after a warm day, the ice goes hard once again, and the men come and heft the little houses up into the beds of the pickups and drive them away. Or drag them on runners off to the edge of the lake to await transport. The skaters vanish. The kites are put away until spring. The cars and trucks go back to driving on asphalt. Overnight the village is gone, as if it had been our midwinter hallucination.

At this point I've heard it called prayer ice. I've always assumed that prayer ice means that it's so thin that you have to say your prayers when you go out onto it. But maybe it means you say your prayers that the ice will come back, at least for a week or two. Almost every year, there's a truck or a car or a snowmobile that goes through, plunging through the thin layer into the cold depths. These are the ones who don't want the party to end, the ones who can't quite believe how short the ice season is, and how long the winter.

FEBRUARY 1999

The Frozen Ones

THERE IS SOMETHING that comes up this time of year known as frozen pipes. I've heard lots of stories about frozen pipes or, worse, broken pipes. Once, not so long ago, I drove by a house in a nearby town during an excruciatingly cold period. A frozen cascade of ice was emerging from the open door. That's not frozen pipes, it's broken pipes to the most nightmarish degree. I'd never had to deal with either situation, though I'd had plenty of friends who had, and their descriptions had been good enough for me. In truth (a truth I carefully kept to myself) I felt like one of the Chosen Ones, to whom Such Things were not going to happen.

Plumbers are fond of saying, "There's always a first time." My turn came last year. There had been a lot of cold weather. Not too unusual. We had a mountain of snow and then a fast melt. Snow acts as an insulator around the foundation, and that was gone. Maybe that's what did it. Who knows. The mysteries of cold weather and old houses. All I can tell you is that I came downstairs early one morning, before sunup. I usually glance at the thermometer first thing, especially when it's cold. That morning the mercury read 20 below, and the windowpanes were iced up to prove it. I padded into the kitchen in my thick socks and pulled open the faucet to fill the teakettle. Nothing happened except that I got this sinking feeling, this deep absolute certainty of why there wasn't any water coming out of the faucet. I went into the bathroom and turned on the faucet. Same thing. Not so much as a gurgle. It was enough to make a grown woman cry.

I turned on all the faucets in the house. All of them were bone-dry, frozen solid. I left them on, as I had been told, to decrease the pressure and make it less likely that the pipes would break. I put on my heavy coat over my nightgown, pulled on my felt-lined boots, and went down into the cold place we call the cellar. I had with me the only weapon I've ever heard of in the battle against frozen pipes: my hair dryer.

For the next four hours I waged war, training that little blast of heated air onto the crystallized pipes. My arms ached. My feet were frozen. My spirits were worse. The sun had long since risen. The temperature inched up above zero. The pipes stuck to their guns. While I was at that task, I thought about all kinds of subterranean things. I thought about where the water comes from, how it comes into the house. I had never before given my pipes so much thought. I also thought about how much I take for granted. Now that they had frozen, I wondered why they never had before. The frozen pipes began to seem to me to be a kind of psychic condition, a physical playing out of our feelings when the temperature drops way below zero. The frozen pipes are us: "No, that's it. I'm not going to go anymore. It's just too damn cold, I'm done. You can just wait it out till spring."

I couldn't wait until spring. I wanted my tea. More, I wanted my shower, my wonderful, unbelievably curative hot shower.

At last (and it seemed like decades later) there was a slight gurgling sound, which I took to be like a voice at last responding to my pleas of the past hours. I went upstairs. Trickles of water made music coming from each faucet, something so ordinary, so simple, and yet, that morning, so very beautiful. I laid aside my hair dryer, filled the kettle, and set it on the burner to boil.

JANUARY 1997

❧ Riding the Ridges

A NUMBER OF YEARS AGO, I worked beside a woman named Millie. We were proofreaders at a printing plant in Vermont and so we worked in silence. But during breaks, Millie liked to tell me about her growing up years on the farm in Dummerston. What she came back to more often than anything was mud season, that time when winter begins its retreat. Mud was what made her hate the farm, she said. In mud season, with the farm way out at the end of a dirt road, they were trapped. No vehicle could negotiate the terrible black ooze that came when the snowmelt and the richness of the Vermont earth mixed together into a perilous quicksand. And so, instead of going out during the day, they went out at night, when the cold turned the terrible mix back into terra firma. "We'd ride the ridges," she told me. "That was our only way out."

Listening to Millie's stories, it wasn't hard for me to sympathize. The only time I've ever been stuck, truly stuck so that there was nothing to do but get out and walk, was not in snow but in mud. And, yes, the worst of the mud visits us at high noon and retreats at night. In mud season, it is wise to think about the temperature, at the moment, before turning onto a dirt road. If it's cool, say forty or below, go ahead. But if the temperatures are up there enough so that you've got your windows rolled down and you can smell the mud, it's best to stay on tar. If you can.

I can't think of any weather — if mud can be considered weather — that does this to us. Like the English in their rain, we maneuver through our snowstorms as if it weren't happening. "Just a dusting," we say, as a foot of snow cascades down upon us. But mud. We love our dirt roads, photograph them, paint them, boast of them but, when the ground squirts out from under our boots we think of it as muck, glop, warm lard, a primeval mix. No one I know rhapsodizes over the advent of the mud. No one I know likes mud. No one I know paints pictures of it or writes poems about it. I have friends who, like Millie, are trapped in their house during the season of mud. And I am talking about the year 1999. Like ordinary citizens suddenly taken hostage, they cry to me over the phone, "We can't get out!" and tell of walking two miles through the squishy stuff after their car sank to its axles.

At the MacDowell Colony, the venerable New Hampshire artists' colony where such luminaries as Thornton Wilder, Aaron Copland and Alice Walker have created their masterpieces, the artists' studios are strung out along a network of dirt roads. Like the U.S. Mail, the lunch there must be delivered to the hungry artists, isolated as they are in their solitary studios. But this noontime endeavor comes year-round, even at High Mud Season. And so, the Colony has begun to create what they call "state-of-the-art" dirt roads, using underlayments of special webbing and crushed stone. In this way, they have averted the potential disaster of mud season and managed to keep the delicious quaintness of their dirt roads.

Though there may be other places where such diligent attention is being paid to the problem of mud, I don't know of any. Certainly, no town could afford such a luxury. In my town, our dirt roads are kept like gardens, tended and graded and raked. They are a pleasure to drive, even and especially in winter when their plowed surfaces of packed snow are smooth and silent as air. But when the mud comes, it's every woman for herself, driver beware, sorry can't help you. Proceed at your own risk. The ruts go a foot deep, causing the kind of swervy, out-of-control ride you might get inside a car wash gone mad and without end. That is, if you are lucky enough to stay on the ridges. If not, you're down, down and maybe for good. The best that our fastidious road agents can do for us at this time is jam a broken-off branch into the sinkholes and put a blaze orange flag on it, a message we all know means: *drive here and you die.*

That's when I remember Millie and the picture she painted for me of her life on that farm growing up in the 1930s in Vermont. If I need to go somewhere, I wait for the cold to come back and harden the earth. Like a tightrope walker, I ride the high ridges, and when the tires hit the paved road, I feel a bit of a thrill and exhale. *I made it!* Escape accomplished.

MARCH 1999

✿ Pelicans and Herons and All That

MARCH IS USUALLY snowstorms and mud, mud and snow-storms but this March has been warmth, thaw, and mud. I have not kept track but it seems we have had warm weather for the past three or so weeks, with a few high wind storms thrown in to keep us honest. In the beginning of this month, we had about three feet up here, the result of two back-to-back storms but since then, I have watched the snow recede from the window beside my desk like a tide going out. I can smell the mucky earth coming forth and watch the ice rot. Some days, I have gone out for walks without a jacket, which feels free and easy, a reward well-earned. My dogs run as if awarded new life.

But so many have cut and run from all this. A friend sent me a photo from her timeshare in Cancun: turquoise sky meets azure sea, a tall palm tree and peach-colored beach umbrellas the only objects in the big blue expanse. Looking at that scene, I could feel the sun on my bare skin, smell the salt air and the coconut lotion, and feel the gentle breezes. It all looked so tranquil.

I heard today from a friend who ordinarily lives nearby but who has spent the better part of this winter in California and Florida. She says she has decided that spending the winter in warm and forgiving climates is quite nice, indeed. I guess she has plenty of company, as the population in places like that does swell sometimes ten and twentyfold during the cold months. So she is not alone in her sentiment. She writes of the easy pace, the sense of peace there, and continues on, as if to convince me: "If you are a person who enjoys reading, movies, sitting with a stack of books by the pool, and a good Sunday brunch at the country club, then it is quite nice indeed. The fact that my parents' house is wide open to the outdoors and perched at the edge of a broad canal creates a sense of air and sky and space. All day, the light pours in; the sliders are open; it is like living outdoors. There are fish flopping and pelicans perching on the dock and herons stalking through the yard. I wake up in the dark, and work for a bit, go to the health club down the road to exercise, do yoga by the pool, read a lot."

It all sounds idyllic. There must be something wrong with me but I can't be sold. For one thing, I couldn't bear to be gone that long, to miss the tiny increments that move us toward spring. We have gotten through Town Meeting and throughout the long weeks of Lent, I rehearse, with the church choir, the joyful songs of Easter and we look forward to sharing that day of renewal together. And, of course, like hungry pilgrims searching the horizon for land, we all notice the little signs of spring, and cry out the news. Crocuses in a lawn in Keene. The first green shoots of the daylilies emerging. One friend tells of all the robins who seem to have "come out of nowhere, so suddenly." I've observed the bobolinks returning — soon they will be nesting in the hayfield. I have heard the soulful, two-note cry of the redwing blackbird, always the first call of my spring and, most celebratory, the return of the bluebirds. There is so much at this time of year to keep me busy. My woodpile is down to the point where I start making bets with myself if there will be any leftover (which means I will have to move it out of the way so I can use the porch for summer) or if I will run out and have to use the oil burner. I like it when it comes out just right, which it sometimes does. (That whole process, by the way, has a dual purpose, not just the resultant heat but bringing in the wood, a daily chore, is a combination of squats, weight-lifting, and curls. And the air is better than what it must be like inside the health club.)

The snow is almost gone but they are talking about a possible snowstorm next week. It's been such a mild winter, I say, let it snow, I haven't quite had my fill. And a spring snowstorm never lasts very long. I do have a stack of books here, towering in fact, waiting for me to read them. The mild winter deprived us of those luxurious snow days, nothing to do but bake beans and stay home and read. So I am way behind. I don't know. One warm day after the next, the unbroken azure sky, pelicans perching, herons stalking. My friend's seamless, azure day is nice to think about, but I'd sooner be here, mud, sleet, wind, whatever, each day different and the drama of it all.

BLOG ENTRY

🌀 New Crop of Rocks

SOMETHING HAPPENS to our roads at this time of year. They rise up. They open. They crack and break as if they were made from delicate materials mistakenly left out in the weather. This can be explained, of course, this rending of our pavements. It's the frost, moving up out of the ground. Those of us who are gardeners understand this strange phenomenon. We discover it in our soil every spring, new stones, rocks we *know* were not there last year because we dug there, we raked and we sifted all of them *out*. No, these are newcomers, boulders that have worked their way up from deep down under, nudged their way upward to break the surface of the earth.

We shrug and say glibly: *new crop of rocks*. But what is this that happens beneath us every year? Of course, all this movement is happens everywhere. We discover it in the garden because that is where we dig. We discover it in our roads because that is where we drive.

The roads that wind around near where I live are said to be the worst in New Hampshire. I am sure there are other contenders, but we'll accept the crown, or carry the cross, as it were. In the summertime these roads are lovely, meandering macadam that lead from one little town to the next. But sometime in early February, the earth begins to stir. Almost overnight that good, smooth, even roadway becomes a monster of buckled slabs of tar and menacing cracks, crevices big enough to lose your baby in, chasms that yield a sudden, shuddering, teeth-clenching cah-*rash!*

Driving these roads is like entering the rodeo, *yippee-ay-oh!* we cry out as we lurch and soar from one mogul to the next.

84

The road crews are busy. They post laconic signs that warn "Frost Heave" or "Bump," great literary understatements that bounce between our cars as we fly into the air and land on our axles. Our cars shudder and occasionally fall from these encounters with February's release. An accident with the road is how the insurance companies explain the damages that result without true collision.

Most of us who travel the same routes every day relearn the pavement's terrain in early spring. Perfectly sober drivers are seen swerving from one side of the road to the other as they seek to avoid the nauseating, head-lurching ride that can come from meeting these potholes head-on. Certain stretches of road excite hyperbole in young people, especially boys. *Wahhhhoa! That one is awesome!* they crow. The time has not yet come for them to worry about their suspension.

Cracks open as if a big iron plow had rent the pavement. Rocks, as big around as beach balls, emerge from the tar and create launch pads worthy for hot-doggers. It is so strangely like a seed, growing forth from the earth, almost like a blossom. But it's nothing of the kind. Unless this truly is our crop of rocks, the road our furrow.

But the miracle is not the rising up but rather the falling back. As the temperature moderates, what heaved the road up dies back. Newcomers to the area sometimes rail about these February roads: why don't they *do* something, why don't they *fix* these roads?! The road agents know. These roads are elastic. If the road crews fill that sinkhole with tar, in June it will become a permanent bump. If they fill it with sand, when the road springs back, the sand will disperse and the pavement will return to that smoothness of summer.

It is like some strange kind of poetry, some unnamed force of nature: The earth rises up (breathe in), the earth falls back (breathe out). What kind of tide is this? What kind of sea? For want of a better name, we'll call it the Rock Tide, which brims up just when we most need something to talk about.

FEBRUARY 1996

🌀 On Fire

FARMER JAY HAS been clearing trees from around the edges of the big field to the southeast of my house. He's gone back into the cordwood business, he tells me, after a brief hiatus. He did not say why but I assume the favorable price of cordwood might have something to do with it. Cordwood is expensive (I can remember paying $45 a cord, years back, but I've heard prices as high as $275 a cord more recently) but there's a lot of work in it. I don't think the hourly wage of anyone who cuts cordwood for a living is very high. Plus it's dangerous work. And Jay, like myself, is no longer young.

So the familiar whine of the chainsaw began. He works alone but within sight of many of my windows so I glance out from time to time, an interesting diorama to watch as I work. He works with a skidder, cutting the trees first, limbing them and then dragging the trunks across the field, stockpiling them up by the road. Standard logging practice. Looked to me like a lot of maple and ash but I didn't look too closely. I could see from the fir boughs that were mounting that he was also cutting pine. Though these fields belong to my neighbor, Jay manages them, keeping the edges trimmed and picking up trees that go over in wind and ice. This makes it easier for him to get as much hay as possible from these big and mostly productive meadows. I don't know of any nicer fields in this town or the next. Aside from the fine horse hay it produces (I am told it is very good quality) and now the harvest of hardwood, these fields provide a great beauty, which is no small product.

So he spent several days cutting and I watching. The pine boughs out by the edge of the stone wall were mounting and the day that I wondered what he would do with those also brought my answer. With his skidder, he pushed the boughs into a big high pyramid and lit fire to it. The fields were covered by a very thin blanket of snow. The pile let up a big plume of smoke and for several hours, that was what it was, a green pile with smoke rising from the center. With his machine, he pushed more limbs and branches toward the pyre. At one point I walked out to the center of the field to get a closer look. As his yellow growling machine revved and rammed, I could hear the snap of wood, perhaps being broken by the force of the blade or maybe just the heat of fire inside the burning limbs. It sounded like a massive hearth fire, snapping and cracking as flames finally burst freely up through the pile. At moments, it seemed he was driving the skidder right into the fire. I stood in the cold and watched. Dense near the earth but thin above the treetops, the gray tower of smoke rose high into the air, visible, I'm sure, for miles.

The day was ending. After darkness fell, I looked out to see the brush still flaming, a big cozy red circle in the blackness. It was a clear night, stars bright. A satellite drifted silently overhead. I wondered if Jay's fire was visible from space. The morning brought a snow squall, dusting the fields and every branch. Flames were no longer visible but smoke still moved slowly upward, a lazy climb, like a tired runner. When the workday started, Jay returned. With the blade of his skidder, he scoured the edges of the fields, pushing long branches into the pile. The fire burst up again, muscular and inspired. The smoke regained its ambition, arrowed into the sky. Throughout the day, the tower of brush alternately flamed and smoked, a physical, vocal, theatrical presence in the otherwise still, silent field.

Last night, I could still see a bright pile of embers glowing in the darkness of the night. Today only a wide charred circle in the white field remains, the end of the week's performance and a mystical footnote on physics: that massive amount of matter, vanished. Where did it go?

Some of the long logs piled up by the road will be my cordwood next winter.

BLOG ENTRY

🌀 Sap Bucket Blues

M Y HUSBAND HAD one bucket and a spigot. Even though it takes 40 gallons of sap to make one gallon of maple syrup, it can be done with one bucket. It is a great deal of work. Eventually we felt that buying the syrup somehow made more sense.

I am changing my mind. Come spring, I see changes along the roadsides, and at the risk of sounding like a curmudgeon, I am having a hard time getting used to this. I'm talking about the new method of collecting sap with blue plastic tubing.

Drive along the back roads in early March — to see the buckets hanging off the trees represented so much: the beauty of our woods, as brought forth in countless paintings and photographs, seemingly never enough to capture that interesting bucket poised midway up the thick trunk of the incomparable maple. It also represented the mysterious way that the sap begins to move up into the branches, long before there is any other sign of spring. The buckets were the cheerful reminder in the midst of the high snowbanks that always defy our hopes: Spring is coming!

Sugaring was the great remedy for cabin fever. There are endless stories of the springs when the snow was still hip deep and what it was like collecting buckets on snowshoes. So many stories told, so much hooch consumed in the wee hours of a sugaring morning. As one who travels the back roads of New England at odd hours, I can say that there is not a more cheerful sight than coming upon a sugarhouse before daybreak and seeing the huge clouds of steam billowing from the roof vent. There used to be any number of these backyard sugarhouses, ready all year for this one brief, glorious season.

It's all part of our history, and I'm not saying it is gone. But it is changing. This quiet revolution surely improves our supply of syrup, but it leaves an aching hole for all of us who simply loved the beauty the process brought to our woods. This tubing is clever and definitely of the late 20th century. The tubes are spliced together like intravenous lines, running from one tree to the next. Where there was once the *drip-drip-drip* of the sap, a sound with the musical elegance of a metronome, there is now a rushing sound, like a faucet turned on high. This is the preponderance of sap, not from one tree but from, perhaps, 20. It races, gravity-fed, gathering speed down the hill toward a humongous covered aluminum vat, placed as close to the road as possible. From there it is an easy pump into the refrigerated tanker truck that comes to collect the sap.

I know we make just as much syrup as we ever did, and I am sure that this job has been made easier for the syrup producers. I believe that the bucket method came to us from the Indians, and there has not been any significant change since then. So we are overdue.

Still I miss those buckets. I recently went to an estate auction. A lot of old wooden sap buckets were sold. There must have been 200, stacked up like custard cups, one stack after the other, the stacks as tall as a man. The buckets had a reddish stain on them and made me long to see them once again, hanging from the maples near my house. An interior decorator bought the entire lot. I suppose many of these old buckets are already hard at work, bearing sprays of dried flowers in some grand living room far from the silence of a March woods.

I am cleaning our bucket. It is not so much work, I am thinking now. That maple beside the garden hasn't been tapped in years. Maybe on a good day, when the sun is strong, I'll take a lawn chair out there and set it up in the snow, beside the bucket. I can sit back and close my eyes, tilt my face into the warming sun, and listen to the *drip-drip-drip*, New England's Morse code: *Spring is coming*.

MARCH 1996

Daylight Nuisance Time

"**S**PRING FORWARD, Fall Behind," my mother used to say, and it was an easy way to remember this business of Daylight Saving Time. On the first Saturday night in April, we advance the clock, making mornings come earlier and evenings longer. Or is it darker? I get confused about the purpose of moving our clocks forward and backward. Is it to give us a longer day? If so, I can't figure out how it can do that. A day is as long as it is going to be. No moving of the clocks can make a difference in the length of our days.

I know of a farmer in this state of New Hampshire who does not observe this ritual. The cows know milking time, he says, in spite of what the clock may say. He calls this Daylight Nuisance Time and lives half the year out of sync with the rest of the country. The novelist Carolyn Chute doesn't set her clocks back or forward either but keeps them on Standard Time year-round, which raises problems when she has to travel. I have contemplated doing that. It appeals to me. I like to think of time and the arrival of the seasons as something celestial, a cosmic occurrence understood only by the likes of Albert Einstein and *The Old Farmer's Almanac*, rather than something voted on by Congress.

Daylight Saving Time was first suggested by Ben Franklin in 1784, and over time we have waffled back and forth in our appreciation for the idea. The war years and the years 1967, 1972, 1975, and 1987 all show up as banner years for its evolution. In those years Congress and various presidents have gotten into the act, signing bills and changing it around, all the while justifying its existence. One theory is that it saves energy. Another is that it gives farmers more daylight hours in their fields (which, by the way, the farmers refute). The British go along with it, too, though they call it Summer Time, a nicer way of putting it. Still, the fact that all this rearranging of the calendar comes from politicians rather than astronomers (or farmers) makes me somewhat nervous.

But then, time is what we make of it. I like to get up at first light, no matter what the clock says, and often those first hours are spent in the garden. It is cooler than in the hot part of the summer, and it is time I feel is my own, rather than that of my employer. I don't think of it as an hour, but rather as daybreak or dawn or sunrise, the finest part of any day. It is also the quietest, when few cars are out on the road and I am urged on by the enthusiasm of the birds all around me.

And so if we want to work an extra hour in the garden, we can. We don't have to change the clocks to do so. Time and calendar are our own inventions, just a method to keep track of things. The sun rises and the sun sets according to that great astronomical wheel about which we can do nothing. Isn't it just like the politicians to want to get in there and change the hands of time? And when they have made their decree, no one is really sure where the benefit lies.

In spite of my objections, I have grown to like this semiannual occasion. I look forward to it, in fact, not for what it does to my daylight hours, for I hardly notice that. But, more than New Year's Eve, I like it for the demarcation, the new beginning it offers. It's a head start on a new season, a chance to start fresh and get a little bit ahead of myself in the garden. Who cares if it's a politician's invention? To spring forward is a good idea.

APRIL 1996

❧ Waking Up the Truck

I N RECENT YEARS I have discovered another way to open up the spring, one that lifts my heart every bit as much as the retreating ice on the lake or that cheerful two-note call of the red-winged blackbirds in the marsh. When the snow is gone and the roads are dry, usually sometime in the middle of April, I decide to start the truck.

The truck is old, and it belonged to my husband. He bought it right out of the Ford showroom 18 years ago, counting out the cash on the counter for the surprised salesman. Candy-apple red with a black grille, the truck looked positively fearsome in its size and in that shining armor. When he died, Paul had only his carpentry tools and his truck to leave behind him. I sold many of the tools, keeping the few that I knew I could use to make small repairs around the house and the truck. I couldn't imagine anyone else driving it but Paul but I thought that perhaps I could make use of it.

I was right about that, although the truck could be said to be in its dotage. No longer does it haul high stacks of wallboard or plywood or pine boards. No more do the springs sag from that extra half cord of green firewood. Instead, I use it on weekends to take small bags of my newspapers and bottles and cans to the recycling center or sometimes to pick up a load of manure for the garden. When Paul left us, the odometer rested at 76,000 miles. Every year since, I have added a few thousand miles, and now the numbers have turned over 100,000, a millennium all its own.

Because I hope it will last forever, I take such preventive measures as not driving the truck in the winter. In the fall I have it oil undercoated, a questionable ablution but one that makes me some-how feel better, and then I park it beside the barn. It sits there all winter, the snow piling up on the windshield and mounding in the bed so that in midwinter just that classic truck shape is visible, all done in that unforgiving white, a ghost of the truck he left behind.

On warm days the snow slides off the windshield and the hood appears, each year faded one more shade — that fiery red is now almost pink, soft like an old cloth. Then, like the equinox, it's time.

The battery always requires a charge, so I bring the charger out and set it on a step stool beside the truck. I open the hood, a great yawn, and step up to the battery. The truck's engine seems huge to me, the cavity big enough to settle into for a nap. I snap the little alligator clips from the charger onto the big knuckles of the battery terminals. For as many years as I have done this, I still do it gingerly and at arm's length, as if the power of this vernal connection could explode. I stand back and watch the needle on the charger rise, like a slow kettle. Several hours pass. I use the time to poke in the garden, rake away leaves from the corners of the stone walls and see if the red eyes of the rhubarb are out yet. Sometimes there are still discs of ice in parts of the garden. I take a shovel and break them up to hurry their parting. While I putter, I'm aware of the truck's presence. It sits so still, the hood open wide, the black wires snaking out from the mouth. Resuscitation is underway. I can almost hear it starting to speak.

At last I climb up behind the wheel. The seat, with its faded red plastic covers, is the most comfortable of any I know and the cab has been warmed by the sun. I pump the gas pedal a good number of times and turn the key. I'm not a lover of engines, I don't even know how to change the oil in this rig, but it warms my heart to hear that engine turn and catch and come to life, an ignition of the season, the return of an old friend.

APRIL 1998

🌀 A Fool for Daffodils

THERE WAS A famous gardener who lived in this town. She was an elderly lady with the improbable name of Vallie Wells, which always caused me to think of the deep beauty of all outdoors. I'd heard about her gardens that meandered through the woods of her Chesham home. Her specialty was daffodils. Every April I meant to walk up the hill to see her display, for I had heard it was spectacular and I am a fool for daffodils — or are they narcissus? What is the difference? It was a question I wanted to ask her when I went up there to introduce myself and to take in the tonic of her spring blooms.

One of the great contributions that Vallie made to this area was the Northern New England Daffodil Show, which graced the town hall for three April days, a panorama of hundreds of perfectly formed daffodils: yellow with white centers, white with yellow centers, yellow with yellow centers, white with pink centers, arranged singly or in pairs. Daffodil lovers came from all over New England to display their proudest blossoms. On those April days the hall, usually reserved for dour discussions of town affairs, lit up with these cheery colors of spring. I loved to watch the cars arrive and the occupants get out, gingerly carrying a single glorious blossom as if it were a newborn bird. Some entries came from as far away as Connecticut and Rhode Island. I imagined them cutting the stem in the cold of the early morning and cruising north to New Hampshire, the daffodil riding in the backseat, limo style.

I don't know why it is that we sometimes fail to meet our neighbors. One January evening my phone rang. It was Vallie Wells, inviting me to serve with her on a special cemetery committee. Our husbands had died within a short time of each other, and their stones were close together in our town's cemetery. Around her husband's stone, Vallie had planted a gorgeous ever-blooming perennial display. She was concerned about the rest of the cemetery, which was relatively new and unadorned with any ornamental plantings. Already she had taken it on herself to plant a scattering of daffodil bulbs at the edge of the yard, along the stone wall. But that was just a beginning. She wanted to make it really colorful all summer long. "I especially want to get up there, come spring, and get some things planted," she said. And then she added, "Before I get planted there myself." I readily agreed to help her. We ended our conversation by saying how much we hoped we would meet each other, soon.

It wasn't a good summer for Vallie. She took sick and her illness lingered. We spoke on the phone from time to time, hoping to meet and plan the cemetery plantings when her health improved. She was distressed that her illness was keeping her from her garden. I suggested I come to visit, and she happily agreed. We would meet at last! I made a fish chowder and wrapped it hot in a glass jar and drove up the hill. When I got there, however, there was a note on the door that explained that she had to be taken to the doctor rather suddenly. I left the soup on the step, and before I got back into my car, I wandered in her gardens, which were fanciful, in interesting shapes and edged with granite. I had questions and missed the possibility of her answers.

Vallie died in January, the darkest month for any northern gardener. The cold ground is as hard as steel and burial must wait. In the spring she was planted, leaving fresh-turned earth next to the garden she had made for her husband. It was a place of beauty, her place. Gardeners leave us the most gracious of legacies. When I went up there in late April to visit Paul's grave, I noticed that her daffodils were in full bloom all along the wall.

APRIL 1997

🌀 Consider the Lilies

CONSIDER THE Easter lily, a potted plant with the brief season of a weekend in April. Here in the Northeast, they grace our altars, rarely our gardens.

Our church has the custom of asking parishioners to order Easter lilies that can be placed on the altar in memory of a loved one. About six weeks before Easter, we can sign up for a lily, or two, and say who it's for. The church charges $10 a lily and they are able to raise a little money this way.

On Easter Sunday, you can smell the lilies as you come up the path, even before you enter the church. Since the Chesham church does not have a traditional altar, only a small table large enough for the brass cross and perhaps a vase of flowers, the lilies are placed all around the church. Their white trumpets fill the windowsills, the blossoms touching each other, and on top of the piano, underneath the high arched stained glass window. The pots are wrapped in purple foil and the bright yellow pollen from the center stamens smudges the floor and the white linens like stains of concentrated sunlight. Ours is a small church and this giving of the lilies is a popular thing which probably contributes to my feeling that, on this day, all the lilies on earth have been brought together into this one place.

Last year Easter came almost in the middle of April and it was a warm day. There was a good crowd at the church. Often Easter draws more people than Christmas, and this was one of those years. To make sure everyone had a seat, folding chairs had been set up in the back. It was a year when I had an abundance of people I wanted to be remembered and so I had ordered four lilies and, once I settled into the pew, I was comforted to see the names of my departed friends printed in the back of our bulletin. Morning light spilled in through the long side windows and I enjoyed seeing my neighbors, who are rarely out of their jeans, dressed in their colorful clothes. The little girls, especially, seemed proud in their frocks, in all the colors of the Easter eggs.

And so, we rose together and sang and the minister delivered her message, the cheerful news that there is hope after dark hours. This particular service always goes by too fast and, for my taste, it can never provide enough of the happy music. After the last note was played and the words of blessing spoken, I went forward to the lilies and chose four. I clasped them around like a bushel and made my way down the aisle. Others carried lilies, too, and so we undressed the church and brought the fragrance and the sheer whiteness outside, into the sun.

On the lawn, we stood and talked, for we do not see enough of each other, and then I set the pots onto the back seat of my car and started off, my wagon filled with that special Easter scent. I delivered two to friends who were recently widowed and I kept two. I placed them in my kitchen and held the aroma there for as long as they bloomed, which, in this case, was well into May. By that time, it felt safe and so I took them to my new house, where I would be moving soon. I planted them there, in the east light, beside the back door. People say these plants that come to us in pots from greenhouses in California won't survive outdoors. They say it's not the right climate here for lilies like these.

In the next couple of months, while I began to tear the new house apart, the leaves of these lilies turned brown at the tips and in general the plants looked poorly. I was too busy to tend them and felt it had probably been foolish to plant them. It wasn't until September that I saw a change. The leaves turned a vigorous green with a distinct sheen. One day I walked in through the back door and caught a sweet scent that I at first had trouble identifying. It reminded me of another time, something special. I went back outside to see what this was and saw at once the white trumpets, four of them, facing east, broadcasting the fragrance of Easter into the autumn air.

APRIL 1999

A Dog's Name

PEOPLE THINK that I named my dog Mayday because she was born on the first of May. She wasn't. She was born on February 20 which, in New Hampshire that year, was the day of the presidential primaries. In honor of that, all the puppies in her litter of miniature schnauzers were named after the aspiring candidates. Female puppies were named for candidates' wives. Mayday, then, was originally named Sabina, after the wife of Steve Forbes, champion of the Flat Tax. I wanted a different name but, as time passed, I sorted through a host of names but none of them seemed right.

I was to claim her in April and so on the appointed day, I woke up and the first word that came into my head was "mayday." I lay there for a while, wondering what that meant and suddenly realized it was to be the dog's name. However, I envisioned it as *"m'aidez,"* French for "help me" and the derivation of our word "mayday," military code for emergency. I was not thinking of the emergency so much as the help. I had decided to get a puppy because I was depressed. Dune, the terrier who had been the dog my husband and I shared, was then 15 and frail. I dreaded her leaving. And so I thought that a puppy could help. I picked Mayday from her seven siblings because she hopped out of the box and jumped all over me. Some of the other puppies tried to do the same but lacked the zest. The others continued to sleep. I liked this girl's eagerness.

And so she became Mayday, or *m'aidez*. I don't very often spell her name out but, from the start, she was more of an emergency than a cry for help. First, she chewed up a stick of firewood and clogged her innards enough to require triage. Next she consumed a small rug and we had to go through that all over again. In her first year, a large black lab lunged at her and tore her throat. Big emergency. I began to picture her with a small whirling red light on top of her head. She became infested with more than one thousand ticks, prompting the vet on call that weekend to remark that in his 35 years of practice on Cape Cod, he had never seen anything like that. More recently, she was mauled by two large and vicious dogs, causing another ambulance-style ride to the vet's. Other instances have been less medically oriented. She once followed a jogger almost five miles down the road to the next town — just enjoying the run — causing me and my two friends to wander several hours across woods and fields, calling *Mayday! Mayday*! — the three of us feeling we were not only calling to her but expressing our feelings as well. And the time she got loose from her leash on board the ferry to Block Island. As a result of my running after her, calling her name, we almost caused the boat to halt and turn back to shore.

Can a name determine one's fate? Sailors sometimes believe that about the names they give their boats. I wonder what kind of dog Mayday would have been if I'd kept the name Sabina.

MAY 2006

No Greater Mystery

M Y MOTHER WAS terrified of thunderstorms. We lived in a valley that caught storms and kept them. Whenever thunder rumbled in the distance and yellow light flickered through the curtains, she would herd my sister and me into the center of the house where we would sit, gathered in her arms, through the storm. Huddled together on the staircase, she would tell us about the time she was in a house when it was struck by lightning, how the blazing bolt shot down the chimney, snaked around the room, and connected with the chandelier that burst into a thousand shards. To me, there was no greater mystery, nothing more fearsome than lightning.

In kind, I spent the early years of my married life sitting out thunderstorms on the cellar stairs. Even the sight of lightning evoked fear in me. My husband, who moved through storms without noticing them, found this amusing. As I grew older, I gradually lost the intense fear my mother had instilled in me. Although I'd envisioned that house she told us about so frequently, I truly believed I'd been there when the chandelier exploded; the truth was, I had never *personally* witnessed a lightning bolt up close.

In more recent years I've been moving closer to the storms, observing them from the window and even on occasion sitting on the screened porch, watching them come out of the west; the powerful black clouds eclipsing the pale humid skies, the rumbling thumping march of the thunder coming closer, the telegraph of light, frantically signaling the coming storm. From my chair on the porch, I watch the corn rows in my garden, the tangle of tomato vines; the upturned broccoli heads dance in the quickening light.

The past few years, what this has signaled more than anything has been water — water for the gardens. The dryness here has been worrisome since our old well prevents me from really watering in a dry spell. It simply doesn't draw enough water. So I rely on soaker hoses and rain barrels and other innovative methods of getting moisture to my plants. Because of this, I've come to anticipate thunderstorms, almost eagerly, I'm reluctant to say.

As they were in the valley where I grew up, the storms here are strong. Not many years ago, the Chesham church steeple was struck and badly damaged. Lightning blasted a hole as big as five men in a barn roof not far down the road. Last summer a house in the next town went up in smoke from a lightning strike. My mother's story has not faded; in fact it is buttressed by these tragic events. Yet somehow my fear has been transformed to wonder. I still believe it is wise to be wary of thunderstorms. But I have a different image now when the storm is raging. I no longer think of the reckless bolt of light blasting down the chimney. I imagine the lightning grounding out into the earth, out near the garden. I imagine light touching the roots. I sense something nourishing about it, not just water but energy. When the storm's fireworks have given their grand finale and the drumbeat passes into the distance, I go out into the garden and walk the rows, checking for wind damage. Usually there is none — only a glow, a sheen to the leaves. It's all in my imagination, of course, but I feel my vegetables have been charged, given a new burst of strength from the storm. I feel it, too. There is still no greater mystery.

JULY 1994

When Haying Meant Love

WONDER HOW MANY courtships began on a hayfield? My husband's and mine did. "I'm haying tonight, if you'd like to ride along," he used to suggest, and that evening, with the late summer sun giving the field a deep angle of light, I found myself riding beside him on the axle of his old, faded red Farmall, the tines of the tedder whirling behind us: *ca-chunk, ca-chunk, ca-chunk.* "Isn't this relaxing?" Paul would say. "I can't think of anything more relaxing than this." We moved at a stately pace, turning the cut grass into rows.

As anyone who has ever hayed well knows, haying is anything but relaxing. Hectic and nerve-racking are words I hear most often in regard to haying season. First you wait for the right moment to cut, when the grass is ripe but not gone by. Then you wait for a stretch of dry weather. Even on the fairest of days, hot weather can change in an instant. Beyond that, it's just hard work, all of it, ending the long evening stacking bales onto the truck in the light of the headlights. But as we wheeled around the rows, talking our shy talk above the clattering sound of the harvest machinery, it seemed like the best kind of work at the best time of year. What could be better than this, he seemed to say: the smell of fresh-cut alfalfa, the cooling breezes of a summer evening, the feeling that a harvest has been gained this time around. Not only the harvest but maybe even a kiss.

That was almost twenty years ago, a long time anyway, and my husband is gone and that field now grows houses. Still, there is another hayfield surrounding our barn, a small but lush field of golden timothy. A neighbor takes the hay from that field now. I refer to him as the phantom farmer. In the spring I can see by the wide imprints of the tractor tires through the new growth of the emerald grass that he's been there to fertilize the field, not alfalfa but horse hay. The summer passes. He cares to take only one cut from this field, from which my husband would have taken three helpings. The stalks grow high and tawny, then tassel off, bending to the slightest breezes: the quintessential hayfield. Grasshoppers abound as do their grating songs. I watch the grass and wonder. When will he come? Some years I think he has forgotten or perhaps he doesn't need the hay this year. And then I think of the snow coming down, pressing the long grasses against the cold earth, which saddens me.

It's always late, but at last he comes. If I'm lucky, I'll be there, working in the barn. I can hear the distant sound of his John Deere, closer and closer. Is he coming here? I watch from the window until I see the gleaming green machine turn in. He lowers the mower deck and engages the blade. The tractor is fast, and even at a distance the cutter blades are deafening. A conversation onboard that tractor would be impossible. He wears ear protectors and takes the corners like a stock-car driver. When the cut is finished, he wheels out onto the road and speeds down toward his farm without looking back.

As the day passes, he returns, first pushing the hay into rows and then, with the tedder, spreading it back out into the sun for a second drying. The method is all the same. What is already perfect cannot be perfected. And then, with the sun low at that magic angle, he's here again with his high-speed baler and his wagons and his daughters, who are stronger than boys. Together they load, and in the last rays of the sun, they are gone. They are so quick that I am lucky if I see any of this. More often, I leave the field and its tall, nodding grasses, and when I return, it is shorn to a flattop. I can't imagine how he does it so fast. My dog, Mayday, goes right out and rolls in the new stubble as if to say, well, finally. I stare at it and feel like an old woman, remembering a time when haying meant love.

AUGUST 1996

Something Big Passed By

WHEN THE TORNADO came through Chesham one sultry July afternoon, I happened to be sitting at my typewriter inside the old train depot. I felt the ground shudder and heard a great roar. My hands froze on the keys and my ears popped. Perhaps for a split second I believed that a big train had come through, for that is what it was like, a thunderous, quaking rush of sound, as if the air around us had been sucked away and then brought back. But the tracks that passed by the station had long since been taken up. Still, there was no doubt: Something big had just passed by. I leapt to the window and saw the yellow sky.

In no time, I was in my car, racing toward home. It had been a hot, muggy morning, and I had left our dog, Dune, tied up outside. Now lightning divided the sky. At the house the treetops waved and rain fell in sheets. Dune was gone. In fact, her tie-up lay on the ground, not as if pulled by force but as if someone had untied her and set her free. I walked about in the storming woods, calling *"Dune!"* The wind was shrill and my words were snuffed out before they could leave my lips.

Back in the car, I drove to where my husband, Paul, a carpenter, was working. I told him that Dune was gone. He left his tools where they were and came home with me to search for her. There was still thunder and lightning, and the winds were so high we could not hear ourselves speak. Still, we walked through the woods, calling to our friend, a white terrier mix. Even as a puppy, her ears folded against her head, soft white triangles that waved like wings when she ran.

Tornadoes come seldom to this part of the world, and when they do, meteorologists seem reluctant to call them by that name. "Downblast" is a popular term. But if we can believe the story of Dorothy and Toto, this must have been a tornado. The hay farmer on the ridge reported that a wagon of hay he'd been loading was picked up by the wind and carried 20 or 30 feet before being set down gently, the hay exactly as he had loaded it. Another resident told of his car being lifted and then set down. No damage. On the other side of town, a young couple experienced the terror of having their roof ripped off and the grove of maple trees beside their house scattered like pick-up sticks.

For three days, while we listened to our neighbors'stories, we waited for Dune to come home. During the day we pushed our way through the wind-whipped woods, calling for her. At night we went out with flashlights, shouting, *Dune! Dune!* — her name carried off into the darkness like the pitiful, mystical human cries that they were. In return came only the moan of the wind.

On the fourth day we woke up to stillness. The wind had finally died. Standing outside the front door, we heard a distant bark. It was Dune. We set off into our woods, walking with sure feet toward the welcome sound of her voice. About a quarter of a mile away, in dense undergrowth, we found her, trapped inside a tangle of vines. Did she yank herself free in fear of the great train of wind that passed through our station that sultry afternoon? Or did the tornado carry her up into the sky like the hay wagon and set her down here, in the thicket? We had walked past this place several times in our search, but we had not seen her. Was she here all along, or was she gone for three days, traveling a yellow brick road with a tin man and a soft-hearted lion? She has never said. But ever since, when the wind rises, her ears wing out and she gets a certain faraway look in her eyes. *Toto?* I say, and she comes to me and buries her head in my arms.

JULY 1998

Blueberry Lust

HAVE ALWAYS wanted to grow blueberries. We have good sandy loam here, slightly acidic and well drained — perfect for blueberries. Because my friends and neighbors have such treasure troves, it is easy for me to imagine my patch, the bushes high, and mature, the berries at eye level, clusters of dusty blue orbs easily coaxed into my basket. They would grow beautifully in this soil, in this place. There would be plenty, such a wealth that I could probably gather enough to eat freely of them all summer, keep my freezer full for winter pancakes, and maybe even sell some boxes at the local store. But every year, I plant tomatoes and melons there instead and think to myself: next year, *blueberries!*

Blueberries are something of a local celebrity. Just about everyone has them growing, wild or purposefully, in the yard or farther afield. Yet every summer, my annual vision of my own private patch yields to the hunt, as the berries come due and we go out with buckets and that rare appetite known as blueberry lust. There are several favorite destinations.

About a mile from here, up on top of a hill, is an overgrown farm with highbush blueberries growing like puckerbrush. If you know where it is, you know you can go there and pick, ten cents a container. The owners are full of trust and goodwill. I go with my neighbors and we get caught up on our news as we pick. But we are focused on the berries. They are so profuse, it's like rooting through the bargain basement for the best buy: This bush is *loaded* — but no, look at *this* one! We gasp and rush from bush to bush, our efforts not to elbow each other out of a better harvest thinly veiled. If you think Filene's Basement is a scene, you should visit here on our hilltop some sultry summer evening and see what goes on. When we are finished, we gratefully dump dimes into the pot that sits nobly on a rock and, sated warriors, we carry our spoils home.

I like it there, but it must be what hunting at a game preserve would be like: a bit tame. And the competition is so close by, so present. It lacks tranquility. I like the illusion of solitude for my hunt. My preference is the lake and my boat. I suit up for the journey: bathing suit and old sneakers. I load my flat-bottomed rowboat with plastic containers and set forth by oar. There are islands in the lake where nobody lives. Blueberry bushes lurk high and low amid the foliage, the berries visible only to the trained and hungry eye. I know the good spots. In the early morning, I row across the water, which is flat and quiet, to the first island. I step out of the boat into the cool shallows, tie the painter to a blueberry branch, and begin, wading as I pick. I am kept company by loons and great blue herons who enjoy the early mornings as much as I do. I pick rapidly, efficiently, filling the containers and sealing them with tightly fitting lids to avoid the ultimate berry-picker's heartache: a full bucket, spilled.

I move from place to place, sometimes drifting alongside the shoreline, where branches bend over the water. It's an idyllic harvest, a morning well spent. My job is always over well before the bushes are picked clean. I can't make a dent in this crop. When I'm done, I take the boat back out in the open water, where a breeze is beginning to stir. I let the boat float free while I feast on berries and drink hot tea from my thermos. At home, I freeze the rest, plan the next excursion, and wonder why I would ever want blueberries growing in my backyard.

AUGUST 1995

❀ Dad's Garden

N ONE OF the family albums is a picture of me and my father. I am ten years old and hefting a big, round watermelon. I am smiling and so is my dad. We grew the watermelon together.

My father loved to garden. When my sister and I were quite young, he dug up a narrow strip beside his garden and designated it ours. This made me feel very grown up. Of course, our father continued to cultivate the complicated things like tomatoes and peppers and peas. For us, he bought the simpler seeds — cucumbers and watermelons and zinnias, seeds that will grow almost in spite of what you do to them. The zinnias and the watermelons gave the greatest rewards — the zinnias for the brilliant neon colors and the watermelons because they were so much fun, delicious to eat, and it was always exhilarating to spit those seeds at each other.

My father had showed us where the rakes and the spades hung in the garage and taught us how to weed. He had a two-pronged long-necked fork, and with it he showed us how to prize the roots out of the earth so that the whole weed came up, leaving no tendrils to take root. We worked side by side, he in his patch, we in ours, and occasionally he'd cross over for a bit of coaching. For my father, weeding must have been a pleasant pastime or maybe even some sort of solace. He would often come home from work, get into his bathing suit, go for a swim in the pond, and then slowly work his way back up the hill, pulling weeds, his bare back browning in the sun. He wanted them all out, every one. It was as if he were excising the evils of the world, leaving the good. My mother would call him for dinner, but he'd have to be called twice, three times sometimes, before he'd rise up and leave the weeding at last.

I think of this now, when I see the picture, and realize that most everything I do in my garden harks back to my dad. My garden now is huge, out of control, you might say (I have everything but watermelons — they take up too much space). And, to my chagrin, there are weeds. Whenever he came to visit, my father would survey the garden and tell me how amazing it was that I could grow things so well, as if he had never accomplished anything even close. But then, a while later, I would usually look out the south window and see him, bent in my garden, getting after those weeds.

A few years ago, my parents moved into a smaller place. Outside the sliding-glass door of the porch was a narrow patch of grass. My father dug it up the first spring they were there. He planted lemon lilies. He put tomatoes in a barrel and coaxed peas to climb against the siding. This, his last garden, was a strip not much bigger than the one he'd deeded to my sister and me when we were children.

My father died the next spring. There was still snow on the ground when we gathered for the funeral. Outside the glass doors, we could see the stalks of his last year's Brussels sprouts rising out of the snow. We talked about the way he made things grow. He had other accomplishments in life, but we kept coming back to his garden. Among his things I found the two-pronged fork and took it home with me. When the snow melted and the ground was right, in a small corner of my garden I planted watermelons.

AUGUST 1994

The Rain Barrel

SINCE AUGUST is our dry month and I don't have the benefit of a bottomless well (or that strange commodity known as municipal water), I have, over the years, tried various tricks to give my plants more water without actually using more water. I've discovered that this sleight of hand is easier than I might have thought.

My initial discovery about keeping a garden watered was that the least efficient (and possibly most counterproductive) method of watering is to actually water the garden, as in turn on the hose and aim it at the garden as a whole. When I was growing up, my father would get out the sprinkler, hook it up to the garden hose, and turn on the faucet. And then go about his business. (He *did* have municipal water.) The sprinkler would spurt along, tirelessly bestowing water on the famished garden. Every once in a while, my father would move the sprinkler and a new section of the garden would flood, small pools forming here and there beneath the tomato vines. When he was done, the plants shimmered like jewels.

A few years back, I read in one of my gardening journals that if you water a garden in that manner, for several hours, the water barely penetrates the earth. I could hardly believe it. So I went out and watered my parched square of garden soil for quite a long time. When I finally turned the water off, I went into the patch, where the leaves glistened and the earth was dark with refreshing moisture. With my spade I dug down. It was true. Less than an inch into the soil, the earth was dry. Of course, for me this is all rather a moot point. Even if I wanted to water in this fashion, I could not. For one thing, the garden is too far from the house, and for another, my well would run dry.

From that point on, I tried various methods, including planting my squash and pumpkins in old tires and then, when that proved less than satisfactory, burying large perforated containers filled with water near the roots of my plants.

Soaker hoses were next. I had a rather good, long affair with them, but in the end they proved too cumbersome when it came time to till and weed. One false move with the hoe or tiller and my watering system was severed. After a few years and going through more soaker hoses than I care to count, I forsook that method. I still use them in small, accessible places, but keeping my August garden green remained elusive. Then came the rain barrel. An old-timey method repackaged as a big green plastic barrel. I spotted it in a gardening catalog, and in spite of the fearsome price of $100, I sent off my order. It was rugged and well designed, with a screen top to keep out debris and a hose at the bottom for gravity-feed flow. I hooked up a gutter to the barn beside the garden and aimed the downspout into the barrel.

There it is. My source of water for the garden. It holds 75 gallons, and even a good thundershower fills it up. It solves all my problems, or so I like to think. Around each plant I dig a small trench to hold the water in. In the evening, before dark, I go out to the garden and take up the watering can. From the barrel, I fill up the can and begin my chore. The heat of the day is gone, and I am alone with my garden as it begins to revive. I feel a kinship with my friends on islands in the Caribbean who rely on gutters and cisterns for their water. My thrifty Scot soul stirs a bit as I marvel at the fact that this water was mine for the gathering. Of course, the water from my well costs me nothing, unless you count the complicated assembly of pump and pipe that brings it up from the ground to my sink and tub. The rain barrel is so simple. It saves the rain for a sunny day. Why didn't I think of that to begin with?

AUGUST 1998

Best Motorized Zucchini

I N THIS TOWN, above all others, the very mention of zucchini raises a chuckle, a snide remark. I say that because we had, for a few years running, something known as the International Zucchini Festival, held right here in our town center. The event was a fund-raiser for Harrisville's day-care center. It raised a lot of money, as I recall, and was so successful that it had to be moved out of town. Harrisville (population 930) just wasn't big enough to accommodate all the world's zucchini lovers. Or, were they zucchini haters?

The festival did the squash up in ways never before dreamed of. There were zucchinis dressed up like babies, there were zucchinis made into canoes and into racing cars (a.k.a. Best Motorized Zucchini), and zucchinis as sculpture. The Zucchini Look-Alike Contest. There was even a wedding album, photo after photo, of two zucchinis getting married. If you wanted a good laugh, you went to the festival, held at the end of every summer. It came to be known that many people around here were growing these zucchinis specifically for the contests, grooming them, pumping them full of water, doing whatever weird thing they could think of just so they might come to the attention of the judges. Folks talked about needing roof racks in order to transport their proudest zucchini to the fair, and when the festival was over, there was a rash of zucchini pranks — leaving the overgrown and grotesque vegetable on neighbors' doorsteps or stopping by at midnight and secreting the wretched and incredibly heavy things into the front seats of your best friend's car.

In all, it was an interesting era in Harrisville's history, one which seems to have all but passed us by. Almost.

What remains is the myth, the Incredible Zucchini Myth, that this squash is nothing but a joke. The odd thing is that this all came out of what could have been seen as the wonderful discovery that this vegetable is so versatile — and so prolific. At some point, probably in the late seventies, recipe columns became jammed with concoctions that could include zucchini: soups, breads, hors d'oeuvres, relishes, chutneys, pickles, my goodness, even chocolate cake could be made from zucchini. No longer just a little side-dish vegetable, this Italian hybrid had become Super Vegetable. It was ridiculous, all the things you could do with this little old squash, which is about when the idea for this festival came about. I remain, then, a minority, here in this town at least. I never crack jokes about zucchini, and I grow the stuff with pride. In fact, I am one of this vegetable's loyal defenders. I consider it to be one of my most reliable summer crops. Zucchini is one of the few things that I raise and eat daily throughout the summer. I never put it up (except once I made relish from it that was actually very good) so that when the summer ends, so ends also the zucchini.

The trick is, unlike my fair-going, prize-touting, neighbors, I never let it get too big. Every morning I go out to the garden and nip off a couple of new zukes. They come in overnight (it is true that they are relentless). New like this, they are small and dark almost black green, slightly tapered — beautiful! They chop up nicely into the evening's salad or I slice them and stir-fry with onions and tamari. And the chocolate cake? The best. It's a three-month bonanza for this pitifully defamed vegetable. Trouble is, I've always got much more than I can eat. So I try meekly to offer my extras to my neighbors. It's not nice what they say to me.

SEPTEMBER 1995

🌀 Sleeping Under Glass

ONE OF MY MOST vivid memories of my growing-up years is that of sleeping in a potting shed. I was seven and my sister was eight. My aunt and uncle had built a new house on the North Shore of Boston, on land that had once been a part of a large estate. The piece of land they had bought included the estate's old potting shed and its attached greenhouse. Since their new house wasn't all that big, and since the gardens that went with the potting shed were nothing but windswept grass, my aunt decided the shed would make a nifty guest house. It was a good-sized little shed and it even had plumbing. So she swept out the gardening debris, puttied up the greenhouse windows, and moved in the furniture. When we came to visit, we settled into this interesting space. There wasn't a pot in sight, not to mention a flower or a trowel. My parents slept in the shed, which had rugs on the wooden floors and curtains in the windows, and my sister and I slept in the attached (narrow) greenhouse, in beds set end to end with a lamp in between. The floor was brick, chinked with beach sand, and I remember the feeling of the bricks and the sand on my feet when we got in or out of bed. And the peculiar light that dawned on us first thing in the morning. At night we would read in bed before going to sleep and then turn out the light and look up at the stars. It was the next best thing to sleeping outdoors, but we were under that protective glass, meant to make us grow.

Maybe it was that experience, sleeping under glass, that made me love potting sheds so much. In my adult life I have always wanted one. On this property, which was never an estate but once a chicken farm, there is a shed, one that was moved here from the railroad station across the way. I'm told that this shed once housed the hand-carts used to repair the tracks, and if that isn't true, I don't want to know about it because I like that snippet of history so very much. When we bought this place, the shed was crammed with machine parts and old tools, enormous bolts and metal rods of all description. And grease. But on the outside it was dear, a little square cottagelike building with shuttered windows, shiny tin siding, and a black cast-iron stovepipe emerging from the roof.

When I scouted the new property for a garden site, I found that the very best location just happened to be beside this shed, groaning as it was with the weight of the machine age. This, I decreed, would one day be my potting shed. And I set to work.

One little project at a time, it has taken years to make this into a shed for the garden. Sills have been replaced and the big sliding door rebuilt. Over the years, men who know about such things have come and, at my bidding, helped themselves to the apparently valuable tractor parts. Last year I finally emptied the last of the rusted pieces from the back corners, replaced the broken window, and swept the rugged, grease-stained plank floors clean. On the walls I hung up rakes, spades, forks, and pruning shears. And on the shelves that once sagged with engine oil, I lined up my clay pots, even the ones I never use. It feels good just to have them out where I can see them.

It's a bit like a dream come true to have a potting shed. What's missing still is a greenhouse, which I could add on to the south side of the shed and get seedlings started in those chilly spring months. But I can't seem to clear myself of the idea of putting a bed in the corner, and a reading lamp, maybe. The stars are pretty bright here, and I hear they can make you grow.

JUNE 1997

Mayday! Mayday!

Dogs and gardens do not mix. So say a number of my friends, admittedly those who are not afflicted with that lifelong illness: puppy love. Last year at about this time I got myself a new puppy. For the record, I have a dog, a 15-year-old terrier mix named Dune. Her hair is white, and it hangs down around her sad brown eyes like a curtain. Dune has been my gardening companion all these years. We had to work on it a bit. When she was very young, she thought digging in fresh-turned garden soil was better than the juiciest bone. I taught her the command, "Out of the garden!" and eventually, after a few disasters, she got the idea. When it's time to plant, or time to weed, or when it's time to just *be* in the garden, I always take Dune out with me. There is a certain harmony to it. She roots around in the grasses that grow high around the patch and pounces on little critters that I cannot even see — grasshoppers and ants and anything that moves — and I root around in the rows and pounce on the weeds, which are quite easy to see.

But knowing that Dune was coming to the far end of her life span, I felt I should get a puppy to come up behind her. Eventually I found the puppy I wanted, a little schnauzer with a thick salt-and-pepper coat, coal-black eyes and nose, and pointy ears that come up from behind her head like a devil's horns.

I named her Mayday and I found out as she grew, her name was more appropriate than that. *Mayday!* is what I say when she barrels into the garden, all 20 pounds of her, a blur of energy and enthusiasm and sheer will. *Mayday!* is what I cry when I come home and find the damage.

May, of course, is also planting time. It was as if she came just in time. Like Dune, Mayday took to the garden like a magnet. Mornings, she zooms straight outside, directly into the rich dark square of new earth and begins to rummage. More lettuce seedlings than I can count have fallen to her small but energetic paws. *"Out of the garden!"* seems to mean something more like, *"Go for it, Mayday! Have a ball!"*

Planting with Mayday was so disastrous that I had to exclude her altogether. She stayed inside, crying softly behind the door, while Dune and I laid out the rows and pressed seeds into the earth. However, as the summer widened, I caved in and Mayday joined us. Her favorite part seems to be weeding. When I am out there pulling up the offenders, she waits for me to toss the uprooted plant into a pile. She grabs it by the roots with gusto, growling and hurling it into the air and then catching it, worrying it furiously like dead prey, until I flip another one. She leaps for the new corpse and begins the punishment all over again, furious, determined, officious — *murderous.* With a particularly large one, she dashes off into the field, looking back at me as if she is making off with stolen goods.

I feel like the proverbial grandparent. Dune never got away with such nonsense. She was firmly reprimanded whenever she set foot into my carefully tended rows. And she learned so well that now she never crosses the line between grass and furrow. She knows. Mayday, my devil dog, likes the garden and wants to be in it, wants to be part of it. I know what that is all about. Besides, weeding with such an accomplice is satisfying. Until I saw her do it, I had no idea that I would love to be able to do that to my weeds, snap their necks and carry them off to their graves.

MAY 1997

🌸 A Matter of Thrift

ONE OF THE THINGS I love best about America is yard sales. What could be more egalitarian than a yard sale? My husband and I furnished our first house by going to yard sales. In fact, I've rarely bought furniture from a furniture store. Why would anyone, I always wonder, when there is so much perfectly wonderful *stuff* to be had from your neighbors?

Aside from the appealingly thrifty aspect of yard sales, there are the associations made with each item. I have a high wooden bookcase here in my office that I bought off a lawn in Hinsdale probably 23 years ago for $10. Over the years, I've painted it three different colors, yet I rarely look at it but that the yard and its tall, thin owner don't come to mind. One of my favorite spades came from a place in Vermont. When I look at that smooth, worn handle, I see that man's hands. I have a sky-blue teapot with a doughnut hole in the center that I bought for a dollar from a sale in Ashuelot one day in, probably, 1975. Tea from that pot always makes me think of that spring day, when the river was high in its banks and the old man had his table out in the yard with those few vases. And the teapot. Virtually every chair, every bowl, every tablecloth that I own brings to mind a face or a front lawn or a day, often a day when it was sunny and warm, the kind of weather that smells like a bargain.

It's a rite of passage that has yet to be recognized: go to yard sales diligently for the first 20 years of your married life and then spend the next 20 holding yard sales to unburden yourself.

That second phase took me by surprise. I just couldn't *move* anymore, there was so much in the house, and in the shed, and in the attic. It's like children growing up. All of a sudden, that's *it!* Everybody *out!*

Last year, in the spring, I decided that on Labor Day weekend I would hold a yard sale. That gave me the summer to get ready. First and foremost, I made a vow of yard-sale-chastity. Then I marked a corner of the shed "yard-sale items," and all summer long I placed things there as I mentally culled my collection. On rainy weekends, I sorted through drawers and boxes. In sane and sober moments, I appraised my shelves, groaning with books and tobacco tins and teapots, and took down everything that no longer charmed me. I even looked with raised eyebrow at my doughnut-hole teapot. But passed over it (for now).

The nights leading up to Labor Day, I was up late, pricing and labeling. I fell into bed late and rose early, muscles aching. On the night before, I set the sawhorses up in the driveway and placed boards on top of them. I went through my checklist: prices marked — check; signs posted — check; plenty of spare change — check; nail apron for cash — check; athlete's water bottle for quick refreshment — check. I covered the tables with old (but colorful) bedsheets and arranged the items shrewdly. I positioned the "Everything for 25¢" box in a high-visibility spot. And went to bed.

In the morning, still in my slippers, I put the flame on under the kettle and glanced out the window. It wasn't even seven o'clock and my yard was filled with people poking around. I threw on my clothes and lurched out the door.

That's pretty much the way the day went. Actually, it was like a blur, a blur of making change and answering questions and deciding that, no, I will not take a dollar for that perfectly good toaster oven. It was a full day that netted me $177.25 and left my house a whole lot lighter.

Perfect. An apron full of cash and two days left in the three-day weekend — to check out the other yard sales.

SEPTEMBER 1996

🌀 Waiting for the Stars to Fall

UGUST IS THE MONTH for shooting stars, and last August the newspapers promised us the "sky show of the decades" with hundreds of meteors a minute. It was as though the circus were coming to town. We put the date on our calendar and made plans. This whirl of shooting stars wasn't scheduled to pass through our skies until late, midnight or after. Even with the one weak streetlight out by the road, we can usually see all we want of the sky. Earlier in the summer, the comet known as Hyakutake had come through. This was the comet that everyone described as a big wet snowball, and it was easily seen here just by standing outside in the garden. Night after night we stood out in the warm evening and watched it move across the sky, a slow-motion blur. Its furry tail tapered to a point as if to describe the speed of its travel, and yet it took a month for it to move from horizon to horizon — a leisurely pass from one end of eternity to the other.

But these shooting stars would pass like lightning. As if for a special holiday, I invited friends to join me for late-night viewing of the celestial fireworks. Before dark we set chairs and cushions out on the big stone patio beside the roses. We lingered on the porch over a late evening meal and watched the time until midnight. It felt like New Year's Eve, waiting for the ball to drop. We would gladly have gone to bed, but the thought of the stars kept us up. After midnight we went outside. As we stepped into the darkness, a star streaked across the sky. "Look!" we cried and pointed upward. We settled into our stargazing seats. We propped up our feet and turned our faces to the sky — a great luminous spattering of stars across the inky blackness. We oriented ourselves to the familiar shapes of the constellations: Big Dipper, Cassiopeia, Perseus. A bright light streaked across the sky — *"Wow!"* we cried. Another came in from the east, an arc of white. We hooted and clapped. Out of the corners of our eyes came another, and we turned to watch as it plunged like dropped fire toward earth. *"Bravo!"* We felt like voyagers now, navigating the river of stars.

Between displays we talked quietly but kept our eyes glued to the heavens. Every movement caught our eyes. Twice we saw planes and thought they were stars. Our gasps turned to laughter. The silence of the night enveloped us, and the darkness played tricks with our eyes. In the moonless night, we felt blind and longed for a streak of light.

The night wore on. August is hot but the nights can be cold, and this one was particularly so. I went inside for blankets, and we wrapped ourselves like mummies in our chairs. Dew fell on us like misty rain. At one point we thought the sky had clouded over, but it was the dew settling on our glasses. Where were these thousands of meteors? Perhaps it was not late enough. We kept on, our eyes trained on the same old stars stuck in their places. From the tree line an owl hooted. The roses were fragrant beside us. Lying as we were, looking upward, there was a definite sense of gravity, a sense of what holds us to this earth.

We began to grumble. The show was not as advertised. We wanted our money back! At last, chilled to the bone, we gathered our blankets and went in, our faces wet from the dew, our necks stiff from looking up. What a disappointment, yes indeed. Not the "sky show of the decades," not even the night of shooting stars, but instead a long night of anticipation with few rewards. Unless you count the quiet company of friends, the scent of roses through the darkness, and the silence in the middle of the night, so rarely experienced.

AUGUST 1997

❧ The Smell of Snow

WHAT BETTER STORM is there than a snowstorm, a mighty blizzard? No one (but the perverse) looks forward to a tornado or a hurricane or torrential rains. But a good, solid Northeaster, snow for two days, maybe three? The anticipation for the first real storm of the season is better than Christmas.

Hours before the snow begins, I can smell it, the most peculiar of all odors, more like a sensation than an actual scent. Still, it comes in through the nose, the cold dampness, the gray stillness, the heavy skies, an impending presence, closer and closer. Still in the earth are carrots and parsnips and beets, the last of the potatoes, a whole row of leeks and the brilliant emerald hedge of parsley. With my basket I go out across the brown lawn in my black rubber boots. Using my favorite fork, I dig the potatoes, careful not to spear them. I put them in the bottom of the basket and then dig the carrots and the beets, whose greens have withered but which are still hard and a wonderful deep red, almost black. A wind has started, and the smell of snow grows stronger. I am planning a stew as I dig, thinking of the warmth inside the kitchen. I pull the leeks and cut the parsley, a small portion of which I will add to the stew, but the rest I will snip down and freeze in small bags. I leave the parsnips to be pulled in the spring. There it is: the end, my garden a barren stretch of earth, flat but for the wisps of the parsnip tops.

I go to the fence and take down the bird houses. On some dark January day, I will spread newspaper on the kitchen table and sit down beside the stove and paint these little houses, where sparrows and wrens and finches and bluebirds live through the summer months. They are my company in my garden, my cheerleaders. As I work, they swoop above me like the great aerialists they are, an air show that features not only barrel rolls and figure eights but songs, little cheering songs that seem to be telling me how happy they are that I am there, that we are there together, in the garden.

From the edge of the garden, I carry the big white painted chair into the shed, already stacked high with the winter's wood. The other two chairs go in as well. I take down the clothesline, and using my elbow, I coil it and hang it inside on a nail beside the garden chairs. Using the wheelbarrow, I bring in all the porch furniture. The table and the couch are too large to carry, so I push them tight against the house wall and cover them with plastic, knowing the snow will drift in during heavy storms.

With good warning and that strong scent to spur me, I work quickly against the track of the storm. When I've done it all, I take one last walk around the yard to see what I have missed. Ah, the bird bath. I bring it in to rest with the chairs for the winter.

It's a big storm coming, they say on the evening news. A green blob marches toward us on the radar screen. They show us scenes of the city folk going to the grocery store to stock up on milk and bread, batteries and jugs of water. Everyone seems excited about this first storm, even the reporters who stand at the end of the checkout and ask such questions as: "Are you ready for the storm?" I have filled my lamps with kerosene, and new candles are in the candlesticks. Inside my kitchen, I am cutting the beets and potatoes and carrots into chunks and sliding them into the big pot, where cubes of meat have already browned. I've got the flames in the cookstove licking up the stovepipe. The room is warm, and instead of snow I smell herbs and the simmer of sweet meat. I glance out the window. It is almost dark, and I see that the snow has already begun to fall.

DECEMBER 1996

❧ Ice Flowers

I N MIDWINTER, windows become of interest. Back in the 1970s we were bombarded with frightening information such as the statement that 40 percent of a house's heat is lost through its single-pane windows. And so now most of us have windows that are double- and triple-glazed, windows thicker and more impervious to the elements than walls. This is an old house so, short of replacing all the windows, we put in storm windows, the newer version with screens that slide down in the summer and extra windows that slide into place in winter. They do the job, though they're not as sleek as new double-glazed windows. We are snug behind them in winter, and we don't need extra sweaters anymore when we sit near a window. They are efficient and we are warmer and our heating bills are lower. But there is one thing that we miss with these window walls: Back before we changed the windows, incredible works of art grew on the inside of our windows, especially at night, when the temperature dropped below zero. We could watch the pattern grow, tiny needles of ice making their way across the glass, like brush strokes creating an incredible silver canvas of cold.

On warm days, the ice patterns would melt and water would bead up on the pane. But at night, the painting would return with the cold, and we would read the designs like clouds, seeing feathers and ferns, lace and doilies, palm fronds, star bursts and pinwheels, birds in flight. Through this windowpane fantasy, ice and cold became masters of creativity.

We discovered that if we scratched a message onto the glass with razor blades, the hoary words would appear overnight. Or, if we washed the windows with a certain stroke, the next night's pattern would follow that stroke. I used to look forward to the coldest nights because I knew that in the morning, when the sun came up and shone through the bedroom window, there would be a brand-new design. It somehow made the cold more bearable. I would lie there, still snug in bed, and watch the light of the sun bring the night's frost painting alive. I thought of this window as my winter garden, where blooms came faster and more dramatically than any green plant ever could.

Years ago, in Vermont, there was a man who was fascinated by snowflakes, fascinated enough to try to preserve them. Wilson Alwyn Bentley would walk out into a fresh snowstorm in a heavy coat and stand with his arms outstretched, catching the snowflakes on a board covered with black cloth. Using his carefully constructed, blanketed camera rig, he'd photograph the flakes. A frail little man with a bristle-brush mustache who did his work in his farmyard and in his cold shed and inside his farmhouse, he became known as "Snowflake" Bentley, and he changed forever the way we think about snow and about cold. Bentley photographed not just snow-flakes, but anything cold: frost, hail, rime, sleet, and dew. He also photographed frost patterns on windowpanes. With no scientific training whatsoever, he carried this hobby on for over 40 years, and when he died in 1931, he left behind him more than 5,000 photographs of snowflakes. It is because of his work that we now maintain, with some certainty, that no two snowflakes are alike. His photographs were used to create new designs for tablecloths and window curtains. Tiffany's used his photographs to create designs for gold pendants and brooches. I use his photographs to remember the gift of our window-born frost gardens and a time when we could wake up in the morning and see the beauty of the cold from beneath our blankets, before we had to emerge into it.

JANUARY 1998

Geranium Morality

AST WINTER, on a visit to San Diego, I stepped out my motel door and saw a tree I vaguely recognized. The texture of the trunk was familiar and so were the leaves. It took a few minutes to realize that I was looking at a geranium — with the girth and stature of a tree. I should not have been surprised. The plant is a native of southern Africa, and I suppose what we think of as a geranium is some distant, hybridized cousin of the tree I was gazing upon. Or perhaps we perform a kind of bonsai on our plants and in so doing conceal their true age. I know of some people who, when winter descends, barber the plants back to the stem and set them in their cellar. When the weather warms, they bring them back upstairs for summer. I'm afraid I don't see the point.

I do grow geraniums in summer. I plant them in window boxes that hang from the sills of my garden shed and from my barn. They provide a pleasing splash of color. But I tend to forget about them in the summer rush of all else that needs tending.

For me, winter is the time when geraniums triumph, a time when they alone have my gardening attention. I have tried other plants in winter, but none suits me so well as the geranium. Perhaps it is a sentimental attachment, remembering the big, clay-potted (and probably ancient) geraniums that grew like vines against the windows of my Victorian grandmother's sunporch. Or the little yellow glazed pot in which my mother would plant a single geranium, in the fall, for her kitchen sill. The plant always started as a cutting from her mother's big vines, placed in a jar in the window where my sister and I could watch the new white roots spiral out into cloudy water.

Their geraniums were always red. White geraniums seemed like no geranium at all, and pink seemed merely a faded, failed attempt at red. If there were going to be geraniums, they needed to be red, not only red but Chinese red, cardinal red, siren red, *red-hot red!*

I once met a man who was famous for the geraniums he grew. He lived in Maine, and by the time I encountered him, he had raised geraniums for more than 60 years. He claimed that during the winter months he hardly went to bed at all, so busy was he tending the new geraniums that he would sell in pots in the spring. In the early hours of the morning, in his wood-heated greenhouse, he walked between the rows, watering, fussing, coaxing his youngsters into the splendid, upright maturity his customers had come to expect of him. He had the kind of old-fashioned geranium morality that pleased my sense of history. His creed was: always use clay pots, never plastic. Start plants from cuttings rather than seeds. Give them air, give them light. And most of all, leave them alone.

I took that last bit to heart. On the night of the first frost, I bring my geraniums in. They are a bit tuckered out from the heat of the summer, and the last of the red petals bleed to the floor. In the first days of their transition, many of the leaves wither on their stems. I pluck them off and trim the biggest branches back, leaving my fingers scented with their pungent, exotic odor. If the soil is dry, I fill the watering can, add a few drops of store-bought nutrients, and soak the roots. And then I walk away, leaving the pot to get used to its new place.

And they rest. And slowly grow. By February they have risen, the thick, scalloped leaves as big as saucers, as green and soft as velvet. The blooms are balls of African fire, a brilliant alarm against my cold, whitened windows.

FEBRUARY 1998

❊ Half Buried

L AST FALL I WAS pruning the lilacs that grow on the east side of my barn. Since they are easily fifteen feet tall, this is not a simple task, and it requires the use of a stepladder. I was making good progress, taking away the old growth to let the new shoots come in more strongly and, where I could reach, snipping off the withered blossoms to encourage better flowers next spring, I worked on one section for as far as I could reach and then moved the ladder over. When I set the legs into the grass, burned down then by frost, I spotted something underneath the earth, something a bit shiny. It is not unusual to find pieces of old bottles, broken at the neck, rusted pieces of farm equipment, even occasionally shards of pottery, in our grasses, in our fields, and most often, beside the old stone walls, where our forerunners, in their innocence, disposed of their trash. But this was not the usual find. It was thin, delicate.

With one finger, I pushed aside the dried stems. It looked like a Christmas ornament, half buried in the ground. I worked it free gently, assuming the underside would be broken. With gentle persuasion, the little ball came loose from the earth's grip. To my surprise, it was whole. Not even a crack. I turned it in my hand. The green color had faded, leaving a silver, mirror-like finish on one side and clear glass on the other. Bits of grass and earth clung to the sides, like an egg just out of its nest.

I took it inside and held it to the light. Where had it come from? How long had it been under the earth beside the barn like that? How had it survived the storms and the cold, the heat, and the rains? Did my predecessors decorate this old hay barn at Christmas-time? It seemed so unlikely. But then, so are most Christmas deco-rations here, where the midwinter is bleak. We are noted for keeping our holiday lights up longer than we need to. It isn't unusual, in mid-July, to find a wreath or two, needles red-brown, as dry as tin-der, still adorning a front door. I know of at least one family in town who continues to light their Christmas lights, long after the day has passed, long after the cold has gone. I'm not sure this is so common in other parts of the country. Why do we do it? Perhaps there is no simple explanation. Maybe we just like to keep feeling the warm, excited anticipation that Christmas brings us. Maybe we find it an effective way to fight off the darkness of winter, which has only just begun. Maybe it's an answer to the craving for color that sets in around January, when our world here is so black and white. Probably all of those things contribute, but I tend to think it's a family thing. Those of us who live alone don't tend to go in for the decorations in the way that families do. I pass a house, all lit up, and I think somehow that inside there lives a big family, an excitement building, tantalized by the strobes of the season.

I suppose it can't be analyzed, only acknowledged. I put the lit-tle ornament on my shelf, without cleaning it or even wiping off the flecks of earth. As the winter closed in, I kept my eye on that little ball. It seemed to have something to say. When Christmas came, I bought myself a string of lights and went out into the woods and cut a little fir tree. I brought it inside and dug out the box of orna-ments my husband and I had collected. The last time they'd seen light was the year before he died. Each one I unwrapped reminded me of another time, another place. When I'd hung them all, I put a little wire loop inside the tiny gazing ball, its mysteries intact, stories untold, and hung it on the highest branch.

DECEMBER 1997

Leaving Chesham Depot

B Y THE TIME I CAME to Chesham, in the spring of 1982, I had already lived in more than a dozen places for varying lengths of time. Coming to Chesham was not a deliberate decision, more like chance that I ended up in this particular town, in this particular part of the world. At that time I did not have any way of knowing the crooked path my life would take from there to here, and I don't think it's anything I thought about at the time. I was thinking more about a marriage lost and how I would support myself alone.

But Chesham became a place of new life as I found new love. The little house that we shared, nestled in the woods, was our refuge. My new husband was a carpenter and I a writer. In search of more space for our work, we rented the old abandoned train depot that had essentially given this town its name as a stop between Keene and Nashua.

Our stay there was brief, a bit more than two years. We sought another workplace in town, a building we could own rather than rent. It is not a big town, and there was only one building for sale at the time, a run-down old hay barn in the midst of wide fields. The barn had once been a part of a much bigger farm, a farm we always called Mary's farm, though Mary and her late husband had come only lately, in the 1940s. The man who first came to this land did so more than two centuries ago. But his barn, which had been built to house the hay from the fields at the far end of the farm, and which had long since been divided away from the farm, was falling down.

The value of the property was supposed to be in the small hayfield with its glimpse of Monadnock — or, in a realtor's eye, an impressive building lot. We didn't want to build, but Paul saw hope in the barn and so we bought it. He jacked the swayback building up and set it to rights and then made a shop for himself in the hayloft, and from two of the old horse stalls, he created a writing studio for me. It was a peaceful place, the only steady noise the distant sound of the tractors working the surrounding fields.

Some might call us restless, but we would say we were just trying to find our place. Two years later the old chicken farm near the depot came up for sale, and Paul and I went to see it. Paul had just come through three years of cancer treatments, and we were under the illusion that he was well again at last. Perhaps impulsively, we bought the place, which carried with it a huge old chicken barn, a tin-sided tractor shed, and six acres of field, woods, and a wide flat river for a back boundary.

In the time that we had, we tore the place apart and put it back together the way we wanted it to be.

Less than a year after we moved in, Paul was taken by his cancer, a theft that left me stunned and alone in that house. It was May and the cherry tree beside the house was in full bloom the night that he died. There never is enough warning for these exits. I almost literally sank into a chair on the screened porch and sat speechless for several months.

A whole year went by before I started a garden there, a long pause for one who needs a garden in order to feel right about things. The earth at the old farm was good, rich and loamy and easy to work. I began with one garden, and then a couple of years later, I opened another. And another. Gardens marked my time there as I gradually discovered the contours of the land and the way the sun ran from side to side. Beside the first garden my great-aunt had a lilac tree planted in memory of Paul. I planted lilacs and rhododendron, mock orange and wygelia, apple trees and crab-apple trees. In the lee of a stone wall that held back the ramp to the garage, I planted lilies and astilbe and peonies, a small rosebush called "Icicle," and Paul's favorite: pink hollyhocks.

Inside I continued the work that Paul had begun, painting and papering and modifying the old house. It was a work in progress, with the smell of paint and sawdust always hanging lightly in the air. The house was in the village, and as time went on, neighbors shared bits of the house's history with me. It was built in 1858, as the parsonage for the Chesham church, which explained why the cemetery was next door. At the turn of the century the house burned to the ground, and it was rebuilt, an exact replica. In the 1920s a young, newly married couple named Ralph and Uriel Bemis moved into the house, and Ralph began his chicken farm, the biggest in the county at that time. Hundreds of chickens ranged across the fields like little cows, and the big barn to the south of the house sheltered the peeping baby chicks.

Ralph and Uriel lived into their eighties. They had no children. Ralph died first and then Uriel, who was wheelchair-bound from arthritis by the time her end came. Paul and I were the next to live in that house, and we noticed that the thresholds had been taken up so that Uriel could better maneuver her wheelchair.

A nephew of Ralph's, who is also named Ralph Bemis, visited once and walked through the rooms like chambers of his memory: This was where Ralph slept, this was where they had the kitchen table. Later he sent me an old photograph of the house, taken in the early part of the century. It showed the house, almost identical to the way it looked then, in 1995, but stark of trees or vegetation of any kind. On the back Ralph had written the names of all the people who had ever lived in the house. I studied the names and realized that many widows had lived in this house. In the photo, Fidelia White, a widow, stood like a sentry in front of the house.

In time I began to write about those gardens and that house for *Yankee*. The monthly column was called "The Garden at Chesham

Depot." I was never short of something to write about, for the house and that land offered themselves up like a story needing to be told. I took it one chapter at a time and told what I knew. I had not come there thinking I would write about that house nor the land around it. But that is what happened. I became its voice as it spoke of its past and perhaps of its future.

It wasn't as if I never thought of leaving that house. I did. My life in Chesham had been my life with Paul. I was not born in Chesham and I had not grown up anywhere near here. And now, with Paul gone, I was alone here in a way that made me feel singled out. A small town can do that. I felt vulnerable, as if I did not have a right to my place in that town. My feelings about the house in Chesham were decidedly ambivalent. In many ways the house was my retreat. I nestled between the safe, warm walls that Paul had crafted, giving me shelter from the cold winds and hot summer days as well. Still, my mind busied itself with the project of discovering exactly where it would be that I would feel right, exactly where it was that I belonged. Why was I here? I kept asking myself. Where would be better? I traveled to North Carolina on vacation and considered buying a condo in Chapel Hill, envisioning myself living there, walking to the neighborhood shops and cafes, joining a totally different community than where I had been living. And I went out to a writer's retreat in Washington State where I met a real estate agent from northern California. Over dinner one night at the retreat, I told her of my restlessness and she sent me a link for a bungalow in St. Helena, a town I had once passed through and been charmed by. The price was amazing since the real estate market in California was in a depression. I daydreamed about living there, a town where M.F.K. Fisher had once lived and written books I had admired greatly. But it was all so far from where I then lived, from the people I knew and loved. I felt somewhat paralyzed, as if I had been silenced in the midst of song: I could not finish it — nor could I start another.

In the meantime, I had kept the barn. It was only three miles from the house and the triangular path between the two places became my life, to write during the day at the barn, to live and garden at the house.

I could not have known that it would be the barn that would offer me the solution to my conundrum, but in late summer of 1997, word came to me that the farm around the barn was for sale. Mary had died the year before, and her farm was being advertised in the paper, the farmhouse and a big chunk of land, much of it cleared fields and most of it with grand views of Monadnock.

Envisioning rows of houses along the smooth slopes of those fields and the noise of such a development already ringing in my ears, I called my neighbor nearest to the barn, who was already in motion. He had called the rest of the neighbors together that Sunday afternoon.

We gathered, some dozen of us, in the living room of this man, whom I had never known very well. In fact, I was meeting most of these people for the first time. In the barn I had led a writer's life, which is to say a monastic one. But we came together with one mind. In this town there are no other places so open to the mountain as on this hill. We wanted the land to stay as it had been for almost 250 years.

Someone said that if we pitched in money together, we might be able to take the farm off the market long enough to be able to come up with a plan. At once, we brought forth our checkbooks.

It was clear from that moment that this was not something any of us could have done alone, but only something that we could do together. Anne Howe was another neighbor I had never met. She lived in the city but kept a house near my barn for summer retreat. It had belonged to her parents, and she grew up knowing this land. She knew the land better than she knew any of us: At the meetings she met many of us for the first time.

Anne sat quietly through that meeting and left without saying much. But at the next meeting she stepped forward with her plan. She would buy the land. Someone else could buy the house. In buying the land, she would put it all under a conservation easement: The land would never be built on.

The meetings continued. At one point, and I am not even sure what made me say it, I blurted out that I would like to buy the house, if Anne bought the land. Saving the land from development was our goal.

I flinched at my boldness in suggesting that I buy the house. Mary's house needed a lot of work. I could not buy another house, just like that! I would have to first sell my house in Chesham. That would take time. We had only a few days left before our right of refusal would expire. And the door would reopen to developers. I feared I had made an offer I could not carry forward. After the meeting I told Anne of my narrow financial circumstances.

At the next meeting Anne told everyone she would lend me money to buy the house. Who would join her? Like thoughtful poker players, the rest of the neighbors in the room stepped forward, one at a time, to join Anne's offer. Within 20 minutes I had a loan, on faith, from my neighbors, to help me purchase this farmhouse and the land that surrounded it, until the time that I sold my house in Chesham. The spoken word and handshakes were all that transpired to seal our deal. I was stunned to silence. In essence Anne and I would unite to save the farm. Together we, who hardly knew each other, signed a purchase-and-sale agreement.

I went home and walked into my house, Paul's and my house. Paul's time in that house had been very brief, and yet in his spirit and in his woodwork, he had left his presence so strongly that it never faltered, never weakened. How could I even *think* of leaving this house?

Nearly frozen with confusion, I hesitated to list the house for sale. It seemed like an unimaginably huge step to take. But I remembered the faith my neighbors had in me. I felt something was in motion, something bigger than I. I didn't really feel that this was something I was deciding to do so much as it was something that I was meant to do. I kept thinking: I am not really doing anything and yet, *this is happening.*

By the time I called a real-estate agent, it was the end of September, not the best time to list a house. Still, the man came eagerly. He marked things on his pad and scrutinized the rooms. He measured and asked questions and ran his fingers across the smooth contours of Paul's kitchen cabinets. When we came to an agreement, he stepped back out into the crisp fall air, walked to the front of the house, and pounded his For Sale sign into the good Chesham soil.

The house did not sell right way, and I took up my neighbors' loan offer. They mailed me their checks, and on a dark day in the middle of December, I drove to the bank in Keene, and with my neighbors' money and a lot of trepidation, I bought my part of Mary's farm.

Within two weeks of that purchase, the temperatures plummeted below zero, and the pipes in Mary's house froze and broke. The plumber responded, "Oh, yes, that happens there a lot." My heart sank ever deeper. I could not move into the house until I sold the one in Chesham. To stave off further damage, the plumber drained the pipes and the old house sat empty and cold.

Meanwhile, I kept the Chesham house scrubbed clean for showing. I spent late nights sorting out closets, and in the morning I would fill my car with boxes and bags and drive my leftover life to the local church for its rummage sale. In every closet there were things that had belonged to Paul, things I either had not wanted to dispose of or things I had not found until that moment. In the short months of that winter, I relived our brief life in that house together. And felt I must have lost my mind to want to leave this house — so perfect, so right, so warm — for a house with a crumbling foundation and broken plumbing.

In early spring of 1998, before the snow had left the ground, the real-estate agent called to say that a young couple from Boston had come to look at the house. They returned again. And again. After their third visit, they wrote me an offer in the form of a letter, which ended with a poem by Maxine Kumin called "Homecoming," which ends with the lines:

> *we will hang up our clothes and our vegetables...*
> *on our hearth we will burn splits of silver popple...*
> *the soup kettle will clang five notes of pleasure*
> *and love will take up quarters.*

I knew then that the right people had found the house.

Appropriately they wanted a closing on May first, May Day, and I hustled to comply. The house at Mary's farm would have to be torn apart, and so I arranged to have all my furniture put into storage. I kept out only my clothes, a bed, and a table and chairs. I would live in Mary's house like a camper until all the work that needed doing had been done. I knew it would be a long time before I could once again enjoy the comforts of a home.

On the appointed moving day, as if it had been scripted, rain began to fall. A huge silver truck slowed outside the house and then I heard the shrill beeping, like a warning or an alarm, as it backed into the driveway. They were tough, no-nonsense men who entered my tender dwelling, and we went from room to room and, as I instructed them, they lifted the furniture and took it from the house. I kept my composure until they emptied the room that had been ours. When they rolled up the rug, I saw the grain of the old fir floor, just as it had been the day we moved in, and a wave of sadness swept over me. I wept for what had not been. And I wept in fear of where I was going. The young men moved around me and seemed not to notice my tears. Perhaps they see them on every job.

I shrugged on my rain slicker, flipped the hood up onto my head, and walked outside through the rain to my gardens, which were deep brown squares against the faint green of the new year. I spoke to them as if they could answer and told them of my fears. The lilac tree my aunt had planted in memory of Paul was now as tall as the shed it stands beside and there was new growth on the ends of the branches, "as big as mouse ears," as Paul would have said. I turned and watched as the men carried item after item into the truck. I wanted to run to them and ask them to take it all back inside, to put it back just as it had been, tell them that there had been a terrible mistake. But they kept moving and I said nothing.

When they finished, the only things left were my futon and my suitcases. I slept that night in the echoing empty house, and in the morning, I got up and got dressed and mechanically drove to the lawyer's office in Keene.

When the papers had been signed and the lawyer had had his say, I hugged the new owners and felt grateful that such good people had come to the house at Chesham Depot. I had brought with me the old photograph of the house, the one that Ralph Bemis had given me, and on the back I added my name and Paul's to the list of its owners, and the dates of our stay, 1988 to 1998, and gave it to them.

It rained then for what I am sure were days and days, and a heavy mist shrouded the mountain. I moved my table and chairs into Mary's old farm kitchen and the bed into the back bedroom. I put food on the old wooden shelves and started a fire in the little stove in the kitchen. In the yard, the dormant bushes began to open in the spring rain. I had never seen so many lilacs in my life, and in a slow, mesmerizing choreography, they opened. Outside, the fragrance was overpowering. I opened the windows and the scent of the lilacs moved in. It seemed like forever until the sun came out once again and I could see, at last, the view from Mary's farm.

MAY 1999

Photo of Mary's farm, circa 1940. The connecting sheds are gone. The big English barn (circa 1760) was disassembeled in 2002, the timbers sold to be reassembled elsewhere.

Mary's farm today.

PART TWO

The View from Mary's Farm

The view from Mary's farm, Mount Monadnock rising above the hay field.

🌀 Child of *Dune*

WHEN DUNE FIRST came into my life, I was struggling with my love for Paul and the dying end of a marriage that had never worked. My first husband and I were separated and thoughts of Paul entered virtually my every waking hour. One weekend, I went to Block Island with friends. It was the last weekend of June and the island was already at its summer best. On the beach, a boy, no older than ten, approached us. He held one black puppy under one arm and a white one under the other. At his feet, a bouncing, wiry white terrier looked on anxiously as he inquired of us, "Would you like a puppy?"

Of course, we all eagerly took the puppies in our arms and held them and smelled the distinctive sweet, milky odor of their breath. But, no, no one wanted a puppy, thank you.

"My mother says we have to get rid of these puppies before we sail tomorrow," the boy said, pleadingly.

Now I was curious. "You're on a boat?"

"Yep."

"Where have you come from?"

"We sailed here from Connecticut," he told us.

"Were the puppies born on the boat?" I asked.

"Yep."

I took the white one in my hands again. She barely filled my palms. The mother was small, skinny.

"Edie!" one of my friends said. "A puppy is just what you need right now! Why don't you take one?" The night before we had talked about my divorce and the empty feelings inside me.

If I could have imagined a worse time to take a puppy, it would have been then, as I was housesitting for a woman who had a long-term illness and would be hospitalized for some time. She had lovely Oriental rugs. I had not yet moved out of the house my husband and I shared but it seemed to be an inevitability. And I did not know where I would move from there. Having a dog often presented problems when looking for a rental. But as I held that small package, I thought of Paul, a lover of dogs, a lover of animals. I thought of how surprised he would be if I came home with a puppy. Paul never seemed to think that situations like that could not be handled.

"OK," I said and I gathered the white ball of fluff into my arms. The boy turned and walked away, with only the black one. At his heels, the mother ran and leapt, ran and leapt, a mother deprived. I never forgot the sight of the boy leaving and the mother dog leaping. I often said later that I wish I had taken both the black and the white. On the ferry home, the little white puppy nestled in the front pocket of my hooded sweatshirt and my friends and I tried to think of a name for her. She was a sandy color. She had come to me on the beach. The first real book I had ever worked on in my budding editorial career was Frank Herbert's futuristic novel, *Dune.* I liked the sound of it on my tongue. I liked the mix of the real and the imagined. I named her Dune.

Paul was indeed surprised. I called him when I got home and invited him to dinner. The look of surprise and love that came into his eyes when he saw the new puppy was one I won't forget.

After we married, Dune became Paul's dog, accompanying him to work every day in his truck. I was always amazed at how Dune grew up to look just like the mother who accompanied that little boy that day on the beach. Wiry and thin, Dune could jump in the air like no dog I've ever seen, except for her own mother. Whenever

Paul would get up to go out to his truck, Dune would leap like an aerialist. We expected that any day, she would do backflips and mid-air pirouettes.

When Paul became sick with cancer, Dune seemed to know. She rarely left his side. During his treatments, he often spent long hours sitting on the couch, reading, and Dune would sit beside him, her chin resting on his thigh. We had taught her to sleep under our bed and the night that Paul died, Dune lay beneath our bed and it took days to coax her away from that place. Her eyes were glassy, as if she had gone into shock. Several months passed after his death, before I started his truck, and when I did, Dune raced in a delirious circle, at the very sound of his engine.

After Paul died, Dune and I settled in together, just the two of us and she took on a protective stance, charging viciously at visitors who came to my door. She peed on the rugs and acted out like a petulant child. At times I grew impatient with her regression.

But, when grief overcame me and I sat down and sobbed, Dune would come to me, from wherever she was in the house, she would come and put her chin on my knee and look sadly into my eyes as if she knew exactly what I was feeling, and wanted somehow to muffle the terrible sounds that came from my core.

As it turned out, Dune nearly lived her entire life in the house that Paul and I had shared. She was 17 by the time I moved to the new farm and I worried about the transition. I never thought she would live that long. There had been a few close calls, including the summer she was run over in the road in front of our house. There was that terrible yelp and the sight of her being tossed aside by the speeding car but by the next morning, I knew that it was just a dislo-cated shoulder and a few scrapes, nothing she couldn't recover from, and did, quite quickly.

A year before the move to Mary's farm, I decided to get a new puppy. I wondered if it would be good for Dune or if it would make her feel angry and hurt. I knew losing Dune would be a terrible wrench, one more in a string of losses. But the silent contract we enter when we take in a dog is the knowledge that we will likely lose them before they lose us. I started looking. I went to shelters and found only dogs who had been abused, none that seemed friendly and anxious to be with me. And I didn't want to take that chance with my elderly friend. It seemed we have all done such a good job in neutering our pets, there were no mutt puppies to be had. All the dogs I've ever owned had been mutts, like Dune, taken off the hands of desperate mothers. I looked and looked, asked here and there but, no puppies were going begging. Only strays and large Rotweilers. I heard about a litter in Keene, a litter of miniature schnauzers. I went to see. It was too much. Their little faces looked so much like Dune at that age. The litter had been born on the night of the New Hampshire presidential primary and so all the puppies in the litter — I believe there were ten — were named after the presidential hopefuls. In the case of females, they were named for the candidate's wives. The little one I selected was named Sabina. I wasn't thrilled with the name but I loved the rest of her.

So, two months later, I brought home the puppy I renamed *M'aidez,* or Mayday. I simply thought of that word when I woke up on the day I was to go pick her up. Mayday. What did that mean, I wondered as I came out of a sound sleep? Oh, I realized it was to be the puppy's name. *M'aidez* is French for *help me.* I felt it was appropriate. I needed help and this little one would answer the call. Instantly, when I brought her home, Dune came to life. A completely revived dog, she took Mayday on like the mother she had never been, herding her around and tolerating the almost incredibly annoying things the puppy would do, such as take hold of Dune's lovely fluffy white tail and pull her across the kitchen floor. It was humorous because Dune might be asleep or even awake and not realize what was happening until she became aware that she was moving — backward. But she was patient, even indulgent of the little salt and pepper beast who had come to stay.

At the time I got Mayday, I did not know I would be moving so soon. The move became one more reason to worry.

When it came time, I worried about the move. As we began the move, packing up boxes and mothballing trunks of linens, Dune went into a decline, oddly like a depression. She would sleep for hours, curled in a tight circle and sometimes it was hard to rouse her. Once we moved, I could see that it had been hard on her. I'd taken to calling her "the oldest dog on the planet."

At the new house with its open fields, the dogs had freedom at last. They could range about the farm at will. It was a delight to watch.

Throughout that first summer at Mary's farm, Dune had been failing, the gentlest and slowest retreat imaginable. I think that my friends were shocked to see her, so frail and thin, but I had grown used to her shadowy presence. Hazy blue cataracts shielded her wonderful brown eyes. She was almost completely blind and deaf as a stone. As I moved about the kitchen. I'd step to get something from the refrigerator and there she'd be, under my feet. Without seeing her there, I'd stumble over her. She moved like a phantom, making not a sound so that, no matter how many times it happened, I couldn't seem to anticipate her presence or prevent myself from tripping on her. It was disheartening to think that in her failing years, some of her last experiences were to be tripped over.

In many ways, it was like having a hospice patient in the house which brought back those last weeks of Paul's life. She had her good days when she would play with Mayday and act like a young dog, and then she had her vague days when she would lie curled in one position for hours until I would draw close and touch her side to make sure she was still breathing. Mayday began to take center stage. It was inevitable.

My vet, Andrea Nealley, suggested two new drugs for Dune, one a "miracle" drug for arthritis and the other, a "miracle" drug for what amounts to Alzheimer's in dogs. "It works on the brain," she explained, "and they've had remarkable results with it. Try it. What have you got to lose?"

I went home with the arsenal and began to feed Dune her pills three times a day. It wasn't a good chapter for us as she struggled while I pried open her mouth and tried to get the pills down her throat. I tried all the tricks, hiding them in ground beef, but when I swept the floor, I often found the pills on the floor later. Even so, she must have taken some of it in as she really did begin to improve. For a while the results were remarkable, truly a "miracle." She pranced and leapt like the young Dune and often outran Mayday. I was amazed. But then Dune had always had the ability to amaze me.

All this time, there were men working on the house, which had to be nearly gutted almost as soon as I moved in. I was living temporarily in the back ell and most of my furniture was in storage. A big man named Ethan was working on the foundation at that time and he and his helpers watched for two weeks as I carried this nearly lifeless body in and out of the house. She must have looked like a parcel of white fluff. I noticed them watching me, as if with pity for the widow and her devoted pet. Poor woman, they may have been thinking, that's all she's got to love.

Perhaps. But then, one by one, they were all startled to discover Dune rushing out to their trucks, jumping up to greet them as they arrived. "What happened?" they asked. "What did you do?"

There is always the down side to these drugs and for Dune it was horrendous runny diarrhea, which began a week or so after the miracle had taken hold. I kept a bucket of Spic and Span ready beside the door at all times. If I thought these drugs could ultimately help her, I would have gladly endured the smell and the work involved but she was clearly getting no nourishment at all. I cut the dose and then ended the drugs altogether.

As if I had taken the hanger from a suit of clothes, she collapsed back into her decrepitude. She wandered the house, in search of some mysterious something, stopping to stare at the floor for long periods of time, as if she might have found it, *there*. And then she would move slowly on. She continued to appear under my feet in the kitchen and pushed herself into corners and behind doors. She was like a phantom, always here and yet never here. When she went outside, she moved the same way and I began to find her wandering in the road. It's not a busy road but she was, by then, almost completely blind and so deaf I could have shrieked in her ear and she would not have heard. I worried about the coyotes that howled so loudly in the fields here at night. But what would they want with her? She was just bones and thinning hair.

I called Andrea, probably three times, in despair over what to do. Dune had her moments when she seemed fine, but she was more often a pathetic creature, long overdue to depart. Andrea suggested that she could come to my house and put her down or I could bring her to her office. She suggested cremation and I consoled myself with the thought that I could take a small amount of her ashes to each of her special places, including the beach on Block Island. It was with some irony that I realized that she was my longest relationship. Those daydreams fed me for a while and I was comforted that I had a plan: all I had to do was pick up the phone and we could end our long time together.

But finding that time was not so easy. I kept my eye on Dune, every day assessing her condition. Not bad, I'd conclude. She's just sleeping. She's not in pain. There didn't seem to be any true misery to put her out of. And there were still moments, brief as they were, when she seemed truly happy. It wasn't time yet.

Still, she wandered. I became used to going out to find her. Once I found her in a drainage ditch, trapped by its depth, too weak to pull herself out. Another time, she was deep in the woods, running in circles and yipping for help as she apparently could not get herself out of the thicket. Once, while we were at the lake with my cousin George, she walked into the water and stood, underwater, completely still. George saw her and leapt to rescue her. He brought her, dripping, out of the water and she didn't even snort. She just looked at me with her sad, clouded eyes. I couldn't fathom what she was trying to say, except perhaps that she was born on the water and intended to die there, too.

And so went the month of October. She would disappear and I'd go out into the woods to find her. When I found her, I'd carry her back out to the open fields and set her down so she could walk back home with me, which she had always done, trotting along in step with my feet. But now, when I set her down she would walk a ways with me and then arc back into the woods, as if a magnet were drawing her back. I knew what this was all about but I couldn't seem to make myself allow her to go.

Still, I knew that she wouldn't be able to navigate snow and ice, which was on its way. I was going away at the end of October, flying to Washington DC to visit friends, and I decided that I would make that call to Andrea that week, so that Dune would not have to go to the kennel again. And I could go to DC and distract myself from my sadness.

But, the week before I was to go, she perked up. She played and the spring in her step returned. Instead of calling Andrea, I called the kennel.

The morning I was to leave, I got up at 6 and let her out. It was still dark and Dune, being blind, always stayed within the circle of the floodlight. I had been awakened at 4 by the eerie cry of coyotes, which is common here but nonetheless unsettling as they sound as if they were drunk on the elation of tearing raw flesh. I went back inside to start the woodstove and then went back out. Dune was gone. Completely gone. It was too dark to look for her but I made an effort to look around the usual places. No sign of her. I called my friend Debbie for help. She came and together, as the day dawned, we walked the fields, which are extensive here.

I spent much of the day looking. My friend and colleague, Mel, came at lunch and helped and then, at 2, I had to get myself to the airport. Mel promised to gather a search party and come back.

I boarded the plane with tears in my eyes, feeling I had deserted my friend in her hour of need. Over the weekend, Mel called several times to report that they had found nothing. I thought of all those people combing the fields, calling her name, which I should have told them would be pointless, since she cannot hear. Still, I liked imagining all those voices, calling her name up into the big sky above this hill.

When I returned, two days later, I continued to search, knowing by then that I would not find her alive, as the nights had been very cold, but wanting to be able to find her body. I simply couldn't bear the thought of her being eaten by coyotes. I retreated into the knowledge that she was gone. Two weeks passed. It was hunting season by then and I hoped that perhaps a hunter would find her little body and at least bring me her collar.

One afternoon, a cool but bright day, I was planning dinner for a special guest that night. I had been meaning to pick some of the winterberries that grew beside the pond. I had never seen such big red berries and thought they'd look nice in a vase on the table. I got my clippers and went over to the pond, which is near to the house. The berries were growing close to the water so I walked carefully through the marsh grasses. I had grown used to looking for her, everywhere, it was habit now, and as I walked, I looked down into the dried grass, which was by then colored so very much like her. At the edge of the pond, I balanced myself beside the water and reached for the berries, which were growing in an awkward way so that it was hard to get near them to cut. I stretched with my clippers toward a good full stem and started to lose my balance. I grabbed a branch to steady myself and as I did, I looked down into the water. There was Dune, adrift, floating. Startled, I jumped, and ran back to the house in a kind of weird panic, as if I needed help to save her.

Michael and his helper Henri were working up at the house. Michael was my ex-husband who had become, at that point in our lives, a good friend. He had, of course, known both Paul and Dune very well. Now he was working to help me renovate the old house. I burst into the room where they were putting up sheetrock.

"I found Dune!" I said, out of breath and holding back tears. Both Michael and Henri had been looking for her, along with every-one else and so at first they thought I meant that I had found her alive. They turned, facing me, with looks of astonishment on their faces.

My emotions were preventing me from speaking very clearly. "She's in the pond!" I wailed.

"We'll get her," they said.

They went out and brought her in. Henri, through his daily work here and through his affection and kind ways with my dogs, had become a dear friend. He removed her collar and hung it to dry on the fence post.

Michael said, "We'll bury her for you, if you just tell us where."

I thought and thought. From all the work on the foundation and plumbing, the whole place was dug up and I knew that more earth would be moved and pushed around in the spring. The hay-fields needed to be clear for the haying machinery.

"What about if we bury her up beside Paul?" Michael asked.

Paul was buried in a small cemetery on an isolated hill less than a mile from Chesham Depot. I never would have thought of burying her there and if I had I would have assumed it would be illegal to do that. Which it is.

"Great idea," I said. It suddenly seemed so very right.

He asked if I wanted him to build a little box for her but I said no, let's let her be with the earth. I had been to a rummage sale that weekend and there had been two like-new baby blankets for 50 cents. I bought them because they were so bright white and perfect and knew I would find a use for them — as polishing cloths if nothing else. Now I brought them out from the closet. "Here," I said, "let's use these."

Henri wrapped her in the blankets and set her gently into the back of Paul's truck and the three of us climbed into Paul's old truck and drove over to the cemetery in Chesham.

Michael and Henri dug and I watched. Over the ten years, Paul's grave had become a garden with abundant daylilies around the back edge and a bed of pachysandra in front. There were stones and small clumps of forget-me-nots at the edge of the pachysandra. When I bought Paul's plot, I had also bought the one adjoining for myself and they were digging in the space between the two plots. They dug down four feet and then Henri went over to the truck and lifted Dune into his arms and set her gently into the deep hole. He folded the white blanket carefully around her, as if he were tucking a baby into a crib. With equal care, they replaced the earth, setting it carefully on top of her remains.

When they were done, I set a small bunch of winterberries on top of the hump of sod.

Michael gathered fallen leaves and placed them on any broken earth so that our clandestine interment would be hidden.

I thanked them — how can you thank anyone for such a deep kindness? I never would have thought to bury Dune next to Paul and there's an amazing comfort to think that, whenever it is that my time comes, I will be next to Paul, and Dune will sleep between us.

Soon after we found her, we had torrential rains and the pond nearly doubled in size. It's a small pond with a springfed source but in spring and during heavy rains, it acts as a watershed. From where I sit in my kitchen chair, it's like an eye looking back at me from the field. If it ever had a name, I don't know of it. I call it Dune's Pond now.

I felt that maybe I was meant to find her, or that she meant me to find her. There were so many people who had looked for her. And we had all thought of the pond as a natural place to look, although there had been no sign of her there, at that time. It was only after I found her that I remembered how she had submerged herself in the lake just a month earlier, like some tragic heroine from a romantic novel. And why did she disappear on the day I was to go to Washington? It all seemed so weirdly deliberate as if she wanted me to go so that she could really disappear and not have me snatch her back, as I had so many times before. And then that she wanted me to find her, so that I wouldn't wonder.

She was a mysterious dog, who experienced a lot of passages in her life. Born on a sailboat in Long Island Sound, brought here to New Hampshire to live in the woods and then at the last to the fields of Mary's farm, she seemed to know so much more than I. Was she really carried away in a tornado? It always seemed impossible whenever I thought about it but there seemed no other explanation. So many mysteries. She lived to be seventeen, a late age for any dog. I believe dogs know instinctively about death and about a life's span. They know when it's time. I know I selfishly held her back from her mission, needing her, wanting her to stay on, but I think she was perhaps a party to my desires. My futuristic, mystical dog lasted those extra years to make sure I made it through my grieving time. Whatever time it took, she waited to take me there and once she knew I had settled safely into my new home, she knew it was all right for her to go.

❦ Blessings

WHEN I FINALLY moved in to my newly constructed rooms here, I had a blessing for the house. That was not something I would have thought necessary, as Mary's good spirits were all through the house when I bought it. But in the first months that I owned the house, it was necessary for me to rent it out, as I had not yet sold my home in Chesham.

The family I rented it to displayed almost every bad behavior known to tenants: they didn't pay their rent, overflowed the septic tank, and, I was to find out too late, their children were in trouble with the police even before they moved in. When the rent was due, I'd knock on the door. While I stood on the doorstep, they'd tell me their troubles, and I'd come away empty-handed. What I feared the most was that they would not leave.

No amount of talk on my part would have helped but at last, what levied in my favor was our winter, a bitter, icy lock on our landscape that would not let go. In March, I arrived to collect the rent and the place was empty. They were long gone. I walked cautiously through the silent house, stepping over the heaps of garbage and peering into a refrigerator full of spoiled food. Upstairs I found the walls of the bedrooms had been defaced and the sink in the bathroom broken by the blow of a hammer. I felt a chill, deeper than the wintry winds that lashed outside the door.

I hired a dumpster and swept out what I could. I scrubbed, especially the floors but also the walls and the windows. But I was astonished at how powerfully the presence of these people persisted.

The renovation helped. The walls with their vulgar decorations were torn out. The men who worked on the house hurled the hunks of grafitti-ed plaster into the dumpster with extra energy and I helped, with gusto.

On the advice of a friend, I hung bundles of dried sage in corners and placed saucers of fragrant oils in the bedrooms. A friend with Native American roots sent me a tribal feather to carry through the house and then burn, which I did. But the creepy feeling clung like a fungus inside a dark cellar.

A year passed. When the first stage of the renovation was completed, I all but leapt into the freshly painted new rooms. For days, I carried boxes in from the barn, where everything had been stored. The renewal felt complete. Almost.

It was my friend Richard who suggested the house needed a blessing. Richard ministers to a lively congregation in Bolton, Massachusetts, and he not only enjoys the pageant of religion but he knows that I do too. Ceremonies, like baptisms and marriages, provide doorways through which we can safely pass.

"Invite your friends and tell them all to bring their favorite dish," he instructed and then added that I would need to provide him with a bowl and an evergreen branch.

We planned the service for early July and we were lucky that the day dawned in brilliant colors and the afternoon was warm, with just a slight breeze. Richard arrived first, dressed in the black of his priesthood. One and two at a time, my friends joined us, bearing hot dishes and salads and plates of cakes, which they placed on my kitchen table.

I had selected a small yellow ware bowl that had been in the house before I and I had cut a sprig from the towering blue spruce out behind the barn. From the kitchen faucet, Richard filled the bowl with water and asked us to follow him.

We trailed Richard outside into the sun where he anointed the garden, the fields, the barns, and then we circled the house, as he dipped the branch into the water and flung the droplets around him. Inside the house, he stopped in each room, saying his words like any priest. Except that the temple where he arched the holy water happened to be my house and the water from my well. There were words for all of us to say together and there was surprising power in the joining of the voices of my friends. We even crowded into the bathroom where Richard sanctioned the "water that cleanses us."

When we had said the last words of the service together, we took our places around the table, which was set and loaded with the good food everyone had brought. There was no shortage of talk and good feelings and within the communion of all that, it seemed unlikely that misguided spirits could ever again penetrate these walls, bright as they were with the new paint and the benediction of the afternoon sun.

JULY 2000

❀ The Glenwood

MY GRANDMOTHER's gray and white enamel gas stove had many burners and sat up on long slender legs. The white boxlike stove we had at home fit flush in with the kitchen counters, as if it were meant to blend in and not be noticed. Nanny's stove was proud, the center of her big kitchen where good meals kept on coming. We were always warmed by it and I found it especially interesting that she could fix oatmeal in the evening and leave it on the stove to cook overnight. If we tried that with my mother's electric stove, we would have a burned mess in the morning. But Nanny's way yielded oatmeal that was creamy and smooth like pudding. A cold night never ended quite so well as it did coming downstairs in the morning to Nanny's oatmeal.

It's been a long time since I've seen that stove, but it comes to mind surprisingly often. When I set about to find appliances for the new kitchen here at Mary's farm, I strolled aimlessly through one appliance center after another. I wanted nothing that I saw.

When I finally found the Glenwood, it was something like love. I discovered it in a shop in Littleton, Massachusetts, set back against the wall, the green and cream enamel longing to be wiped clean and polished. In fact, the stove had been made over, like new. The legs were long and slender, reaching the floor with rounded catlike feet. The sultry black cast iron burners winked at me. I pushed the hood of the rolltop warming oven open. In spite of the metalworking shop that surrounded me, I could smell biscuits; I could smell pie.

I brought this stove home and designed my new kitchen around it. Everything in the kitchen depended on the size and graceful reach of this big range. For months, it sat off to the side, cold and mute, while the work on the kitchen progressed. Every once in a while, I ran my fingertips across the smooth green enamel. When they carried her into the finished kitchen, I felt there should have been a drumroll and a great clash of cymbals as her elegant legs were set down gently onto the newly painted floor.

The first really big meal I cooked on the Glenwood was Christmas dinner. By then I felt confident enough to tackle a leg of lamb in her big oven. As I often do, I invited friends who had been left alone that year. My friend Judy had died the year before, just days before Christmas and so I invited her husband Tom and their two children, Taj and Lydia. Another friend was enduring a painful divorce and was facing his first Christmas alone, without his children.

The day before Christmas, I went into the woods behind the barn and found a good looking little spruce, not too far from the edge of the field. With a bow saw, I cut it and I brought it inside to set it up in the corner of the kitchen. That evening, chutney simmered on the Glenwood's back burner while I dressed the branches. The tree was small so I hung only my very favorites, the elf in a swing, the tiny chalet dusted with glitter, the hand-blown glass star.

In the morning, I lit the oven, setting the blue flames dancing. Not only did the lamb have to roast but there were pies to bake as well. The stove gave off a welcome warmth as I rolled out the dough. When the pies were done, I slipped them into the warming oven and slid the big roast into the hot oven. My friends arrived, smiling and hungry. They were drawn to my stove, exclaiming over its color, its age, its marvelous shape. From inside my cream and green friend, the fat on the lamb popped and sizzled. Lydia gingerly lifted the rolltop where the pies waited.

We all needed an extra boost that day. Sadness lingered at the edges of our conversations. The food seemed to be what made us smile. After the main meal, we bundled up for a walk through a biting wind, then hurried back for hot tea and pie, still warm in the overhead oven.

It's not my grandmother's stove but it's the center of my kitchen, the source of warmth and hearty meals and it seems to have the mysterious ability to provide a good ending to all kinds of cold nights.

DECEMBER 2000

Weather or Not

N EW ENGLAND IS not known for its hurricanes. We had our 1938 doozy, which had been predicted as nothing more than "strong winds." Bricks, firewood, even apples from the ripening trees became bullets, puncturing walls, felling cattle. After the storm had passed, farmers one hundred miles inland told of saltwater streaks on their windows. Nearly 700 people were killed by this unforecast nightmare. 300 million trees were lost or damaged, giving rise to the term "hurricane lumber."

With each hurricane season that comes, there lurks the possibility of a rerun. The weather channels track them, the Glorias and the Bobs, as if they were the criminally insane, escaped from their hold. On the nightly news, forecasters pinpoint the storm, days, sometimes weeks away, give it a name and mark its progress. Like an unfolding drama, we watch the great wheel of catastrophe that rolls up out of Africa, careens through the Caribbean and wobbles onward up the East Coast. With the camera's eye, the TV tells the story, so far. In the tropics, roofs lie scattered. Palm trees bend and touch the ground. Waves crash through living rooms. But Septembers come and go and the storms blow away or change course before they reach us here in southwestern New Hampshire.

Last year, though, they felt sure we were in for it. It was early September, a beautiful mild time here. We had not yet had a frost. The air was close. Sitting outside in the evening still seemed like the best idea we could think of. It seemed much too early to carry in the lawn furniture and evacuate the porch. But Floyd, an enormous coil of thick clouds with a hole in the center, was on every channel we can get. "This is a *huge* storm," the forecasters admonished. And the map showed its fury could reach from Maryland to Maine.

Inside, I flicked on the evening news. Aerial photos showed a traffic jam leaving the coast of North Carolina like a line into infinity. Heavy surf crashed through the kitchens of oceanside cottages and flattened garages.

In my TV-charged imagination, I pictured uprooted trees and felled power lines; my innocent lawn furniture became lethal weapons. And so in came the chairs. And the tables and the birdhouses and feeders. Even the wind chimes, which are made of clay and have the contemplative sound of Buddhist bells, were taken in. Like a bankrupt cafe, our summery outdoor living space went dead. I walked around the house and barn one last time and on the final circuit, hefted the birdbath and set it in a horse stall in the barn and latched the doors.

That night, it rained. There was a bit of wind. And, in the morning, the sun lit up the garden. Could that have been it? On the television, the big wooly wheel of Floyd was turning toward the Maritimes. That evening, listening to the radio, I heard a man who had evacuated from Florida say he would never, never leave again, no matter if he had to be arrested. His home in Florida was completely untouched by Floyd, which collided with the coast of North Carolina and then veered out to sea. The people who suffered most were the inland farmers of North Carolina who were completely unprepared for the flooding that followed the storm. It rained for days and their houses filled like empty buckets. In spite of the days and days of watchful advisement, no one warned this would happen.

Do we really know how to do anything but photograph the weather? In the clear, post-Floyd morning air, I set the chairs outside again and hung the feeders and the wind chimes. There would be another month of summer, surely. I carried dinner outside on trays and we ate into the warm darkness, to the sound of the crickets. I felt a sense of relief mixed with sadness for those who had been so devastated by the unpredicted floods. A week or so later, I woke in the night to the howl of high winds. Rain rushed against the windows with hurricane force. The house timbers creaked and wind chimes rang wild. In the morning, the lawn chairs were scattered in the field, as if from a night of reckless partying. My wind chimes lay in pieces on the ground. The forecast had been for rain, some wind.

SEPTEMBER 2000

🌺 Loving Harriet

MY TWO-YEAR-OLD border terrier, Harriet, has been a big
discipline problem since day one. Black with a white star on
her chest and brindle legs and face, she is curious, rugged,
and wicked cute. Good thing. She once chewed on the emergency
brake handle in my car so vigorously that the town fire chief had to
come to my rescue to disengage the brake. It has never worked since,
just an example of the many naughty things she has done. Perhaps
worse, she has an affection for Diet Coke cans, which she consumes,
completely, except for the pull tab — the proverbial oink. She sur-
vives it all, with aplomb.

Over the summer, she was sprayed directly in the face by a
skunk. When I went out to rescue her, I found her in the road, grinding her face into the pavement. I could hear the pebbles scrunching
under her agonized face. I tied her to the run. As soon as the day
began, I took her down to the groomer (windows rolled all the way
down on a cold morning) to have her shampooed and shaved. Nothing else would do. When I brought her home, she looked pitifully
naked and still smelled but at least being near her no longer made
my eyes water.

A few weeks later, I was awakened in the middle of the night
by a strange sound, like a shrill bird or an animal in distress. At first
light, I heard the cry again and went to the window: through the
dusky light, I could see a very large porcupine walking down the side
of my big apple tree. She was making that very sound. I immediately panicked. A faceful of skunk juice is one thing but what would

happen if Harriet got into a big old porcupine? Those quills can go into their mouths and down their throats and the ingenious fish-hook barbs at the end of the quills make it very hard to remove them. As soon as it was a decent hour, I called Brian, who often comes to my rescue. I was hoping he would come and whisk the porky away. But he was very busy. Instead, he offered to loan me his Hav-a-hart trap. Better than nothing. The trap is designed to catch the animal in the cage so that it can be harmlessly transported somewhere else. They come in all sizes. Sometime later, I found on my porch a huge Hav-a-hart, surely big enough to house a child. I had asked Brian on the phone what kind of bait I should use. He suggested a carrot. So I peeled a lovely fresh carrot to bring the sweet scent out. I took the trap down and set it under the apple tree. With some effort, I set the trap. I stepped back. It seemed poised for success, with its open trap door and the bright orange carrot sitting temptingly on the plate that would trip the door closed as soon as the victim stepped inside.

Harriet had been nosing around the garden while I was per-forming this unwelcome task. "This is all because of you!" I said to her as she poked around in the weeds.

As I walked away, toward the barn I heard the trap clatter shut. I turned and saw in the trap — not the porcupine but Harriet! She looked out at me pleadingly from behind the bars. I rushed to vindi-cate her. So far as I know, the porcupine continues to range free and the skunk has taken up residence in the barn.

MAY 2012

Fruitcake Weather

I T SEEMS THAT the word "fruitcake" can no longer be spoken in polite society. You wouldn't dare serve it. Referred to as a doorstop or a boat anchor, fruitcake has become the object of jokes on late night television where chainsaws and welding torches are suggested as successful cutting tools. One jokester somewhere out west apparently has an annual fruitcake toss, with the current record "toss" being 420 feet. Another man claims to have found in his attic an old fruitcake that he estimated to be pre-World War II. I believe he said he ate it. A woman put an ad in the paper after the holidays, soliciting unwanted fruitcakes, which she then added to her compost, expecting a rich result. When fruitcake was added to the list of things you cannot take on an airplane (it's so dense, a weapon baked inside could go undetected by current technology), it only added fuel to the fruitcake fire. How has this once exalted holiday staple become such a target?

When I was growing up in the 1950s, we often received gifts of fruitcake in the mail between Thanksgiving and Christmas. The powerful confection came to us from bakeries in Georgia or Texas, where pecans are plentiful and fruitcakes are still big business. From inside the rugged mailing carton, the dark cake would emerge, crimped red paper gripping the circle of candied cherries, citron, pecans and apricots. On nights leading up to Christmas, my mother would slice the cake thickly and serve it to us on holiday plates, an exciting prelude to what lay ahead.

At Christmas, for many years, I have read Truman Capote's *A Christmas Memory* aloud, with my cousin George or with whomever I can coax into listening. The set-off line to this wonderful, evocative memoir is, "It's fruitcake weather, Buddy," a line spoken by a woman in her sixties to her seven-year-old cousin and best friend. Thus begins the story of their annual ritual of gathering the ingredients for thirty fruitcakes to be presented to friends — such as Eleanor Roosevelt. Included in all this is a perilous journey to obtain a bottle of whiskey for the cake from the local bootlegger, Mr. Haha Jones.

Early last December, I gathered with new friends who love Capote's story as much as I do. They had just put up their tree and begun to trim it. They, it turns out, always read *A Christmas Memory* aloud at this time of year, a fact that automatically endeared them to me. Along with their two young sons, we all settled in front of a big hearth fire, each of us taking a turn reading. The fire popped and spat sparks and, if we looked outside, it might have been Alabama in the 1930s. We were stuck in a time none of us ever knew or remembered.

Just before Christmas, my new friend baked me a fruitcake, the first one I can remember receiving in my adult life. It was plump and heavy, yes, capable of being a doorstop (though I'd stop short of the boat anchor concept). Later, I opened the tightly wrapped loaf. The wheat-colored cake was dense with citrons and candied cherries, walnuts and dried cranberries and lots of raisins. The fragrance was somehow just as much of Christmas as a balsam tree and a roasting turkey. "It's fruitcake weather," I thought to myself, and dropped back to a time when bootleg whiskey was a secret ingredient and cousins were the best kind of family.

NOVEMBER 2008

❧ Orphan Holidays

'VE BEEN ALONE a long time now, nearly 20 years. It's something I never imagined, and yet at this point in my life, I can't imagine its being otherwise. I guess you could say I've grown accustomed to this life alone. I've figured it out.

My life alone intensified five years after my husband, Paul, died; both my parents passed away, and sometime later, my Aunt Peg and Uncle Jamie left this world as well. It's sobering to be this alone in the world. Being without a spouse, without parents, and without children leaves one in a kind of dangling solitude from which there truly is no rescue. It's simply a state of being. And I figured either I could continue feeling I was at the end of the perilous rope or I could find a family of my own — a family without the traditional ties but one that nevertheless provides everything the traditional family does and, in many cases, probably much more. So one thing I figured out was the benefit of being able to choose this family.

A lot of the rest of what I figured out had to do with food. I realized that by inviting someone to join me for dinner — and on occasion that "someone" may be as many as 21 people — I've accomplished a lot. I love to cook, so I've brought to my home people for whom I can cook. And I may presume that I've been able to provide these people with some good food and company as well. Though I can't be absolutely certain I've done that for them, I can be certain about the pleasure it brings me.

It's a mystery to me why I haven't remarried. I suppose there are many reasons, but I do recall that in those first confusing months after Paul's death, I felt certain I would marry again. I'd been happy in my marriage to Paul, and so I reasoned that I would find that again. I wished we'd had children, but life is so complex, and to those who truly believe that everything in one's life is a result of a deliberate decision, I can only say that I wish that were really true.

Most of what any of us encounters is such a complex stew of circumstance and happenstance that we're truly fortunate if we can choose what we'll have for dinner that night, much less our own destiny. Anything more that seems deliberate is simply an illusion. Paul was 39 when he died. I have many friends who have lost their spouses at a young age, and I know people whose children have died, and friends who have had accidents in which they've lost their legs or their minds. No, it seems to me that in many cases we're asked to react to circumstances, not choose them.

And so, for whatever reason, I'm still alone. But I'm not alone in any real way. For one thing, the renovation of this house has consumed me, as much as any marriage with at least three children would have. Constantly, there were decisions to make, budgets to balance, supplies to pick up or deliver — and all for the ultimate well-being of the structure as well as my soul. I needed this house in a way I'd never needed anything.

After I bought the house, the pace of the project quickened, and once the first few boards were torn from the side of the building, it didn't slow for nine long years. And so, within that storm of activity, I found a compelling heart to every one of my days, a rhythm that kept beating and never slowed, until just recently. With the work still unfinished but so close, I can rest a bit now and reflect. For a long time, reflection wasn't possible. Or even desirable. The work was a kind of frenzy; if it had been set to fast motion, as is popular now on house-building shows, you would have seen siding and roofs flying off, additions and dormers magically appearing, walls disappearing, doors moving from one opening to another, and windows vanishing as new ones zoomed into place. If Mary were to come back from the dead for a visit, she'd be lost in her own house.

But within all of that, there was always time for a meal. The first really new parts of this house were the kitchen and the dining room. And so these two spaces became almost sacred as other spaces were pounded into place. And there were meals, gatherings, parties — something for which I wasn't particularly well prepared. My Aunt Peg had given dinner parties on occasion, and as a child, I sat there uncomfortably as the erudite conversation wafted high above my head. But the food was good. That was always something to look forward to.

And there was something else, something much harder to grasp. The dining room in that old Colonial house had a big fireplace; in the winter, the fire was always lit, as were the candles, which gave the room a glow and a cozy feeling, as if we'd all come in out of the cold to gather there. Of course, we had, in a sense, but to my way of thinking there was something more primeval about it — a kind of bonding together against the rigors of the wilderness of an ever-more-confusing world. Maybe, in some vague way, that's what I'm reaching for when I invite friends to dinner, a solution to the puzzle.

My first bit of fortune came with the table that my parents left me. It had belonged to my great-grandparents. My great-grandparents, I should explain, had a lot of money — money that never made it past the year 1929. The money was gone, but the furniture stayed with us, passed down and down into ever-smaller homes. In our modest house in New Jersey, the table was a circle with four grand chairs around it. The table had a beautiful mahogany finish. As a child, I loved to hide under that table and was always slightly awed by the fierce nature of what held it up: a grand base carved into fearsome gryphon's claws, grasping big wooden balls.

In the basement, my father had stored four more chairs to match the set and four leaves that could be set into the expandable table frame. I'd never seen it with more than one leaf in it because my parents' dining room had been too small. But, once the table made its way to this new house, I was able to expand it completely and set all the chairs around it. I'd already envisioned it many times as the workmen were demolishing two old bedrooms and putting the new wainscoting into place: *This is where the table will go. This is where the fun will happen.*

The appearance of my new dining room and the banquet-size table must have seemed absurd to anyone watching this process, as this was a home for one person. Who was going to sit around this table? I'm sure it's a question poised on the lips of anyone who enters this house, especially all the men who come to do various jobs, wiring and plumbing and flooring. I can see them glance into the big room and then glance again.

My dinners began some years back when, weary of trying to figure out what to do for Thanksgiving and Christmas, I hit on the idea of what I called "orphan holidays." Gradually, I noticed that I wasn't the only one around who was alone at Thanksgiving and Christmas. Not only were there those who were truly alone, but there were others who weren't technically alone but were in transition — friends whose spouses had died, friends in the midst of divorce, friends in some other kind of despair. I realized we could all come together on those days, and hosting the holidays fulfilled my need to cook a big meal for many hungry friends.

At the most, I've crowded 25 people around the table (with an extension), and at the least, I've hosted seven — all grateful for a good place to go to share what can otherwise be deadly days of remorse or sadness while (you're certain) the entire rest of the world is celebrating with their big happy families. An exaggeration, of course, as I know there are people with large families who grit their teeth through the whole ordeal — but, truly, holidays can be so difficult for anyone alone.

I love the holidays as a way to try out new recipes and to re-experience the joy of bringing out old favorites. I also love this time as a way of loving my house. You could look at it as something very similar to dressing up — that wonderful outfit just hanging in the closet, waiting for the right occasion. Well, I love dressing up my house. It's a chance to decorate. (I'd never unpacked even a single Christmas ornament before I started hosting the orphan holidays. It seemed so pointless. Decorate for what? For whom?) And it's an opportunity to get out the good china and silverware, use the gravy boat, change the tablecloth, put new tapers into the candlesticks.

It's no different from what everyone else loves about having family over for Thanksgiving and Christmas; it's a chance to change gears, see the house through different eyes. I love every part of a party: planning the menu, cleaning the house, setting the table, cooking the meal — which I insist must be almost completely ready before the first guests arrive. All I want to have to do once the party starts is put the food on the table. After all, I want to attend this party, too. That's why I'm giving it!

And so, out of the somber puzzle of how to cook for one came the joyous process of cooking for 20 or more. I recommend it highly. My favorite moment of all comes at the height of the party when I like to sit for a moment and listen . . . listen to the talk, the laughter, the joy within these walls.

NOVEMBER 2007

🌀 Santa's Home

N THE DOWNSTAIRS of the farmhouse here, I have a small furnished apartment that I sometimes rent out. Last year I rented it to Santa. A portly man in his fifties, he was serious about this Santa business. No fake beard and rented suit for him. He had a big full bushy pure white beard that flowed to his chest, a cloud of white hair and a big round body. When he came to look at the apartment, he explained that he would only be here for a short while, that he had many bookings across the country and would be traveling quite a bit during the Christmas season. As an example, he told me that he was to be the Santa on stage for the Boston Pops. He was extremely believable.

When he came that day, he did a song and dance routine for me in my kitchen. He danced lightly across my kitchen floor, a heavy man with nimble feet. His voice was a soft tenor and as he moved across the old floorboards, he sang the Santa songs (*you better not pout, you better not cry, you better not shout, I'm telling you why, Santa Claus is coming . . .*) His red suit was exquisitely tailored, the black boots made by a cobbler of old as was his belt, shining black leather and a bold brass buckle that held in his ample waist. Oval rimless glasses half down his nose completed the picture. It seemed to me he really must have come down from the North Pole for this short while, to stay in my house and tend to his duties around New England.

So he took the apartment. Perhaps he had a sleigh and eight tiny reindeer stabled elsewhere but so far as I could see, to get around to his various commitments, he drove a red Prius. Glancing out the window from above, I could see him leave the apartment in full regalia, tuck himself into the little car and set forth. I would sometimes pass him on the road, not hard to spot, the big red man behind the wheel of the little red car, his white beard glowing from within.

Even when he was not playing Santa, he seemed like Santa. On the rare days when he took a day off, he dressed in red and white striped long underwear underneath a pair of dark green woolen overalls, red piping running down the side of each leg, and red clogs. He would sometimes emerge from the apartment, dressed like this, his dog on the leash and together they would walk up the road. That is to say, I rarely if ever saw him dressed like an ordinary fellow, doing ordinary things. After a while, I wasn't sure what was real.

I hoped my guests might catch a glimpse of my Santa when they came here on Christmas. But, for days before and after Christmas, as snow sifted down, he was gone. I never saw him. And then, sometime after New Year's, he came home, and it seemed to me that he slept for days. Sometime in February, he left for good. He never said where he was going. When I was cleaning up, getting ready for the next tenant, I found tinsel on the floor and a big box of especially nice looking candy canes in the closet. So I knew Santa really had been here, at least for a while.

NOVEMBER 2010

Kindle Your Warm Hearts

T SEEMS LIKE the beginning of December is often like the beginning of a marathon. I start keeping checklists: write cards, buy gifts, wrap gifts, mail cards, plan Christmas dinner, put up decorations. . . the list is long and sometimes complicated by a snowstorm or bad weather. At times, I stop and think: wait! There must be some way I can eliminate some of this. In all the frenzy, there's hardly time to stop and think about why we are doing all of this.

A few years ago, mysterious messages began to appear along the roadsides of this town. The messages were written on thin strips of wood, painted white. The letters were black, painterly, drawn with an almost Oriental brushstroke. Like the old Burma Shave commercials, there were sometimes three little signs, nailed to successive trees or telephone poles. Signed "phantom haiku," the words almost always left me pondering the message. I recall one that appeared along the main highway, near a little gift shop, sometime in the fall: "Red, orange, yellow, brown/ Leaves are falling like gifts/ Remember this day." I felt the message, more than the falling leaves, was a gift, and, oddly, I have remembered that day.

Some time later, another message appeared, down near a place known to us as Mud Pond: "Endeavor to put yourself in the way of wandering miracles," the first panel read. The rest of the message was gone, perhaps blown off by the wind or torn away by someone with a hard heart. But that first line was enough of a poem for me. I took in the sentiment and remembered it later, kept it near for spiritual triage.

A side road that runs beside the lake comes to an end at the main highway. Turning safely onto the highway is a bit of a challenge, as the curve in the road obscures the fast-moving, oncoming traffic. Sometimes the best way to know if someone is coming is simply to roll down the window and listen. In the winter, the winds coming off the lake are particularly cold and forbidding at that intersection. Snow piles up and visibility is even more obscured. On a day close to Christmas, I was in the heat of my Christmas frenzy, my brain in the pressure cooker. I was driving to see an elderly friend but needed to be somewhere else at the same time. I was late getting the Christmas cards mailed, forgot to answer several phone messages. And so on. If my memory serves me right, this was the Christmas after the 9-11attacks and an additional anxiety clouded everyone's face, a mix of fear and anger and confusion. Even though, way up here in New Hampshire, we were so far away from so much of the threats, we felt it all heavily and with deep concern. On that day, I pulled to a stop beside the lake. The traffic on Route 101 whizzed by me. The day was cold and bitter — not snowing but the snow blowing off the lake made it seem like a blizzard. I leaned over to look to the left and then to the right and when I looked right, I saw another of the phantom haikus, nailed to the trunk of a birch tree. It had not been there the last time I went by. This one read: Cold winds of change blow/Prepare and be mindful now/ Kindle your warm hearts.

Kindle your warm hearts. I drank these words in like warm broth. The frenzy eased, just long enough for me to be grateful for the surprising beauty of these words and for the generosity of the anonymous poet who had released the words so artistically into the outside world — an act of faith that they would reach the right heart.

DECEMBER 2003

❈ The Wheel of Christmas

So much of Christmas is about traditions. We hang the stockings from the same hook, brew up the same favorite recipe for cranberry sauce, and bring out the ornaments that, in some cases, have been hanging from family trees for three or four generations. We always linger a bit over the oldest ones, gazing at them, conjuring up the magic they have bestowed in the past.

There are so many stories. There was the amazing Christmas when our entire family gathered at my aunt's house in Ridgefield, Connecticut. My recollection is that the Christmas tree that year was as high as the roof. I wonder how tall it really was. I remember that my cousin put Christmas candy at the foot of our beds, the night before, a prelude to the loaded stockings we discovered hanging from the mantel the next morning. Did anyone on earth, ever, have such a wonderful Christmas as we all did?

There was the first Christmas my husband and I spent in New Hampshire. We went out into the woods behind the farmhouse we were renting and cut a small fir tree. We dragged it back to the house, across the snowy field, and decorated it with popcorn and cranberries that I strung together with thread and red ribbons we had saved from last year's gifts.

But then there was the Christmas that my grandparents' chimney caught fire when we burned up the wrapping after we'd opened all the gifts. I was five but I still remember the black-hatted firemen coming into the living room, their boot steps resounding on the floor as they entered, as if they were there to escort the spirit of Christmas out into the cold.

And the Christmas Eve that our neighbor's car caught fire. His cat was with him and when he smelled the smoke, he jumped free of the car just before it went up. He had his cat in his arms and he was unhurt. The car was later replaced. But I always wondered why something like that, which had never happened before or since, would happen on Christmas Eve.

In fact, I can recall as much sadness on Christmas day as merriment. My grandmother's father died on Christmas day and she often told the story as an explanation why she could not enjoy Christmas.

My husband underwent radiation treatment on Christmas Eve, just one day in a long series. We knew, from the crowded waiting room, that this is a sad experience many people endure.

The first Christmas after the death of my husband I stayed home alone, fasting and meditating. I remember the white of the snow outside and the silence in the house, except for the sound of cars going by out front.

For the past fourteen years, on Christmas Eve, I've sung Handel's *Messiah* with a local chorus in the same place, with the same conductor to the same appreciative audience. It has become my favorite part of Christmas. The words we sing were taken straight from the Bible, familiar words and yet words I always listen to as if I hadn't heard them before. How can so many millions of people hear the same story over and over again and still listen with new ears?

Like all good stories, it is never enough to hear them once and in fact the more we hear them, the more meaning they seem to have. And so we hear them, over and over, in a revolving wheel of significance. In spite of all the ways we try to make Christmas into what we want it to be, the day changes and moves, much like the turn of the seasons or the shape of a growing tree, the same and yet ever so different.

DECEMBER 2002

🌀 On an Evening

L AST YEAR AT THIS TIME, which was to be the turn of the great 20th century to the 21st, I had a good supply of kerosene and candles as well as a hand-cranked radio stashed into my broom closet. My biggest concern was my computer, around which many things in my life and work revolve. It was probably eight years old and not compliant with anything that I could think of, including my wishes at various moments. What would happen when I turned it on on January 1, 2000? One of the most persistent rumors about Y2K was that our computers would crash, unable to make the momentous shift from one century to the next. All these oppressive concerns had all but erased the thought of celebrating this amazing once-in-a-life-time transition into a new century.

Then an invitation came into my mailbox. In red letters, the elegant script read: Millenium Celebration! A New Year's Eve party, to be given at one of the grandest houses in this town, a great sprawl-ing white mansion across from the lake and with a full view of the mountain. I had only ever glimpsed it from the road. Soon, word spread that the hosts had invited *everyone* in town to this black-tie-optional affair. There are more than a thousand people in this town. And, according to the invitation, we could bring children and guests. I hurried a favorable reply.

Our New Year's night was mild and the sky was clear. Before I left for the party, I turned off my computer and unplugged it. Who knew what the next morning would bring? All day long, on the television they had been broadcasting celebrations from around the world. As I dressed in black velvet, I watched monks dance around the Parthenon. It was a rare moment when I felt as if the entire world had stopped to join together in one happy event.

Up the long driveway, the big house was lit like a birthday cake and inside, not even at town meeting have I seen so many towns-people in one place. We have our quota of wealthy citizens and they were all there. Many of the men were in tuxedoes, women in long gowns, but just as many of us were in jeans and corduroy shirts. I saw a lot of our guys from the fire department and the road crew and our wonderful postman, Willie, smiling and rosy-cheeked, dressed in a suit and tie. There were lots of friends to hug. Everyone seemed happy that the big moment we had thought about all year had finally arrived.

Tables were laden with food and drink. As midnight approached, word spread that we should bundle up and go outside to the lawn which looks down across the lake to our mountain, the great arched blade of rock called Mt. Monadnock. With seconds to go, together I stood with all my neighbors known and unknown to me and we began shouting the countdown, *ten! nine! eight!* We were hundreds of voices and I thought at the time that we were shouting in unison along with millions, billions in our time zone. I looked out at the mountain, which is always black, and at the peak I saw a red flare, and from that light, came a distant brilliant silent shower of sparks.

There was no time to contemplate how or why the mountain had erupted. Other, much grander fireworks burst so near us, we could practically see the fuses. They flew up over our heads with that exciting *phhooooot!* and then BAM! the explosion and the rain of sparking colorful flowers came down into the magic of that night air. As the rockets went up and gently fell back to earth, we, this great crowd of our town, some leaning on canes, some hoisting chil-dren in their arms, were standing in the cold air, screaming like children, our faces lit by the glare. At last, the finale was shot off like the cannons of war. As everyone began to hustle back inside to dance, I looked back at the mountain and the red flare was still there and then came another small burst of distant fireworks from the peak, as if whoever was up there was sending an answer to our big show.

I never look at the mountain now but that I don't think of the fireworks flaring up out of the peak like a little volcano into the darkness of a new century and I never think of the term Y2K without remembering the generosity and optimism of our neighbors, Tom and Anne, who gave us a reason to celebrate and be with each other on an evening truly like no other, anywhere on this earth. The next morning, I switched on my computer. One century knit seamlessly into another and I was back to work without a single moment lost.

JANUARY 2001

🍥 The Art of the Trades

Last New Year's Eve, I bought a new car, something I do every ten years or so. Two days later, I had to drive three hours north, to the White Mountains to teach a workshop. In a blizzard. Baptism by fire. The car charged through it like a filly heading for green pastures. I passed accidents along the way but I arrived without incident and felt lucky to have gotten there only a couple of hours late. The hotel was a grand historic structure from the Victorian age, all restored to keep the feeling of the old yet offer the luxury of the new. The car was whisked from me on arrival and put into a valet parking lot. In the morning, I took in the breathtaking view of the Presidential Range which seemed to advance outward in every direction. Two or three days later, temperatures plummeted to 30 to 40 below zero. Maintenance men were on their knees in the hallways, applying blow torches to frozen pipes. I called a friend at home to ask her to please check on my house. Her report was what I feared: the pipes were frozen. I called Glenn, my plumber who has always been there for me at times like this. This time was no exception. He happened to be working near my house and went right over. Yes, he reported to me by cell phone, they were frozen and cracked and needed to be replaced. He set right to the task and by the end of the day, everything was in order.

This isn't what usually happens. When the temperatures fall below zero, finding a plumber who might be available is like looking for a ripe, sun-warm tomato in the dead of winter. Over the years, I've had two plumbers. The first one was Dan, whose wife was a friend of mine. They had met in college, both of them art majors. While in college, Dan worked as a plumber's assistant to help pay his way through school. When he got out of school, he kept on plumbing. The pay was good. He never returned to the art but his work became his art, pipes aligned and plumb and tidily labeled. People noticed. After a while, he was in such demand, I couldn't get him so I switched to Glenn, who once worked for Dan and whose work was just as lovely. But I wonder what it's like for the artist to labor in obscurity like that, the result of his work hidden behind a wall. Eventually, Dan's wife, who had a career as a graphic artist, joined Dan in his business and now goes out on calls with him, leaving her art behind the way Dan did. Apparently, art is a dangerous profession.

A friend of mine, who once taught English and drama to high school students, tells me that he used to counsel his students to be able to find a job in the trades, even in spite of high aspirations. "Something to fall back on," he says.

Is there a lesson here? Arriving home from the White Mountains, in my eager new car, I managed to back into my porch, a sickening crunch in the dark of an icy moonless night. In the morning, I called Michael, another artist in the trades who is there to help when I need him. In time, the porch too was fixed: an erasure of the fact of my late-night miscalculation.

At the time, it all felt catastrophic, a lightning bolt from God, but in retrospect, everything has been restored, as if nothing had ever happened. I don't know if there is a lesson but certainly a reason for me to be grateful.

JANUARY 2015

🍥 The Winter Breakers

WINTERS TEND TO BE long here, a fact we all acknowledge and live with, just the same. One day, probably forty years ago, a man who is no longer alive came up with an idea to make the winters pass more quickly. It struck him one day that all he did during the winter was wave at his neighbors at the post office. He thought it would be good to have a party every Friday evening, an informal affair that would have a revolving location. The host would supply the drinks and the guests would bring snacks. This way, every week there would be a place and a time to gather and catch up on the news. He called the group The Wave because it would be a bigger way to experience that "wave" across the parking lot. His tradition stands to this day: ready-made Friday night parties that require only one person to keep track of who is giving the party and on which Friday. And getting the word out. The rest is just fun.

In the next town, rumor of these parties reached a woman who decided her town also ought to have such regular opportunities for gathering and conviviality. And so she started what she dubbed The Breakers, a play on The Wave.

This woman has also passed away but her innovation carries on. I live on the border of the two towns so am sometimes invited to both shindigs. And, just as the generations have cycled through the town rosters, so have the guests at these winter parties. I especially like being invited to homes I have never been in before. New England homes are inherently unique. There are no tract houses in either of these towns so the individuality of each home is outstanding.

This past winter, we partied in a house that has three large living rooms and décor that rivals Winterthur — in fact, the owner is a benefactor of Winterthur. Another home is a converted mill house, one of the small houses given to mill workers back when the mill was operating. This little house has not changed its size or shape but has been polished like a piece of furniture, with ceilings that reveal old timbers and a front room window that frames the mill pond. One, once the town's post office, and another, the town's store, have both since been made into gracious homes. Another is an old farmhouse that's been handed down through the generations, complete with grandma's iron stove and her furniture, couches and chairs frayed and comfy. The most fun: a house built in the shape of a car, complete with headlights and fins.

See what I mean? The rich heritage of our towns emerges in these winter gatherings. Sometimes to reach the front door we may have to walk around signs advertising political candidates we may not endorse and inside, we skillfully maneuver around such subjects. Instead, we open our houses to each other and reveal our leanings, left or right, and our furnishings, retro or antique. There is a lot to that, if you stop to think about it.

Friday nights, we plow through snowstorms and in mud season, we squish and wiggle our way to arrive at the solid doorstep. Inside, asparagus canapés and pigs-in-blankets await. What brings us together more than anything is a desire to ride out the winter together. Before we know it, it's spring for which we rejoice a bit less, knowing the parties are over.

JANUARY 2012

Waking the Dead

WHEN I WAS growing up, a funeral was considered a somber event, one too gruesome to allow children to attend. As a result, I was not allowed to attend the funerals of my grandparents nor my great aunts and uncles. Maybe this was a good thing, I don't know, but I do know that for the past several years, I have attended the most wonderful, entertaining and heartwarming memorial services I ever could imagine.

One old auctioneer who lived in these parts threw two "funerals" for himself before he passed on. He didn't want to miss the party, he said. He also prepared for the event by painting his town's church (white) so that everything looked good for that inevitable event. I missed his service but I bet it was a good one. A service I attended on a bleak day in February last year took place in a bar because the dearly departed had spent most of his time there. There was guitar music, jollity, and plenty to drink, as hoped. But most of these events take place in churches, which have blessedly lifted the bar on allowing fun in the sanctuary. Most still include readings from the Bible, a few hymns, soothing words from the minister but there is a lot more that goes on now.

A few years ago, to celebrate the life of one Floppy (*née Florence)* Tolman, who lived past 100 (some say she was 104 but no one seems to agree, one of the risks of not being honest about your age), the town band oompahed, thumped and tweeted from the balcony of the church, as everyone knew how much she loved to hear the band. At another, also in February, we celebrated the life of a quirky lady who had made her living in the world of fashion. In cleaning out her house, her heirs discovered a vast trove of expensive perfumes. In a generous gesture that had more than one purpose, they devoted an entire table to these fragrances, new and old, so that any mourners could help themselves, which we all did, lingering over our choices. Again, a recent celebration of a dear friend who loved to contra dance, included a performance by one of the great contra dance callers (he himself no spring chicken) who walked to the front of the church, carrying his accordion, alongside a fiddler. Together they took seats in the choir pews and began to play a reel, calling it as if the dance were taking place right then and there. We, packed into the pews like sardines, could only clap and stomp our feet to the beat. The dance, we all knew, was not for us but for our friend in heaven.

What comes in between all these blessedly inspired elements are the stories. Everyone has stories to tell and we laugh and cry and learn a lot more about this person than we thought we ever knew. Recently, the lives of a couple who were devoted to each other throughout their lives came to an end. After an uplifting service that included a jazz band and lots of stories, their ashes were packed into a small cannon, usually reserved for celebrating the Fourth of July, and shot in a fiery blast toward their beloved Tolman Pond. We all screamed and laughed and blew kisses to them in departure. This is a lot closer to what the Irish would call a wake, which I believe is meant to wake the dead, in case they were only sleeping. I wonder what my grandparents would have thought.

JANUARY 2012

Not My Grandmother's Paperwhites

M Y GRANDMOTHER had a sunporch and around the edges, in front of the windows, she had copper trays filled with pebbles where she grew paperwhites, small white trumpet-shaped blooms emerging from bright green stalks. It seemed like a miracle to me, to see such beauty grow up out of gravel.

When I rented my first apartment, a small studio on the second floor of a brownstone in downtown Philadelphia, my grandmother came to visit — a long journey, carefully planned and bravely executed. She carried with her up the stairs and into my new home a brown bag with marble chips and four big bulbs. My first paperwhites. She also brought a wide blue bowl. "These will make you feel like you aren't in the city," she said as she emptied the chips into the bowl and nestled the big papery bulbs down in. She set the bowl under the kitchen faucet and turned on the tap. When the water was just visible among the stones, she carefully carried the bowl to my windowsill. "There," she said, "these will make you think of spring."

The bulbs gave up quickly and grew tall, then bunches of small, pure white blossoms opened, dots of bright yellow in the center of each one. My tiny apartment soon filled with that strange, exotic fragrance, not sweet, not spicy, I can't put my finger on it, but distinct, nothing quite like it. I can never smell paperwhites but that I don't think of my grandmother, her copper windowsills and her journey up the stairs with the brown paper bag in her arms.

Ever since, I can't imagine winter without paperwhites. First thing after Thanksgiving I go to Agway and buy ten or twenty bulbs, choosing carefully. I want bulbs that are hard and weighty, ones with a bud of green pushing out of the top. At home, I prepare several bowls. I keep the marble chips, year to year, and hunt yard sales in summer for interesting and colorful bowls. A dish of bulbs just starting up make nice Christmas gifts and I prepare several but mostly, I want them for myself. I repeat the whole process about three times over the course of the winter, keeping my windowsills cheerful and my kitchen filled with that grandmother fragrance. On good years, I have paperwhites right through March.

Sometimes, though, in those early years, my paperwhites used to grow up so tall that I would have to tie them with a ribbon to keep them from falling over. Then one day, an older woman came for tea and, casting a practiced eye on my windowsills, she said, "You should give your paperwhites a bit of gin. That will cure them." She was a member of a prominent garden club and I always listened to what she had to say to me about plants, indoors and out.

"Gin?" I asked. I wanted to be sure I had heard her correctly.

"Yes," she said without so much as a smile, "when they are up about three inches, add about a half a shot glass of gin to a cup of water and give it to them. Next time you water, repeat and you'll find that they won't get so leggy. The gin stunts their growth and they'll bloom more in scale with their stalks."

So I went out and bought some cheap gin. And gave it a try. It worked like a charm. Later, I learned you can also use vodka or whiskey, tequila, even rubbing alcohol. But somehow I prefer the gin. The only trouble is, instead of that mysterious fragrance, they make the room smell slightly boozy, which can be a little embarrassing when folks come to visit. So I tell them it's the paperwhites, which, of course, if they know anything about paperwhites, they know that's not what they smell like. Still, I like to add the gin, it works really well. But with that nip of booze, they are definitely not my Baptist grandmother's paperwhites.

JANUARY 2011

🌀 Mount Trashmore

T USED TO BE THAT the best view of our village was from the top of the mound at the dump. Every year as it grew taller, more buildings below came into sight. Once, more years ago than I know about, this mountain was nothing but a deep crevice. But then, along with all of these endless fickle desires, rose this pyramid created from what we no longer wanted.

Our weekly visits were a seminal part of our life here: the dump became the one place where we met up with our neighbors. Often we stood on this peak, having flung our garbage (*yeehaw!*), and talked over issues that concerned us. Our local politicians knew to set up headquarters and pass out campaign literature at the dump. Animals grazed on our leavings and occasional fires broke out. Artists prowled, looking for interesting objects. The mound itself was like a living organism. Each week, the powers that be designated a new area where we could hurl our trash and, at the end of the day, loads of sand were added to cover our sins. The next week, the area for disposal might be on the *other* side of the mound, an effort to create balance. And thus the size and shape of the hill would change, slightly. Like time-lapse photography, we could almost see Mount Trashmore rise. Though no one ever kept such records, in a year's time, it seems that the mountain would grow ten feet, maybe more, our ability to see ourselves ever increasing.

We could put anything into the old dump, anything at all. Of course, there was ordinary garbage, the scraps and bones from our meals. But there were also boxes, bottles, chairs, lamps, teapots, books, couches, stoves, tables, beds, doghouses, shoes, car fenders, air conditioners, rugs, cribs, skillets and crockery. What was brought in could also be taken away. Which one of us does not have a prized possession retrieved from the dump? (I myself have acquired a sterling silver tray and a copper colander from the town's leavings.) But if these old pieces of our lives were not claimed, they were buried, pressed and compacted ever downward into a weird geologic time-piece that someday an archeologist might view like the riches of a Roman ruin.

It's changed now. Five years ago, we were closed down by state authorities who viewed our dump as a waste site, leaching ugly substances into our groundwater and possibly polluting the wells of those who live downhill. Of course they were right. How could we have been doing this all these years? We repented and brought in engineers who assessed our unrighteous burial ground and instructed us in how to make amends. Experts arrived in shiny red trucks and the work began. Somehow, they moved our mountain and put a tray beneath it, then covered it with a layer of impervious material that no one of us had ever heard of. They graded and shaped the mound so it looked like a perfect cone and then planted it with grass, which is how it stands now, isolated by a wire fence, the great green pyramid of Mt. Trashmore. Though it was not, it somehow seemed ceremonial, almost sacred. Our lives and all the evidence of who we were lay within and beneath that pile. If we had a face, this was it.

We performed penance. We washed our bottles and separated our papers. We learned to know No. 1 plastic from No. 2. We no longer "go to the dump", we "visit the recycling center." If we want to discard chairs or tires, we have to pay, $2 for a chair, $5 for a tire. It is a sober and sterile place now, a place with order and rules. When we forget the rules, we are scolded, or fined. Our visits with each other at the new facility are shorter, less impassioned. The odor has evaporated. The politicians and animals have gone elsewhere. Everything we bring is later taken away in containers, hopefully to be reused and returned to us in another form. When I built my new deck, I used boards that are not made of wood but of recycled plastic bags and sawdust. I felt slightly liberated by such a notion but it wasn't like the glee of the old Saturday fling, more like an old person's memory of a good time.

Terrible things were going on beneath Mt. Trashmore — leachates were leaching and gases were building — but on top, like Romans, we pontificated and admired the view. In spite of what we know now, some of us miss the old place, for all that it hid and for all that it revealed.

MARCH 2001

❦ Piano Forte

WHEN I BOUGHT this house, there was a piano in the front room. It was an old player piano that I hoped to keep but it was judged to be ruined by mold and dampness and so, when we opened up the walls of that room, we strapped the piano to a bucket loader which lifted it gently into the waiting bed of a pickup truck. And off it went, to someone who thought he could restore it. Previously, I've given away two pianos that came with houses I have bought. Maybe I've been too hasty.

At a gathering of neighbors, I recently told the story of that player piano being removed from my house by a bucket loader and one among us recalled that once, many years ago, he had been called upon to remove a grand piano from a cottage on Silver Lake. The cottage sat sweetly beside the water but access was down a steep embankment. He gathered together three of the brawniest men he knew and then they all puzzled through the mechanics of carrying the instrument up the hill to their truck. It was winter time. They first removed the legs and then they strapped up the big sound box and endeavored to haul the body up the embankment with pulleys. The icy slope made this an easier task, or so it seemed at first. Halfway up the slope, however, the straps let go and the grand piano slid like a big sled right down the bank and whizzed across the ice, which gave way and the beautiful instrument sank to the bottom of the deep lake. Some oldtimers around the lake know the piano is there and occasionally someone dives down in search of the sounding board, which is probably all that's left of what went down maybe fifty or more years ago.

Another, similar story has to do with Babe Ruth's piano, a legend that comes out of the town of Sudbury, Massachusetts, on Willis Pond, where the great slugger once rented a cottage. The legend is that the Babe hurled an upright piano off the porch and into Willis Pond. A dogged Red Sox fan named Kevin Kennedy came across the story a couple of years ago. He believed that if he could find the piano and bring it back to life, the Curse of the Bambino would finally be lifted and the Red Sox would win the World Series, which they have not done since 1918, the year that Babe Ruth was traded to the Yankees — which is, for those of you who were just born, the root of the Curse. Kennedy recruited the help of divers and on several different occasions, they searched the lake with magnetometers and sonar. They found interesting looking "masses" under the silt but no definite piano, no keys, no harp-like image.

Could the great man have actually thrown a piano? A more likely but less dramatic version of the story was that, in a partying mood, Ruth pushed the piano out onto the frozen pond and played rousing tunes while friends gathered around and sang. Soon after, the ice thawed and the piano sank to the bottom. Mr. Kennedy is apparently still searching the pond's bottom for the instrument and the Red Sox are still searching for the win.

So, if you happen to find a piano at the bottom of a lake, you can imagine that it landed there by sliding down a slippery slope — or that it was thrown there by the great slugger himself. If, on the other hand, you find a piano in search of a home, by all means give it shelter. It might very well provide you with not only music but legends to last a lifetime and more.

MARCH 2004

🌀 The Snow Bunny

WAITING FOR EASTER sometimes parallels the wait for warmth. What is going to happen? We never know. Last year, snowstorms came, woven in with warm days, some in the 80s. Our family Easter plan was for my cousins to gather here at the farm for an Easter feast that included lamb and egg braid. My cousin Mac and his wife Marcia had been living in Nepal for the past 8 years and this was their first Easter at home in all that time, so that year seemed particularly festive. Mac grew up on the North Shore of Boston and a couple of weeks before our gathering he called to ask if I had the photo of the Snow Bunny. I hadn't thought of that picture in years but it was a family favorite, an enormous rabbit made of the snow that had fallen that Easter morning in 1955. The Bunny was as big as a grown man, ears straight up like fresh corn, haunches strong: a masterpiece. They had truly made the most of that April surprise.

At one time, I recall that my grandmother kept that photograph in a frame on a table in her living room. I paged through the albums, looking for the old favorite, going deeper and deeper into the trough of memory as I went. My cousins' mother, my Aunt Peg, had died the month before and so each photo I came across of her demanded particular study. She had great zest for life and her wonderful laugh could almost be heard, coming from the images stuck to the pages. At last I found what I was looking for. In fact, there were several photos of the big bunny. In one, my cousins, in their snowsuits and galoshes, are posing proudly in front. In another, my uncle, in tie and jacket, is putting the finishing touches on those wonderful ears. And in yet another, my cousin Susan is propping a hockey stick against his perfectly formed paws. The sun is full and in the background, Manchester Harbor is visible, a single lobster boat the only thing afloat. I pulled the best one from the album and put it into an old frame.

All week I found myself wishing a snowstorm would come on Easter, so that we might create a 21st century version of the Snow Bunny. But the day dawned, bearing warm sunshine. There was still a lot of snow at the edges of the fields and here and there where the plow had piled it high through the long winter. In the morning, with the smell of the lamb roasting in the oven, I opened the windows and let the breezes in.

I enjoy setting the Easter table, perhaps more than for any other time of year. I keep a collection of decorated eggs, some I made myself and some I bought on a side street in Prague many years ago. I also have a collection of little bunnies, which emerge from the drawer and decorate the table. I like the colors of Easter, too, yellow and purple and bright greens and I always try to include them in the setting. Sometimes, I have cultivated a small pot of green grass for the center of the table. We are so hungry for it. Our gathering was to number 15 and so the chairs at the table were close and cozy. I took time to place the eggs and the bunnies around the table and various other places in the room. When I was done, I put the framed photo of the Snow Bunny in the center. As we gathered, everyone studied it and recalled that day as if it were yesterday.

After dinner, we went out and sat on the screened porch, enjoying the spring warmth. No Snow Bunny this year. Thank goodness.

APRIL 2004

✣ The Irony of a Tree

A ROUND THIS TIME of year, I start thinking about pruning my fruit trees. A few years ago, I planted a couple of Macouns, my favorite of all apples, and a Reliance peach — known to be rugged in cold climates. I still worry a bit about mice chewing on their trunks at ground level and then, there are the deer who do the pruning for me in ways I don't approve. So these trees are at risk, probably for several more years. Last year, I got a budding yield of four apples and one peach, a delicious start.

What I have come to count on for harvest are three old trees, a Seckel pear and two enormous apple trees. These big trees have taught me a lot about the resilience of nature.

When I came here in 1997, I thought of these trees as the anchors of the house. I had no idea how old they were but their impressive size made me think they dated back at least a hundred years, perhaps more. The irony of a tree is that one cannot know its age until it is dead. Or perhaps that is the beauty of its being. In any case, these two apple trees rose up beside the driveway like proud guardians, each of them easily twenty feet tall, one of them maybe even thirty. On the other side of the drive, the tall pear stood in balance. But only a few short days into my ownership of the property, a horrific ice storm visited this hilltop and brought down many trees, including two thirds of one of these big apple trees. That is just a very short list of the damage, which also included the pear tree, so badly damaged, I almost cut it down. In my first year here, that tree looked as if it were made of coat hangers and it bore no fruit. At that time, I felt these trees would never recover.

It was the apple tree that worried me most. When I had looked at the property, that tree had had an endearing reach, the branches undulating outward in a kind of longing to escape its roots. After the storm, most of the tree was cut up and removed but there was what one might call a sucker, a hefty trunk that had grown out of the base and probably should have been nipped in the bud but it had grown outward like a branch, with that poetic stretch. The lean was sufficient so that the tree man was afraid it would not stand up on its own so he found a suitable crotch and wedged it up into the tree, a kind of life support. By doing that, the man likely saved its life and restored the poetry to the tree. In the years that have passed, the apple tree has developed a graceful goose neck and a lovely well-shaped crown. Eventually, the Seckel pear recovered as well and in the late fall I can stop under the tree and enjoy a snack of its small, yellow, blushing fruit, sweet as candy.

Somehow, this long, slow process restored my faith in nature. The trees are far too tall to pick, even the lower branches require a ladder, so I rely on drops. Good enough. I've found, by mixing the apples with the Seckel pears, a wonderful sauce results. The only thing I add is a cinnamon stick. I make sauce in the fall and freeze the many quarts, which last me all the way to spring. I don't prune these trees or worry about the mice or the deer. I do hope they live forever. Or rather that by the time they die, I'll be gone or else too old to count the rings.

MARCH 2012

Middle of the Road

E VERY MEMORIAL DAY since just after World War II, the townspeople in Dublin have paraded from the town center all the way to the cemetery, a good half mile. It used to be what I thought of as a quaint tradition. When the town policeman stopped the traffic in 1950, I'm sure it involved a few cars, if at all. It was a quiet road back then, barely paved. But now, the town police stop the traffic on one end and the other, and the world appears to go silent.

The band, bussed in from a bigger town nearby, consists of young people, on tuba and drum, horn and pipe. They step out into the empty highway along with the honor guard of retired military men carrying flags and rifles. Behind this snappy regiment come the men of our town who have fought in previous wars, marching, or, more frequently with each passing year, riding in convertibles, waving to all of us like the heroes that they were, decorated or not. They are dressed, most of them, in the uniforms they wore during their service. Many served during World War II and some in Korea or Viet Nam. When they have rolled royally by, grandmothers, dogs, babies in strollers, and all of us in between, fall in behind them. The parade that starts with pomp ends with our commonality, our union as a town.

What I love is that these men who served for us — and in this town, they are all men, so far — are here for us to see. They are the embodiment of why we are doing this. Once we get to the cemetery, we gather around a small podium that has been set up for this moment. Our war heroes come forward from the cars that carried them here, one of them on a cane and another on a walker. To see these uniformed men so frail brings tears to my eyes.

On the highway, the police allow the traffic to begin again, and the sound of the passing cars resumes, providing the background for the minister's comments that follow. We are reminded then of the sacrifice that was made by those who have fought overseas. When I was growing up and, in fact, until very recently, this was always a reality shift for me, to think about men going off to fight in distant lands. Since both my parents served in World War II, I used to think, how amazing, that our parents did this for all of us and then they came home, gratefully alive, and gave birth to us. Their triumphant return was perhaps a rare meeting of minds in this country, a kind of unrecognized nirvana.

But then there was Viet Nam and people quarreled about the morality of such a war and that feeling of unity seemed to vanish. Since then, the reasons for putting our young men and women in harm's way has changed, again and again. In fact, the very word "war" seemed to transform in its meaning and implications. Now that we are fighting a new kind of war, I wonder how Norman Rockwell would paint the Four Freedoms if he were still alive.

Shots from the rifles shouldered in by the men from the VFW resound across the lake. Salutes are made by all. And our police step cautiously back out onto the highway to stop the flow of cars so that we can return to the town center, where hot dogs and sodas await us. It seems like a longer walk home down the middle of that road, suddenly so still and so safe, and every year it seems that on the walk home, there is more to think about than the last.

MAY 2005

⚜ The Wedding Cake

E VERYBODY HAS their favorite wedding story and we had ours. It so happens that it involved Mary, whose house this was, whose house I did not know I would inhabit as a widow, as she did. But the story goes way back, before any of that.

Some twenty years ago, Paul and I were married in the little church in Chesham and it was to be a gathering of good friends. For the reception, we rented the old brick schoolhouse in the next town and friends provided platters of ham and salads and pots of baked beans. Our friend, Mel offered to provide the wedding cake. That would be his wedding present to us, he said, a cake from a special bakery he knew of in Maine. It made me a little nervous, the bakery being more than two hours away from the little schoolhouse but we were touched by his offer and made no other arrangements for a wedding cake.

On the morning of the wedding, we thought about Mel making his journey to Maine for the cake and were warmed by the generosity of his efforts. There was much else to attend to and, other than hoping Mel would make it back here on time, I didn't think too much about the cake.

I recall that there was some commotion as we all gathered at the schoolhouse, that there was some talk about Mel being late with the cake. Mel was often late, so this was not unusual. At last, he entered with the splendid creation, a cake so large it took two men to carry it in on a big board. We all gasped at its beauty for it was not only swirled and tiered but the top was bedecked with a veritable garden of flower blossoms, mostly lilies. They set the cake on a table in the center of the room, where everyone could admire it.

When there had been a goodly amount of eating and drinking and dancing, Paul and I took to the task of cutting the cake. As is the custom, we removed the top tier and put it aside, to freeze and eat on our first anniversary. And then the sumptuous cake was divided among all the many guests present. I don't recall that there was much, if any, left. It was good cake, well worth the trip to Maine.

Many months later Mel told us the story of the cake. On the morning of our wedding, he had set out for Maine. He made it to Saco in plenty of time and acquired the triumphant confection. He carefully set this sweet tower on the passenger seat beside him and drove cautiously, down the Maine Turnpike and across New Hampshire all the way to Peterborough, which is about ten miles from here. As he approached the local shopping mall, a car darted out in front of him. He braked and, *splat*, like a pie in the face, the cake hit the dashboard. The top of the cake was destroyed.

After he had assessed the damage, his mind raced. He had only two hours to spare. How do you repair a wrecked wedding cake? He called a friend for advice. She suggested Mary, who often baked for special occasions. It so happened that Mary was home and he carried the big, sorry-looking cake into her kitchen, requesting triage. She immediately began the operation, sweeping and shaping, trimming and tucking. From her garden, she cut flowers and brought them back inside, arranging them delicately on the crown of the cake. Back into the car it went and off to the schoolhouse where we were already dancing, oblivious to this flurry of activity that had just surrounded our cake.

When Mel told us this story, we laughed at the circumstance and were amazed that we had had any cake at all for our wedding. It wasn't until we took the top layer out of the freezer and unwrapped it for our first anniversary that we were really able to see the extent of the damage to that cake. The flowers had truly hidden just how badly it had been damaged. If we told that story once, we told it a hundred times.

Now the story of the cake has another layer as I marvel once again that it was Mary who performed the emergency surgery on our wedding cake and, some thirteen years after the cake hit the dashboard, it was to Mary's house that I moved. And that it is now Mary's flowers that I tend.

JUNE 2001

The Legend of Edgar's Rhubarb

T USED TO BE THAT not too many folks in this town planted rhubarb. Why plant rhubarb, they reasoned, when they can get it from Edgar's field? Edgar was an old farmer who lived up near the lake, keeping a marginal farm, with most of his revenue coming from the hay crop. Below the house, on a slanting bit of the field that never got hayed, he kept a big patch of rhubarb. Edgar died in 1978 and his house fell to ruin as the heirs bickered over the land and the farm. Every year that passed, the roofline sagged a bit more, another dormer slouched and the barn roof let light shine into the loft. But the rhubarb seemed to thrive. Edgar's rhubarb was thick-stalked and tall and, as it grew, you could see the leaves rise up, like big green hands waving, signaling that picking time was here. I knew when I was eating a pie endowed with that stealthy harvest. Where did the rhubarb come from, I would sometimes ask, already anticipating the one word answer: Edgar's.

In June, eager pickers made a path through the grasses from the roadway to the patch. I don't ever remember seeing anyone up there picking but I could see from the heavily traveled path that they had been there. Before we had a rhubarb patch of our own, we helped ourselves as well. As the hayfields grew up with milkweed and the edges of the fields began to close in with saplings, there were times when the rhubarb at the farm seemed like the most vital thing there. What the farm began to grow more than anything was legend. Stories abounded about Edgar and the legal battles that raged over possession of his farm — a rhubarb all its own. For some reason, Edgar's spirit would not let go of the place. I remember someone telling me that the teacup he had been drinking from the day he died remained on the table beside his chair. For years.

Then, a few years ago, came a young couple — interested in farming, it was said. The girl was the daughter of a local farmer and she had, quite remarkably, gone to college to study farming. The young man held a job somewhere but he was big and strong and seemed ready to tackle just about anything. No one knew what arrangement had been made for them to be living at Edgar's. The first summer, they parked their travel trailer in the farmyard. At night, driving by, I would look in and see the lights glow from inside the trailer and I realized how long it had been since there had been any lights in that barnyard at all. Those soft, yellow lights seemed especially sweet. That spring, they tilled up a big garden beside the old chicken house. Signs of life at Edgar's farm provoked conversation at just about every neighboring dinner table. Soon, the farmhouse began to revive, as if life had been blown into a skeleton. The clapboarded Cape transformed almost magically, not in the way we now do renovations but in that simple way that pays homage to the old place, respects what was there and re-uses it if it can. The changes were so subtle that some people did not really notice. The farm simply resumed.

Now the young couple is married and they live in the old but revived farmhouse. They have reroofed the barn, where they keep cattle and chickens and pigs, and to all of us grateful townspeople who know where to go to find them, they sell eggs with bright-yellow yolks and freshly slaughtered chickens that taste "the way chickens used to." They even offer beef, pork and homemade sausages. The rhubarb patch, however, is gone, the path to it erased. We accept that some progress requires sacrifice. And closely tend our own expanding rhubarb patches.

JUNE 2005

In Heaven

I N THIS ISOLATED PLACE, the woes of the rest of the world sometimes seem very far away, quite imaginary. But I have an apartment in the downstairs of this house that I rent out in the summertime. Guests come from all over — California, England, Belgium, New York City, Saudi Arabia — proving to me that I need go nowhere; the world can come to me. I meet the most interesting people this way. A weaver. A documentary filmmaker. A writer of scripts for real-life TV dramas. An artist.

The apartment was home for some time to the grandfather of the big family who once lived here. I've scrubbed it up and painted it over but there are still residues of its antique beginnings — the old brick chimney that passes through the kitchen to the upstairs, the deep pine cupboards, the light over the kitchen sink that keeps vigil. Guests seem to enjoy this bit of antiquity. They sit on the porch rockers and take in the untainted air, the silken quiet, and the unadorned view of our mountain.

Last spring, a woman about my age called to see if she could rent the apartment for her parents. She was staying nearby but had no room for them. I booked them in for a week in July. When they arrived, I greeted them and showed them around. They spoke to me in the musical lilt of the Deep South. It was haying season, the only time of year when there is a lot of traffic, tractors and trucks coming and going. I apologized for what I knew might be a noisy week. As we spoke, the big green John Deere wheeled into the drive, towing the baler, and headed for the back field. The father smiled broadly.

It seems he had grown up on a farm in Arkansas and had done his share of haying in his day. Evidently he loved nothing more than a farm scene, noise and all.

It was not only haying season but also peak season for berries. I have blueberry bushes and a blackberry bramble that yields good, sweet berries if you can get to them without drawing blood. And a few raspberry canes that came to me from a neighbor a few years ago, humble beginnings for what's now a darn good raspberry stand. Early mornings in July, I like to make a quick tour of these bushes, carrying my breakfast bowl with me as I pick. When I do this, words such as manna and ambrosia come to mind.

That week, I was busy, not home much but whenever I was, it seemed to me that my southern guests were resting contentedly on the porch. The week passed quickly and soon, I looked out to see them packing their bags into the trunk of their car. I hurried down to say goodbye. It was yet another of our glorious blue sky days. The mother stood for a long moment beside the car, looking around her, and then, sounding like a character out of Tennessee Williams, she said, "Yue know, Aah feel as if we ah in *heaven*."

"I know," I replied, "I often tell people that I live in heaven." She turned to me then, a look of surprise on her face. "Yue mean, we *agree?*"

"Oh yes," I said, "we do agree!"

"Well then," she went on, "if we agree, then it must be *true*! We ah all in heaven!" We all grinned and nodded conspiratorially.

The green tractor worked in the distance; clouds drifted across the blue skies; berries ripened silently on their branches. It was hard, very hard, not to imagine that all was right with the world.

JULY 2014

🌸 Red is the Color

L AST YEAR WAS one of the worst years for hay that I can remember. Aside from the need for sunny days to dry the hay before baling, these fields are wet anyway, so if it rains too much, the fields are too wet to bear the weight of a tractor. So the farmers wait and wait for that longed-for stretch of hot, dry weather. Here, we waited all through July — the wettest July on record, according to some reports — and into August before it seemed possible to cut and dry and bale. Even now the memory of that time is left in the fields in ruts so deep, the words of the tractor are written in the earth clear enough to be read beneath the snow.

A bad year for the garden, as well. For the past several years, I've belonged to a CSA, short for "community supported agriculture." The concept is simple: community members purchase a share of the farm and in return receive a bushel of produce. Such a thing is left on my porch each week, the vegetables fresh from the garden. Everybody wins. The basket provides a serving or two of peas or tomatoes or squash, each in succession as they come in throughout the summer. This also answers the call to buy local, which is sensible in every way I can think of. The produce is from the same earth we till here and it has not been shipped thousands of miles to reach my table and forced to ripen along the way. And the person who grew it is a friend who is trying to earn a living as a farmer. I think that person should be supported. Nothing against the farmers in Chile but I like the idea of eating the fruits of her labors instead. Supporting local agriculture is a simple idea, perhaps even self-evident and one once taken for granted, yet it has become a movement, an agenda that stirs passions among the committed, inspires bumper stickers and banners.

Even aside from what I get from the CSA, I still plant a garden, rows of tomatoes, basil, parsley, summer squash, cucumbers, the things I need more of than what comes to me in the basket. I love to can tomatoes, for instance, for use throughout the winter. The year before last, I had such an abundance of ripe tomatoes, I was able to put up 30 quarts plus plenty more for salads and slicing. These tomatoes, in particular, were unusually beautiful, perfect red red orbs, no blemishes or cracks or worms. Some even seemed heart-shaped. In fact, they were so gorgeous, so catalog-perfect, I posed them for pictures, wicker baskets full of happy fruit. I even had a bumper crop of green tomatoes, their season cut short by frost. Wrapped in newspaper and stored in the basement, these went in unripe and came out weeks later, red and juicy. That's what I call the end of a good year.

But then came last year, rain and cold, the tall hay standing in the field, blown over and flattened by each nasty storm. It was all a sorry sight. In my garden, the tomatoes hung sullen from the vine. (Puppy Harriet was no help. She picked them off the vines as fast as I could turn my back.)

Our summer ended with few ripened fruits, certainly nothing like the abundance of the year before. We shivered through many a July and August day, a fact that made some of us a bit cranky. The produce from the weekly basket wasn't much better than what I got from the garden here, that is to say, disappointing. I did no canning. In another time, even 100 years ago, we would have been facing a hungry winter. No matter how technologically sophisticated our world becomes, no matter how global, we still have to rely on the earth beneath us, the unpaved, still-fertile soil to provide, just as Benjamin Mason did when he first worked the soil here in 1763. I'm sure his first crops were meager. But each year must have strengthened the harvest. If that were not so, I would not be here now surrounded by open fields that still bear crops, fields that Mason and his sons opened by clearing virgin forest with axes. It all would have been forsaken by the successive farmers and long ago it all would have grown back to woods. But it's all still here and the hay still grows tall and the tomatoes blossom and bear fruit the color of anger, the color of heat, the color of passion, the color of love.

JULY 2010

🌀 With a Little Luck

ONCE REALIZED with sudden clarity that owning a home, a home that has some land and a few outbuildings, perhaps some animals, is no different from owning a small business. I manage the budget and prioritize the needs the same as any shopkeeper, lying awake with worries as well as hopes for expansion and improvements. One thing I lack in my little affair here are employees. Good help is not only expensive (budget item) but hard to come by (human resources). Especially in the summer months. Once in a while, with a little luck, the right person comes along at the right time. But there is usually a catch. Take, for instance, the Irish fellow who flew in and out of here like a rare bird on the wing. Friends told me about him. "He'll do most anything for a very reasonable price. And his work is good."

I didn't need to hear much more so I called him. He had a gorgeous Irish brogue, the kind that is so easy to fall into, once you hear it a bit. "Howareya?" he sang out as he emerged from his older model Volvo. "Aye, *gurgeous* place here! Yuh've gut a bit o' chores ta doo, have ye?" He was tall with silver hair, spiked up, not a young man but the piercing gaze of his blue eyes flashed intense energy. I showed him the gardens, the lily beds in particular, that had fallen into disrepair. It's hard to give over my garden — only I know what's in there and, oh, how well I know the weeds. "Nuh problem," he crooned, "Oy ken doo that up in nuh time." After I had shown him around, we sat on the porch and he told me the story of his growing up years in Dublin — Ireland. Eight children, hardly enough food to go round. They were hard years, worthy of the teller of *Angela's Ashes*.

The next day, I went away. I hadn't expected him to but he came while I was gone. When I arrived back, the lily beds behind the house were transformed, neat as the squares of a quilt. I was thrilled, even though he had left my garden tools strewn about and the wheelbarrow filled with weeds. It was more than I'd expected or hoped for. His muddy shoes were on my porch and so was his sweatshirt. But he was not.

A few hours later, he drove in. He was in a hurry, collecting his shoes and the few tools that were his. He asked for a nominal sum in return for his work. It was a bargain, by any stretch of the imagination. "Ooo, donchee worry now, el'll be beck and take care of all ye're gardens," rolling those r's to a fare thee well. I couldn't believe my luck. I wheeled the cart out behind the barn and dumped the weeds and picked up all the tools and returned them to the shed. If he came back, even twice, my place would look like a page out of Martha Stewart. I don't, usually, but I whistled for a little while, as if my life had suddenly become carefree. But, summer came and went and I never saw nor heard from him again. My gardens returned to being less than perfect. But I can still hear the musical manner of his speaking, the stories he told, and the promises he made. Aye, in this business o' mine, 'tis so.

JULY 2011

❧ Jazz Night

A THIN BREEZE BLEW UP off the lake as I parked in front of the old manse. It was late summer, most all the summer folk had left but there were a few hangers-on who had not, as yet, drained the pipes and cleared the pantry shelves for the winter. I let myself in, walked through the big old-fashioned kitchen, smell of casserole in the oven, and walked the familiar path toward the voices and the lights that seeped from under the living room door, closed to keep the heat in. Inside, a crackling hearthfire rendered warmth to a gathering of white-haired gentlemen who sat round the fire, cradling martinis. On the big chest, an array of old LPs had been arranged carefully in order, their frayed album covers set to the side. The gents were waiting for me, their year-round neighbor, to arrive before starting. Greetings all around but let's get to the music. Dick, our host and keeper of the cherished albums, scrutinized a center label, peering close through horn-rimmed glasses, to be sure. The turntable, perhaps from the 1970s, wasn't really an antique but it seemed nostalgic, to hear the familiar sounds, placing the platter on the tall spindle, securing it with the holding arm, and advancing the lever that starts the robotic process. The needle arm rose, tapped the record which dropped down onto the turntable with a slap. The needle moved over onto the edge of the thick, vinyl platter and settled there, allowing first a band of rhythmic static, once the prelude to all recorded music, before the drumbeat. Jazz night had begun.

For the past several years, it's been my privilege to be invited to Jazz Night, an otherwise all-male affair. No cigars are smoked but wives are sent off to the movies, jazz not their thing. It is mine and has been since my earliest years. The first LP I ever bought was a recording of The Dukes of Dixieland, all while my contemporaries were buying Elvis Presley and The Supremes. Jazz has always spoken to me, inspiration provided by my Uncle Jamie whose collection rivaled Dick's. With my uncle's help, I built my own collection, learned to dance the Charleston, and understood the importance of Louis Armstrong.

This has always been my pleasure but that night it was my ticket into this exclusive evening. Here we were, a gathering of jazzophiles, rapt by the sweet notes that jammed the wood-heated air. Peter sat back in his easy chair, closed his eyes in bliss. George tapped his foot with enthusiasm and sipped his cocktail, eyes focused on the middle distance of another time. We were no longer in this cheerful room at the end of summer. Peter remembered New Orleans in the 1930s. Were you there? Yes, they had all been to the French Quarter, to the clubs, before the war, but, shhh, we are not here to talk, we are here to listen. We stopped talking and fell into the spell of the music. Bix Beiderbecke, Paul Whiteman, King Oliver, Jelly Roll Morton, Sidney Bechet, Kid Ory, they were all in Dick's line-up. Bix's mellow cornet eased into the room. Singin' the Blues ("Can you hear the difference between the cornet and the sax?" Peter asked), Mississippi Mud, Riverboat Shuffle. Satchmo's infectious scratchy voice and his soaring trumpet took over. From time to time, Dick squinted at the faded labels to tell us who was playing what, which mostly the old guys already knew. The casserole burned but we served it up with gusto, in the spirit of the past, in the grip of a time I can't recall but they surely could. Eventually the stories emerged anyway. War stories, love stories, times spent on foreign shores. Another log on the fire, another record on the deck, till late in the evening, the music carried them off to these faraway times. I felt like an audience of one at a performance of memory, a privileged seat at their life's opera. Stories told, music heard — in opera, one is nothing without the other. I was privileged to have been there for that final act, before the old house was shut down for winter.

SEPTEMBER 2010

❦ Blue Moon

O F A RECENT FULL MOON, a cold, clear October night, clouds raced across the sky as if on a summer's day. The clouds were full, billowing, the moon reflecting off of them, creating a light almost as brilliant as that of the moon's. The sky itself was a midnight blue and the stars that I could see were sharp as steel points. I have rarely seen such a dramatic sky.

On the nights of the full moon, perhaps we are, too often, inside our snug homes, asleep, or stashed in the connected rooms of the city, unable, even if the desire exists, to see past the blazing lights of the metropolis. But here, in the stillness of an autumn night, there are no distractions or interferences and the event of a full moon can exhibit a pull, similar to a tide or an appetite. The moon rises, a big pink disc or cream yellow, blood red — the color always slightly different as it inches up from behind the pines that line the field. I go to the window, as if called. The moon, at the horizon, is huge, a planet bearing down on us. As it moves up higher in the sky, the color drains, fades to a bright white, happy orb, floating up into the dark sky.

Our Native Americans devised their calendar around the phases of the moon. To them, the moon was perhaps the most important aspect of their lives, around which everything that mattered to them revolved. They planted and harvested according to its phases, calculated their days and nights according to its wisdom. Each month was the length of the moon's cycle. Each month the name of the moon identified what mattered most that month. There were many variations but March was the Full Sap Moon, referring to the sap rising in the trees at that time of year. December was sometimes the Full Long Nights Moon, referring to the short days of that month. July could be the Full Thunder Moon, acknowledging the season of fierce storms. That October moon I saw, according to the Old Farmer's Almanac, was the Full Hunter's Moon, the meaning of which is still clear to us.

I was reminded of all of this that night, as the moon created a scene of singular beauty and awe. Soft moonlight spilled onto the floor and created still, silent shadows across the room. From my window, the outline of my house spread across the lawn below in dark moon shadow. The light was bright enough for a walk without flashlight and so I went out. Animals and birds talked out loud, as if either fooled or amazed by the presence of the light.

Standing there, I realized that many people around the world are blind to this moon, the light of their television sets providing a strange parallel. Among other reasons, the Native Americans revered the moon for the light that it gave them. Now we have so many sources of illumination, who needs the moon?

If we were to give this moon a name that would identify what mattered to us, it would not be a hunter's moon. Perhaps it would be the Full Foliage Moon, for the bright leaves that bring tourists that fatten our wallets. Or perhaps it would be the Full Politics Moon, for the flurry of politicians who descend on us, getting ready for next month's election. Whether or not we watch it or even see it, the moon still affects us deeply, architect of our seasons, our tides, our storms. The Blue Moon, of course, is the occurrence of more than one full moon in a single month. But maybe we could borrow this and call all the moons from now on the Blue Moon, sad moon, mournful moon, trying as it does to get our attention and remind us of what really matters.

OCTOBER 2005

🌀 Good Enough for Eve

PPLES. HAVE THEY BEEN with us since the beginning of time? If you believe the story of Adam and Eve then they were here before we were, since quite a few years pass between the time a seed is planted and the time a good apple can be plucked from its branches and eaten.

I love growing apples. Every year I put by a quart for each winter week. When I was young, I pledged to avoid insecticides and poisons. In my early gardens, compost and manure worked well, maybe even better, but with fruits, it was said, it was hard to avoid using chemicals. If you didn't spray, the fruit would not be worth eating. Well, in the various places where I have lived in the past forty years, I have been host to any number of apple trees. Some wild, some cultivated, most of the trees yielded apples with holes, blemishes, rust and sad deformities. Still, I have never sprayed a single tree. Nevertheless, I have been blessed with a ready supply of apples and applesauce, especially applesauce.

The two trees I now harvest are big, maybe twenty or thirty feet tall, gnarled and bent, yet veteran producers. The apples on the tree to the south are ready to be picked in August. These are leprous, deformed, wormy and green, showing only a hint of blush when ripe. The apples to the north come later, late September. These are also lopsided, a little wormy but a faded red, the color of my husband's 1948 Farmall. If I bite into a ripe apple from either of these trees, I might as well have chomped down on a lemon. A sour, puckering face results, the bitter fruit cast away. An apple only a mother could love.

Over the years I have discovered that these unsightly, unappetizing apples make great applesauce. Apparently the heat will bring out the sugar in the fruit. The key is that they are unsprayed, pure. You need add nothing. My trees are so tall, I have to rely on drops, which reduces the harvest — falling from such a height, some of them land bruised. But a lot of them survive so I go out and collect what I can into buckets, baskets and canvas totes. Sometimes I ask a tall friend to wield the apple harvester — a metal basket held aloft on a pole — and bring down more, usually a couple of bushels. In the kitchen, I cut the apples, washed but skins on, into quarters and put them in a big kettle, appreciating the vast colors of their skins against the whiteness of their flesh, cutting away blemishes as I work. The quarters quickly fill the kettle. Into the bottom of the pot, I pour a cup or so of unsweetened cranberry juice (it adds color and keeps the bottom pieces from burning). I push a cinnamon stick into the pile and turn on the heat. When I hear a little activity in there, I turn the heat down and keep it at a low boil. In an hour or so, the entire pot has been reduced to a bubbling mush and the kitchen a fragrant heaven. I turn off the heat. When it's cool, I put the mush into the mill. I turn the crank. Sauce oozes out, leaving the cores, seeds, and skins in the strainer. A surprisingly rosy, organic, all-natural, (not to mention free) applesauce falls into the bowl. It's a kind of alchemy, transforming these leprous outcasts to a spotless, sweet, and virtuous sauce, good enough for Eve.

SEPTEMBER 2014

🐾 Best Dog

WE CAN SEND MEN to the moon and clone sheep but no one has figured out how to extend the life of our dogs to even begin to match the length of our own. In my adult life, I've had three memorable dogs — Gorm, Dune, and Mayday. They all lived long lives, for dogs. When Dune came into that time of twilight, her warm brown eyes clouded into a strange blue. Her hearing all but lost, I despaired of losing her. She had been with me when my husband Paul was alive and after he died, she refused to come out from under the bed for three days, which is what I felt like doing.

My parents died soon after. I found it hard to recover from all the loss. Now Dune was getting ready to leave me. I definitely needed help. The doctor recommended anti-depressants. I was reluctant. What about a puppy? That sounded easier to take so I found a mini-schnauzer with a delicious little face and eager eyes. In seeking her, I was looking for a way out of the unending grief. Of course, as soon as she entered our lives, Dune and I were restored. New life! Mayday entertained us, infuriated us, and brought us joy. Better than Prozac any day.

But, alas, our scientists not working hard enough on the right tasks, Dune could not live forever and she surrendered at 17. More precisely, on the very day I had arranged to have her put down, she walked off into the dawn and never returned. Weeks later, I found her tired old body floating in the pond, a veritable Virginia Wolfe, equipped with clairvoyance to boot.

When they are with me I have called all my dogs, "best dog." Because they are. Mayday was very much my best dog, a sturdy little terrier who could run like a racehorse and snore like an old man. It seemed like no time before she was reminding me daily of Dune at her most elderly, the cloudy eyes, the hesitant step, the occasional lapse in continence. By then, I had brought the puppy Harriet in to ease the inevitable. It took a while but eventually they bonded, under whose terms I will never know.

Unlike Dune, Mayday did not take her own life but instead we drove together, Harriet and Mayday and I, on a somewhat overcast October day to Vermont where their beloved vet, Andrea Nealley, waited. I carried Mayday inside, where she went peacefully and with-out protest, ending it all with only a small sigh. After, Andrea stood back and said, "She was one tough cookie." She opened her file. The first entries: "3 months old, chewed piece of cordwood, developed bowel blockage; 4 months: chewed up rug, bowels blocked, removed fabric 'cork.'" So many other maydays followed. When the black lab tore her throat open; the time the two shepherds ripped her butt off. And no one will forget the evening she acquired 1,000 ticks, in the blink of an eye — a story worthy of Stephen King. I used to say that if we shaved her, we'd find a crazy map of scars and stitches, badges of her tenacity.

I named her Mayday because I was feeling sad and felt the need for "m'aidez" — I didn't think I was christening her with a name that would establish her fate.

Andrea gave me a hug and then gathered my best dog into a soft plaid blanket and bore her away. I swallowed my tears and went back out to the car where Harriet waited — Harriet, on her way to being Best Dog.

OCTOBER 2013

🧠 Waiting

I SUPPOSE THAT WHEN we think we have identified in a dog's eyes expressions of love, anger, sadness, guilt, shame, happiness, we may be imposing our own emotions on them, a bold assumption. But can a dog truly grieve?

Even when Mayday came limping toward her end last fall, Harriet gave me a clue of her deep connection to her friend. As Mayday prepared to leave us, I kept thinking it was my imagination when I found Harriet sitting beside Mayday's bed, day after day. She sat as if sitting vigil. Could she know? At last, when we returned from the vet's where we left our Mayday behind, Harriet went directly to Mayday's bed and not only settled into it, she draped her whole body lengthwise across it, a position I had never seen her take. Though she looked uncomfortable, her head hanging over the edge of the bed, she didn't move for days. Again, I kept rejecting that this could be anything but fatigue or coincidence. That this could be such an extreme expression of grief seemed incredible.

Mayday and Harriet did not start out best buddies — Mayday reacted to the new puppy like an angered venomous snake, lashing out, snarling and snapping at the tiny Harriet. In fact, Mayday was so upset by Harriet's entry into our household, she rejected me as well, deciding to sleep on the couch rather than her customary place beside me on the bed. She was so angry, if I walked into a room, she would get up and walk out, ears back, nose ever so slightly raised. This discord continued for at least six months but Harriet persisted. She wanted a friend. Gradually, Mayday softened and they adopted an increasingly close companionship. Where one went, the other followed, whether room to room or field to field. They were about the same size, Mayday gray with a cropped tail and ears tall like a donkey's and Harriet black with brindle face and legs, soft ears folded down, black tail wagging. They walked the land together, nosing the grasses and exploring the edges of the pond. They rolled in play. At rest, they shared the top of the couch, a favorite perch which allowed them to look out to the field and the driveway, keeping watch, able to survey activities inside the house as well. They ate peaceably side by side, never daring to stray to the other's dish. The backseat of the car became another refuge, Mayday vigilant, active, warding off approaching dogs, Harriet a silent partner, observing, never joining in.

So Harriet and I had to carry on, without our Mayday. Harriet lay across Mayday's bed for three days and finally rose up. But only to change her position, continuing comatose. This went on for days and days. Gradually, Harriet slowly returned to life as she had never known it, a life without Mayday who was her mother, her sister, her best friend, her teacher, her protector. Nothing I did seemed capable of consoling Harriet.

One day, a couple of months after Mayday passed on, I pulled into the post office. In the car parked next to us, a mini-schnauzer that looked very much like Mayday sat calmly in the passenger seat. Harriet saw the dog at the same time. She leapt up, cried out, and pawed the window. "It's Mayday! It's Mayday!" she seemed to be saying. But just as quickly, she realized it was not Mayday and she turned from the window, slumped back against the seat, and dropped her head in what looked like true despair.

Of course, I suppose that could also be my imagination or sheer coincidence. Dogs don't really grieve, do they?

MARCH 2014

🐚 The Approaching Cold

I T IS ALWAYS interesting to unpack the contents of an old building, bits of history spilling out like clues to a shapeless mystery. What is this broken plow doing here? Could it ever again have a purpose? Why would someone save a three-legged chair? Questions like this pop up as I begin the task of emptying the old barn for its demise.

It wasn't that I hadn't tried to save the building. I had investigated every avenue I could think of, queried every possible grant and historical site, but no savior came. To its disadvantage, the barn was not particularly distinctive, but it was indeed a barn of great age, and the posts and beams were blonde and fair and imposing, the pins as big around as a giant's thumb. The roof leaked, the sides leaned as if they were up against a steady wind. I was told it would take $30,000 just to put it back to rights and then what? I have no farm animals to house.

Up in the haylofts, there are still a few bales of hay — how old, I wonder? The wide center loft sags with boards and old doors, evidence of the Yankee thrift I still suffer from, always imagining that someday that door will again find a doorway to fill, that the molding will find a room that needs trim. It is as if whoever put those boards up there was thinking my same thoughts, as I gaze up into the loft and cringe at the idea of pulling all of this down, carrying it to the center of the hayfield and lighting it on fire. So I don't.

But I have to deal with everything down below, as it all needs to be moved out before the barn comes down. The boats come out first. Friends help me lift them bow and stern and walk them out onto sawhorses set beside the woods. Next the old picnic table. I think of the many outdoor meals shared on this pine table over the years but none since the screened porch was added onto the house. Dust and bird droppings cover the tabletop. Out it comes, into the brisk autumn air, where we set it next to the boats. The men will be here any day to begin the process of dismantling this big old building so there is tension in the air, mixed with the chill of the approaching cold.

In the horse stall, a fine porcelain sink rests on the old bed of hay, so surprisingly thick and fresh, it seemed one could lie down on it and sleep peacefully. I stashed the basin there when the renovations were in progress, thinking it might be right for the bathroom. Just looking at it, I feel my back ache. We heft it up into the truck and drive it to the dump, where we set it down gently, hoping someone will rescue it to another life.

And so the days go by, a parade of old stoves, rickety chairs, picket fencing, all of it too rusty or too rotted to really consider doing anything with but throwing away. Some things — skis, a doghouse, boat hardware, lime spreaders, rakes, cultivators, and so many different styles of shovels I feel I could start a museum all my own — I add to the pile for the yard sale, the great American recycler. A few things, like the broken plow, I keep, for reasons I can't explain.

As I carry all of this out from under the big old shelter, it occurs to me that these old barns are like temples now, a place of hope and prayer, where the pieces of our past can be placed, safe and dry, awaiting resurrection. I see then how much lesser my life will be without this great structure, how much I have counted on it for grace and the help of things past.

NOVEMBER 2005

❀ Raging Bull

ONE DAY LATE LAST FALL, when I was out raking, a pickup with a noisy muffler rumbled past. In its wake, a big black beast went raging by, hooves flying, tail spinning. Head down, he rollicked into the field across the way. My dog, Mayday, barked furiously from behind the protection of the front door.

I was pretty sure whose animal this was. I stepped quickly to the phone and called the farmer down the road, who keeps cattle. "I think one of your bulls is in my field," I said. My heart was pounding a bit, as I'm not brave around certain kinds of animals.

There was a pause. "Yup," he said, finally, "that one's been on the run for a couple of weeks."

"Well, I've got him in my sights," I reported cheerfully, expecting to hear him say he'd be right over to get him.

"Mmmm," he said, laconically. "He's awful hard to get, that one. We've tried but he's slippery like a deer. It would take a posse to catch him."

"But," I said, not quite wanting to disclose that I was a bit fearful of having a bull on the loose around my front door. Or state the fact that it was hunting season.

"I'm not too worried," he said. "He'll probably come home through the same hole in the fence he went through to get out."

Sounded like wishful thinking to me. I hung up and went to the window. Mr. Bull cut a fine profile out there, big and black and mighty, flipping his big rope tail as he tore at the late season grass. He fit the scene like a glove. But, when Mayday and I went out for walks, I would have to decide: did I want to wear red to protect myself from the hunters or *not* wear red to avoid being charged by a raging bull? One farm near here has a large sign on the fence that reads: "Don't cross this field unless you can do it in 9.9 seconds. The bull can do it in 10." No need for a stopwatch on that one. I'm not a fast runner.

A few days passed. I hadn't seen him do any more stampeding. In fact, he was becoming rather endearing. Sometimes he'd turn his head and look toward the house, as if tempted to come over and make friends. At night, he'd cry and caterwaul and carry on sadly. Each morning, first thing, I'd look out to the field to find him. If he wasn't there, I'd fret until I spotted him.

Weeks went by this way and the weather turned cold. Frost on the field. Bull still on the loose. Then days of not seeing him turned into weeks. I began to think that maybe the farmer had come to get him when I wasn't home. Or, perish the thought, a hunter had taken him.

Finally, I called to inquire. "Oh, yes," he said. "One day I was standing out in the barnyard talking to a friend and she came walking up the road, right up to us. We stepped aside and she went right into the barn."

"She?" I said. "I thought it was a bull."

"Nope. A cow, a young cow, full of beans."

Whatever. I was surprised how much I missed him, a contented presence who had raged in and settled down, munching on the last greens of a good year.

NOVEMBER 2007

⚘ One Stick at a Time

OVING TO New Hampshire forty years ago was a combination of rebellion and adventure. At that time, I was an editor at a book company in Philadelphia but my husband and I were uncomfortable city dwellers. We moved first to Vermont but soon saw the advantages of New Hampshire. So we crossed the bridge and found a farmhouse to rent. In the dirt-floor cellar, an old stove was tucked into the corner. With Herculean effort, we carried the stove up the rickety stairs and set it up in front of the chimney flue. It wasn't too hard to figure out what we needed to make it work but we missed one important feature: we pushed it flat up against the wall, which was composed of pressed wall board. It's a wonder we didn't set the place on fire.

But we brailled our way through it. A lot of mistakes were made. We perfected a method of building a fire: a nest of newspaper (*New York Times* preferred), plenty of dry pine kindling, then three (no more, no less) sticks of dry hardwood, adjusting the dampers as we went until it was a good, settled blaze that spread heat all the way to our bones. All this came about during the oil embargo of the 1970s and we liked the idea of outsmarting the sheiks. I see now that we were building not a fire but a life.

Our first season of heating, we cut the wood with bow saw and axe, moved the wood out of the woods and up to the farmhouse in my '67 VW Beetle (removing the front passenger seat made it into a dandy woods vehicle) and gobbled up 10 cords in a notoriously frigid winter. An uninsulated farmhouse and a stove with open seams helped in that effort. We were young and strong and our bodies never failed us. The heat, provided by the labor of others, didn't come on just by flipping a switch, another badge of pride we wore for years. We loved the reward found in the work required which provided us with a deeply penetrating heat all winter long. We felt there wasn't anything like it. We turned in the old leaky stoves for beautifully restored antique cast iron stoves that provided not only function but form, the cornerstone of our lives.

Somehow, this method of heat has followed me throughout, transitioning from cutting our own to buying it cut, split, and delivered. There's a catch, though. Time moves on and the aging process sets in. My husbands have been gone for a number of years. Keeping the house warm has been my challenge and delight throughout these years alone. But this is the part I never saw coming. An illness this past winter severely limited my strength. Where carrying a large armload of split wood into the kitchen woodbox had been how I started each day, suddenly this was no longer possible. What once had been my joy became my agony.

The woodstoves went cold and the dread rumble of the basement oil burner became a familiar sound. Recovery was the goal. I once revered a man named Scott Nearing who, at a late stage in life, built a house of stone. He did this by picking up stones from his woods, one at a time. From this, he built his stone house. So I started bringing in the wood, one stick at a time, filling the wood boxes slowly throughout the day. It was a way of building strength and restoring confidence. When the time comes next November, I'm hoping my ability to carry wood in by the armload will parallel the rest of my recovery.

NOVEMBER 2014

Bean Time

I HAVE COME TO LOVE being snowed in, no way out until the storm ends. Deep in snow, the big greystone trees that surround my fields stand watch and I sink down into the release of a day all my own. Sometimes, especially on these days, I get a hankering for baked beans. Last year we had a lot of snow days so I made a lot of beans.

Over the years, I have collected bean pots and bean recipes. I've found people are passionate about beans and you can spark quite a discussion about what kind of beans to use when making baked beans. Pea beans. Kidney beans. Yellow eyes and black eyes, black turtle beans, lima beans and, good heavens, even soybeans.

I'm a fan and defender of navy beans, also known as Great Northern or pea beans. I still use the first bean pot I ever had, which belonged to my grandmother. I've tried all 37 of the pots that I own and this one makes the best baked beans of any of them. It is unglazed on the outside, giving the feel, if not the exact color, of a flowerpot but the inside is glazed, a glossy deep cinnamon color. The lid (the Achilles heal of bean pots — at least half the bean pots I see are missing their lids, the casualty of time and the mobility of the human race) is all glazed, with a small hole for escaping steam,

When a good storm heads this way, I put a quart of navy beans into the bean pot, cover them with water and leave them to soak in the pot overnight. All night, while the storm pounds the house, the beans plump up. In the morning, the road not yet plowed, I parboil the beans, a gentle process to soften the beans. I'm still in my nightgown and the snow outside is still falling. After a while, I spoon up a few beans, blow on them and if the skins crack open, I turn off the heat and get ready for the bake. The oven in the wood cookstove is already at a good low heat — never above 250°. I drain and rinse the beans. Into the bottom of the pot, I put a small onion, cut in half. The onion adds the same kind of sweetness as the salt pork, without the fat. On top of the onion, I pour the drained beans.

Every recipe I have calls for molasses and I used to use it, all the time. But years ago I worked with a woman in Vermont who gave me her bean recipe. No surprise, hers called for maple syrup instead of molasses or brown sugar. This is the recipe I've used ever since. By January, what's left of my year's supply of maple syrup is ready to be emptied into the bean pot. So, with pleasure, I measure 1½ cups of maple syrup into a pint of boiling water and then I add ¼ cup of apple cider vinegar, 2 teaspoons of dry mustard, a teaspoon of ginger, a teaspoon of salt and some fresh ground pepper. I pour this over the beans, which usually covers them. If not, I add some more. I set the lid on. And into the warm oven they go.

I have a pile of books I save for stormy days. I choose one and settle next to the stove. The kitchen fills with the sweet scent of the oven beans. The day goes by this way, the luxury of time like the pleasure of a good dessert. Occasionally, I lift the lid to make sure the beans are not getting dry. If they are, I add hot water and tuck them back in for a while. After about six hours, the beans have turned a golden brown. I ladle a few out of the pot and let them cool before I taste. Sweet surrender. I want to eat the whole pot. Usually by then the snow has stopped and the road is plowed, leaving silence and the brilliance of the new snow. And a pot of beans for the rest of the busy week.

JANUARY 2006

🌀 One Last Good Meal

FOR THE PAST DOZEN or so years, I've sung in the choir of our local church. Each Sunday, we guide the congregation in hymns and sing an anthem, something by Brahms or Rutter. With a clock tower, a weathervane, and Doric columns, the Dublin Community Church is a classic 19th century New England house of worship, such that appears on calendars and postcards. Inside, the painted wooden pews, softened by long corduroy cushions, lead up to a simple altar: a drop-leaf table adorned with a linen cloth. The minister, awaiting the start of Sunday service, sits on a Victorian loveseat that's probably as old as the church itself. Downstairs, a deacon turns up the heat as the church, six days gone cold, takes a while to warm up. These are the stripped down days of winter. But in February, the Sunday before Ash Wednesday, the old furnace has help as we come together for what has become the hottest day of our year: Jazz Sunday.

On this annual event, four jazzmen arrive, stepping through snow to carry their telltale instrument cases into our chaste, high-ceilinged sanctuary, setting up next to the piano beside the choir. Usually, they wear dark glasses and dark suits. Scott Mullet is their leader, a local legend who once played sax with greats like Woody Herman and Artie Shaw, Aretha Franklin and Lou Rawls. For years, he was on the road and then he came home to roost. Our gain. His frequent appearances at clubs and bars and similar Boston-area venues always bring in the crowds. Surely this white-steepled venue is his most unusual — sometimes he has been up till all hours, playing a gig in Boston. But he manages to get to Sunday service on time. He is accompanied by a trumpeter, a bassman, and a drummer. Scott is a man of few words. His tea-colored skin and long black ponytail would make him seem Native American even if he weren't. His language is his sax, which sings, wails, and cries.

The sanctuary fills. Scott snaps his fingers a couple of times and they swing out into "When the Saints Come Marchin' In." Barbara, our choir director, who is usually up in the choir loft turning out the usual Bach or Handel organ prelude, works the piano like Jelly Roll. Close my eyes and I am in New Orleans. This is our faint effort to tie in to Mardi Gras — a way for us slightly uptight northern Protestants to steal a bit of joy from our more fluid Southern cousins. As the service begins, we move on into the hymns, maybe "Precious Lord, Take My Hand" or "Down by the Riverside." Scott and his men listen one verse and then jump in with their harmony. Earlier, we rehearsed our anthem together — "Amazing Grace" or "A Closer Walk with Thee" are favorites. The choir sings a lot of oo's and ah's and amens — we know we are just back-up singers for the main attraction. Our voices blend with their hot sounds. The congregation starts to sway, a bit stiff at first, smiles broadening, and finally they bring their hands together in time with Scott's beat.

Lent is an arcane Christian ritual of self-denial and abstinence. Some people give up something for which they have a weakness, chocolate or alcohol. Some fast. It's a hungry time. Mardi Gras is actually French for Fat Tuesday, being the last day of eating without restraint before the fasting days of Lent arrive. And so we invite these music men in to our church to give us one last good meal. And when we leave the church, our hunger sated, even the snow seems to have melted, just a little.

JANUARY 2013

🌸 A Shock of White

AT THIS TIME OF YEAR, when the ice is disappearing from the ponds and some fields are greening up, patches of snow or ice stay, along the edges of shaded roads and in the north corners of the fields. They are a shock of white in a spring landscape. Sometimes, if it's a warm day, I think it's a shirt or a piece of paper blown into the corner of the field, stuck against a wall by the wind, but when I get up close, I find the cold remains of the winter's snow, clinging.

I have a friend who is an artist. Her studio is in the upstairs of the old tractor barn on her big farm in Ashfield, Massachusetts, and her canvases, large and small, reveal glimpses of brooks and hillsides, hidden corners and open expanses of this farm, which she and her husband bought 20 years ago from a couple of old bachelor farmers who had lived there, the last of many generations to work that land. When they gave up the farm, the brothers sold everything, not just the farm but the contents of the house, which fairly burst with their belongings, along with the possessions large and small of those who came before them. Their past clung to them and when the time came, it was all put up for sale at an auction. People still talk about this day, all the old tools and furnishings carried out onto the lawn, sold to the highest bidder and then carted off, vanishing from the farm like ice on a hot day.

Jamie and her husband Paul have settled in just as comfortably with their horses (nine of them at last count) and their children (three — gone now but a lot of their things have stayed) and their boats and their tractors. They say if you have a space, it will be filled. Jamie and Paul have done the farm justice by using the land as it has been used, filling the barns with animals and haying the fields for feed for the animals. Jamie can run a tractor as well or better than most men. And when they break down, she will take a crack at fixing them too. When she's done with her horses and her children and her haying, she turns to her art. For the past several years, Jamie has been painting what she calls the Last Snow Series. As it gets warmer and warmer, Jamie tells me about discovering these wedges of leftover winter in the corners of her vast fields or along the roads she travels. She is a *plein air* painter, that is, she paints outdoors rather than in her studio. So if she is on her tractor or in her car and she spots these shreds, she hops off and paints — Jamie is always prepared to paint.

She calls me and tells me about this. I tell her I love to come upon these stubborn remnants in my fields too. Sometimes it's not only spring but almost summer when I find the crescents of snow or ice in the north corner, the cold remains of winter, clinging.

MARCH 2010

🌀 Thin Ice

CE FISHING, A SPORT I've never fully understood, is popular among men. There must be some women who enjoy ice fishing but I don't know of any. On the lakes where it is permitted, colorful little shacks known as "bobhouses" appear on the ice. In deep winter, men drive their trucks out across the ice, and park beside their little houses, which creates the cozy impression of a small village.

It was this kind of scene last winter that created a drama on a lake near here. The ice had been unpredictable, as was the weather itself, a strange mix of snow and sleet and thaw and cold. One Saturday, a couple of friends drove their trucks across the ice to their bobhouses. They were following each other, each driving big pickups. The ice was only six inches thick, though they claimed later they thought it was 14 inches. As they approached the middle of the lake, down they went, first one and then the other, the hefty trucks vanishing under the frail ice in a matter of seconds. One observer told me one of the drivers popped back up out of the ice "like a champagne cork." The other driver made his way out of the slurry more slowly, unable to coax his dog from his sinking truck. The men arrived on shore, unharmed but chilly. And heartsick over the loss of the dog.

That left the puzzle of how to retrieve the trucks. Divers searched and found the trucks resting on the bottom, 60 feet below. The trucks, filled with gas and oil and other engine-essential substances, posed a threat to the pristine lake's ecology. There was a sense of emergency about extracting these pollution-laden vehicles before they caused any further damage. A wrecker arrived and started out across the ice to help but, it shouldn't have been a surprise, the wrecker then plunged through. With the news of this third episode, the shores became dense with onlookers and reporters. Signs were posted at the boat launch, warning that three trucks had gone under and "don't be #4."

The problem of how to get three trucks up out from under the ice was posed everywhere, in barns and in coffee shops. Everyone had an idea. Days passed. Eventually, and perhaps miraculously, using divers, snowmobiles, cantilevers, jerryrigged wooden cradles, a little Yankee ingenuity and the help of many men, the vehicles were hauled up out of the depths like monster catches, each one receiving cheers and elations. The men who had driven those trucks out across the thin ice and nearly lost their lives in the process came forward and great helpings of humble pie were shared among them.

We, who stay away from thin ice at all costs and who would never think of doing anything but perhaps skating or walking on thick ice, were given the chance to read about these incidents in the dark winter evenings, after the paper was delivered. We talked of it in amazement, mourned the loss of a good dog and, in general, exercised our enhanced ability to feel superior. Which was just what we needed to break up a winter that hadn't had much else to offer.

MARCH 2006

🌀 The Good Apples

T IS APRIL AND I have just carried the last of the apples up out of the root cellar. Outside, the snow has gone at last and the earth is beginning to warm. The daffodils are beginning to emerge, pushing up through stray leaves, and the farmer who keeps my hay-fields came yesterday in a rainstorm, pulling a big trailer of fertilizer behind him, spreading it across the fields around my house. Within a few days, I will be surrounded by a brilliant green. But, for now, the fields are still muted, a mix of the straw of winter and the coming green. With restraint, I'm singing that good old pop tune, One Bad Apple Don't Spoil the Whole Bunch, Girl.

At first glance, the bag appeared to be full of rotten apples, puffed, mud colored and puckered. Of the two bushels I set down there in October, throughout the winter I had made a steady procession of pies and sauce, cakes and just plain apples eaten in the hand. They had spent the cold months down there in the silent darkness, alongside onions and potatoes as well as a bushel of winter squash, a few cabbages, and a bushel of grapefruit sent to me by a friend in Florida. It is a larder from which I take, week to week, month to month. The apples are not from my trees. Those apples are scarce and lopsided, somewhat bitter, the trees so tall, it's not really possible to pick from the fruitful crown. Instead, I buy from an orchard in the valley. I buy the crop that looks the best that year. With the exception of MacIntosh and Delicious, most upcountry apples are good keepers, given a good cellar. This year it was Macouns, plus a half a bushel of Northern Spies. I use the Spies first, as they don't keep that long but the Macouns live on, seemingly impervious to the passage of time.

By April, the onions and potatoes are still good as the day I brought them into the cellar but the apples are pretty much over. Peering into the bag, redolent of vinegar, I think I see one good apple. I gingerly put my hand down into the bag and the apple-like image that appeared to be nestled into the mush feels hard and sound. I pull it out, like the Crackerjack prize, and find, to my surprise, a perfectly good apple, with a hearty sheen of red and yellow. Looking back down into the sad remains, I see another possible survivor. That too I pull forth and pretty soon, after dusting the skins of flecks of mold, I have more than a dozen good apples sitting on the counter. While the others succumbed, how and why did these survive? A question for the ages.

The skins were still thick and the flesh, a bit pulpy, was forgiven, considering the alternative. These were not eating apples but they were still good for other uses. I sliced them into quarters. I put the wedges into the stew pot, adding a couple of cinnamon sticks and a dollop of cider to keep the bottom of the pot from scorching, and set them on the already hot cookstove. Simmering on the edge of the stovetop, the apples reduced to mush and filled the kitchen with the stronger scent of new apples. When the skins rose, I pulled the pot off the stove and let them cool. While they cool, I carry the bag of rotten apples out to the compost and release them into that friendly environment. The spring wind is high and chilled and I am glad to return to the warm kitchen. I put the good apples through the strainer, producing a big bowl of hot applesauce, the last of the winter, turned to warm comfort.

APRIL 2006

❦ Making Hay

O N THE WALL INSIDE the barn hangs an old scythe. It belonged to my husband, who knew how to sharpen the blade and how to wield the serpentine tool to cut grass neatly and sharply. He was not an old man but rather a young man who appreciated the ways of the old. The scythe handle is itself of wondrous design, contrived to pass straight along the curving contours of the land, to have mercy on the grass as well as the man who cradled it, an ancient dance between earth and man.

Haying quickens the pace and brightens awareness, as we watch the sky and smell the air for the sudden change of a summer's afternoon. I try to imagine the fields here, all cut by hand. I know that the men came out in teams and cut together. I've heard the sound was like a great singing whisper.

Many years ago, I worked in the hayfields in the windy and cool climate of Iceland. The grass was not cut with a scythe but rather with sickle bar attached to the side of a small, squat Russian-made tractor. The cutter laid the grass in rows to dry in the cool Arctic sun. What Icelandic farmers do not have in intensity, they make up for in hours — the summer sun never sets so there's more time for drying. When the hay was ready, we children of the farm were sent out to rake it into windrows. Later, when these rows had dried, we began the harder task of collecting the hay, using rake and pitchfork. We used the fork to stab the grass, bunching it tighter and tighter onto the sharp tines until we had tight bundles at the end of our forks. We'd heft these handmade bales onto a wagon until the overflowing load was pulled back to the barn where we would unload it, one bundle at a time, into the high loft, a precious harvest for the very long winter to come.

Hay is still made here on this farm, though I don't participate. Each year, it seems, the process becomes quicker, more synchronized, more efficient. Jay, a farmer who is also my neighbor, takes the hay from my fields as well as from the fields that adjoin. He and his son-in-law come in on fast tractors and sometimes sweep the fields in a majestic John Deere duet, the two tractors cutting, tedding and raking in tandem. The baler has a kick on it so that as the bales are made, they pop out of the hopper and fly up in a high arc, landing neatly in the wagon behind. On a summer evening, this can make for mesmerizing viewing as the field becomes the stage on which these tractors and bales become the performers. The sound is more a great clatter than a whisper. At last, sun setting, engines straining, gears grinding, the tired farmers pull the harvest home, wagons piled high as a house. The scent of drying grass lingers in the air and comes in my open windows at night. Within days, the fields green up, the beginning of another crop. Making hay, however it is cut and baled, is an eternal harvest, if we can keep the fields and the farmers that long.

JULY 2006

❀ Phantom Dahlias

A MAN DOWN THE ROAD grows dahlias, the magnificent and ancient starbursts of color that only really dedicated northern gardeners will grow. Ted and his wife, Wendy, are schoolteachers in another state. Several years ago, they bought this small dormered Cape for a summer place. It faces the mountain and was at that time surrounded by bare, uncultivated ground. Once they purchased the property, they wasted no time in turning up the soil and planting a flower garden which now rises up from behind the stone wall in colorful display, causing the occasional car to slow as it passes by.

Less prominent but no less spectacular are the dahlias. On a triangle of land across the road from the house, with the full view of Mount Monadnock as backdrop, Ted opened up a long row into which he placed the tropic-loving tubers (once beloved by the Aztecs) that would later in the summer become a broad stripe of color across the cool New England landscape. They grew tall, their flowers opening in almost any color you can imagine — tangerine, lemon chiffon, Mexican orange, blood red, pure white. Some blooms are big as dinner plates, some small as crabapples but all of them blaze in vivid colors. Ted's uncle got him interested in dahlias, way long ago, way before Ted brought his gardening prowess to this hill. His uncle, gone now, gave him some dahlia tubers to start him off. Now Ted grows something like 175 plants in his long thin garden, 90 or so varieties, but the one from his uncle blooms purple.

Ted says that when it opens, it's like seeing an old friend. He believes that flowers are connections, to people past and present.

So when I drive by, I see him down there in his colorful paradise, communicating with his old friends, human and floral. Built like a wrestler, he works steadily, long hours, his bare back browning in the sun. A few years ago, Ted added a beehive and painted it a bright, sunny yellow. While he works, the bees buzz from bloom to bloom as he steps carefully from flower to flower, fussing, tending. During the summer, he ties their bobbing heads to tall stakes to keep them from falling over (some of them grow to be seven feet tall!) and he weeds around their roots, waters them if it's a dry year. His yield is terrific. They are in full flower all summer long.

Most gardeners (including myself) think dahlias are too much work — planting the delicate tubers in the spring, digging them up in the fall, tagging them for variety and color, and storing them in the cellar until spring. It's a notion that Ted scoffs at. He says only, "The earth smiles in flowers." He loves the joy he gets from just watching them grow — and he especially loves sharing the dahlias with others. While he's working, sometimes he's thinking about who in town might enjoy some of this color in a vase on their table. "I like to make people smile," he says. On Sunday afternoons, before leaving to go back to their other life, Ted and Wendy fill their car with bundles of these dazzling flowers and start out on their route. As if on angel's wings, they make their phantom deliveries. Occasionally during the summer, while I'm working at my desk, I hear something on the porch, the dogs bark a bit. By the time I get out there, no one is there but on the table a big showy bunch of dahlias greets me. Or, if I'm not home, this is what I come home to. Believe me, I smile.

JULY 2012

🕸 Kindling the New

RECENT CARTOON IN *The New Yorker* depicts an older couple sitting amidst the construction debris of the interior of their house. The caption is "Our dream is to live long enough to see the end of our renovation." I have often spoken those words here, where, one room at a time, the walls have fallen to sledge hammers, doors lifted off their hinges, windows crowbarred out and thresholds pried up and away from their long service. There is little in this house that is as it was on that September day nine years ago when I signed the agreement to purchase Mary's farm.

The building was sound, except for the foundation, which, I was told by the house inspector, was "one of the worst he had ever seen." Sobering. But, like so many others who have entered into these tumultuous relationships with old houses, I was floating on the river of denial when I imagined that the house could be fixed up with just a bit here and there. One thing always leads to another. Some architects had advised that I tear the place down and start over. "It will cost you a lot less in the long run," I was told, more than once. Houses such as this once was are now referred to as "teardowns," to me, a chilling word. No, I'm too stubborn and frugal. I wanted too much of what was left standing from 1762 and years in between to even consider taking away the whole.

With the many walls and doors between all the small rooms of this big house gone, the incredible light of our open sky spilled into what had been a dark and segmented place. I welcomed the light, a virtual presence that is now every bit as much a part of the house as the old floors and remaining doors.

Fortunately, I burn wood. The water-stained ceiling moldings, the cream-colored baseboards, the treads to the old stairway, narrow as a mountain stream, along with miles of lath — many fires have been kindled with these colorful pieces of the old house. As I cut them to length, the sticks were prickly with nails, heavy with many coats of paint or wallpaper or hunks of plaster, and redolent of the rich lives that walked those floors and leaned against those walls. I sometimes rake the ashes beneath the grate of the woodstove and find not only square-cut nails but hinges and latches. I have saved as much as one person can without sinking from the weight of its heft as well as its legacy. The rest of it has gone up in smoke and the smell of its history lingers in the mountain air.

In spite of all that's gone, much is left. Mostly, what remains is the skin and the skeleton and what is referred to as the "footprint." That word seems especially fitting, as the impression of the old structure is what remains, the evidence that it has stood in this place and left its mark.

We're almost there, the house and I, greatly changed but still standing, still breathing, still bearing testimony, leaving me to wonder what I will use to light my fires as the next heating season draws near.

SEPTEMBER 2006

❧ Hauntings

PEOPLE SOMETIMES ask if I've ever seen a ghost in this house, a reasonable question since the house dates to 1762. Like the flowers in the field that open in spring and fold when their time is over, many people have been born here, lived here, worked here and died here, leaving an invisible tapestry of legacies. Ghosts, I've been told, are beings with unfinished business, unable to leave until it's settled. I believe in ghosts and would not dismiss a ghost or reason it away if I saw one. But, I've never seen or heard one in this house.

Over time, I've heard many accounts of ghosts, including one from the inn in this town: in one particular room, a gossamer woman takes a seat in the rocking chair at the foot of the bed after dark. I've heard the same account from several different guests who have stayed there. The accepted remedy, if you want one, is to put a stack of pillows on the chair, which seems to keep her from making herself at home.

However, the first year that I lived here, so many unexplained and unfortunate things happened, it felt like a haunting. The pipes froze and broke. The heavy weight of a massive ice storm broke many of the venerable trees that had given the property its poetic appeal. Since I was unable to move into the house until my previous home sold, I rented the house to a family whose rent was to cover the mortgage until I could take up residence. The septic immediately overflowed, and then, in spite of their excellent references, their children managed to wreak enough havoc upon the place that my insurance company (fortunately) covered the damage under vandal-ism. In their four months of occupancy, our one-man police force made 25 visits to the house, for reasons that could not be disclosed, because these were minors. But I have a few solid guesses.

When at last I moved in, early on a May morning, I set to work on the renovations, hiring a number of wonderful craftsmen to help me. It seemed then that the curse had been lifted. And yet, within a few weeks, one of the men had a heart attack and a week later another one followed with the same ailment. Fortunately, both men recovered. But as all these occurrences accumulated, they, in them-selves, created a further sense of foreboding. I became convinced that a bad spirit lingered here, giving me the extremely uncomfort-able feeling that I was not meant to be in this house.

Perhaps it was my persistence that ended the jinx. I continued on the path I'd set, brushing away cobwebs, opening up doorways and adding windows. I filled the house with family and friends. Light entered and warm feelings took up residence.

So, in answer to the question, I've never seen a ghostly figure walk down the hallway nor have I heard footsteps on the stairs or harp music coming from the rafters. But if a house is capable of hav-ing a spirit, this one certainly does. A spirit I cleave to.

OCTOBER 2006

The Legacy

MY LATE HUSBAND Paul came from a big clan. His mother was somewhere in the middle of a span of twelve children so there were lots of aunts and uncles and cousins. Paul's favorites were Aunt Elsie and Uncle Stanley who had a little farmhouse on a broad stretch of acreage, a place where the wood cookstove was warm nearly year-round and the smell of pickling spices or apple pie wafted out into the dooryard. The house was surrounded by the Christmas tree farm Uncle Stanley had carefully tended throughout their lives on that farm. We often went there for visits (drop-ins welcome) or Sunday dinner. Elsie could concoct miracles in a kitchen most of us today would find impossible to work in. Uncle Stanley was a logger. He wasn't very tall or very big but he was a strong muscle of a man who kept working well past retirement age. Once, when Stanley was into his nineties, son Gary arrived to find Stanley high up in one of the tall pines that surrounded their house. Something about cutting limbs that blocked his view. He didn't know what all the fuss was about when his feet safely came back to earth.

Aunt Elsie died some years ago, and then Uncle Stanley followed after going it alone for probably as long as he cared to. I don't know how he managed without Elsie's cooking. Their children kept the house. Some years passed before we realized we could all still gather together, even if missing such important members of the clan. So last year, Cousin June called to invite me to join her and her siblings for dinner on Thanksgiving weekend. I was happy to accept. It had been years since I'd been to visit Stanley and Elsie. Stepping from the porch into the old kitchen, I rocketed back thirty years or more. Nothing had changed. Sometimes the past can live right alongside us in the present. Gary and Curtis and Elwood and Douglas and June were jostling around in the space, each at their own task. The smell of roasting pork and apples spiced the air. At this house, you sit down to dinner almost as soon as you get your coat off, which is what we did.

At the same time, the Christmas tree farm was open for business and cars were driving in to the yard, parking willy-nilly. They seemed to know the rules. June and Gary kept watch from the window. Folks got out of their cars, bow saw in hand, and trudged up into the meadow, selecting the perfect tree — these trees were beautifully conical, pruned yearly by Uncle Stanley's expert hand. They returned with their prize, June greeting them at the porch door, depositing the asking price into the jar. It was their father's best legacy to them: they were reaping the benefits from trees they never planted. Still working on our big dinner, we watched from our seats at the table as they placed the trees on top of their cars. A good show. At least one out of four needed Gary to go out and help them strap it to the roof or reposition it, gently explaining the aerodynamics of it all.

We finished our meal and our string of family stories and memories. As always, laughter prevailed. I suddenly realized this was my opportunity to get Aunt Elsie's recipe for Soft Molasses Cookies. I always regretted I had never asked for it. Scraping back their chairs, everyone went rummaging around to find this wonderful receipt that produced a soft, cake-like cookie, a high dome of ecstasy. Recipe card in hand, I went home happy, knowing that, in their absence, the essence of Uncle Stanley and Aunt Elsie lives on.

NOVEMBER 2013

Aunt Elsie's Soft Molasses Drop Cookies

These are wonderful, cake-like cookies, beloved in the
Phelps family. Bet you can't eat one!

> 1 egg
> ⅔ cup shortening
> ½ cup sugar
> ½ cup molasses
> 1 tbsp. white vinegar
> 2 tbsp. cold water
> 3 cups flour (scant)
> 2 tsp. baking soda
> ½ tsp. ginger
> ½ tsp. salt
> 1 tsp. cinnamon

In large mixing bowl, mix together first five ingredients until well
blended. Whisk together dry ingredients and add to the big bowl.
Bake on a cookie sheet in a 350 degree oven for 8 to 10 minutes.

Do not overbake!

✿ Days on Ice

DECEMBER 11, 2008. Freezing rain was forecast. I prepared in my usual way, setting aside jugs filled with water, and checking my supply of lamp oil. I filled my woodboxes, made sure my pantry was well stocked. The dreary rain reminded me of the day in January 1998 when the sound of gunshots resounded around me as big trees snapped in two and fell on my house and barn roofs. It was like the world was falling down all around me. Since that time, any forecast for ice has traumatized me. They called it the "storm of the century." Nothing like that could happen again in our lifetime. We hoped. But this rain, falling heavily through the night seemed like déjà vu all over again. At one o'clock in the morning, I woke to a still darkness and the instinctual knowledge that the power was out. A call to the power company revealed that virtually the entire state of New Hampshire was without power. I stoked the stove and returned to bed. In the morning, still dark, I lit candles and brought my hand-crank radio down off the shelf. The radio had little news, except to say that 400,000 households (a substantial portion of the state) were without power, from Berlin to Winchester. A power company official used the apt analogy of a tree to relay the news of when we could expect our power restored: "There's the trunk, the branches, the limbs and then the twigs. If you live in an outlying area, you are a twig." I knew it would be a long wait.

Morning light revealed my car, every tree, every branch, every blade of grass imprisoned in ice. Icicles hung from branches and power lines like prisms from a chandelier. The power and phone lines that connected my house to the utility pole on the road lay on the ground across my driveway.

Soon, my neighbor who lives about a mile down the road called to ask if I had lost power. Her house is all electric. I invited her to come to my house where I have woodstoves and a gas range. She said she would be right up. I waited a while but she did not come. I pulled on my ice creepers and set forth onto the newly arctic land-scape, everything coated in ice white. I traveled about on my tundra, every step resounding in the still air, careful to avoid the wooded areas where trees continued to fall. It was a completely new world. Tree bowed, trees broken. Limbs lay about as if a tornado had come through. On the icy sheath I crept out onto the road. For the first time I could see tree after tree lying in the way. I knew then why my neighbor had not come. I was completely cut off. From where I stood, it looked like Armageddon.

For two days, I sat at my kitchen table, watching out the big window that faces the mountain. Rain hammered the house like a summer storm but the thermometer was stuck on 30 degrees. Every ten minutes or so, a branch or a tree snapped, giving that dread sharp crack, and then shattering on the ground like broken glass on a concrete floor. Rain continued. I felt like a captain on the bridge of a ship keeping watch in a big storm. Visibility was poor, naviga-tion pointless. On the second night the rain ended and a full moon rose, lighting up the crystalline world like a stage set for Fantasia. I strapped on my ice cleats and walked out into the welcome, almost blinding light. The shortest day of the year was only a week away and the darkness brought on by the storm had felt punitive. The beauty of this ice-covered world seemed magical, suspending reality.

Driving was a unique experience, slaloming around felled trees, broken telephone poles and downed wires. The tops of many trees had snapped off, leaving naked trunks standing like so many raised swords in the forest. Trees, too big around for me to hug, had been snapped in two like twigs. Some had been reduced to a bundle of splinters, the tree torn as if by the huge hand of a giant. Enormous splinters stabbed the ground like javelins thrown. Of all weather phenomenon, ice is the most serenely destructive. No shrill wind, no thunder or lightning or shuddering of the earth. Just silence but for the piercing reports of the breaking trees.

So many back roads were closed it was easier to tell us which roads were open than which ones were closed. Out on the main highway, I saw a tractor trailer loaded with generators parked by the side of the road, selling generators out of the back like a street vendor. When I reached the town of Peterborough, I found what looked like an abandoned village, stores dark, few cars parked on the street. It turned out that some stores were open, in spite of their lack of power, and customers could come in, using flashlights to scan the aisles and cash to purchase their items. At the post office, workers sorted mail in their heavy coats by the light of big flashlights. The impression of End Times continued.

Shelters were set up in schools and in fire stations. Volunteers, most of whom did not have power at home, cooked for their neighbors in the school kitchens. Bathrooms with flush toilets were much appreciated but hot showers were the scarcest commodity. A mobile trailer with stall showers was set up at the town fire station, offering showers to anyone who needed them.

I hauled water in five gallon jugs from the local spring into my kitchen. I read by candlelight, gathered hunks of ice fallen from the trees and melted them in pots for wash water. I cooked and washed dishes by the light of my (indispensable) headlamp and fed all my woodstoves an astonishing amount of wood. My bedroom went cold so I slept beside the stove in the living room, a considerable gift. The real meaning of a three-dog night became apparent but I had to be content with just one.

The days went by. My hand-cranked radio worked well but the radio stations seemed clueless. The public radio station continued with their usual programming, referring listeners to their website for information about the storm. Who among us had a hand-cranked computer, I wondered. We were also warned to "stay away from downed power lines," but they were everywhere, scattered across the icy roads like so much spilled spaghetti. Most of us had become used to driving over them and even walking over them. There was no such thing as a live wire for miles and miles. Those toxic cylinders known as transformers lay about as well, some of them sitting in the middle of the road day after day. It was not only a physically frozen world but everything else seemed frozen as well. If help was on the way, we had no way of knowing. Shipwrecked sailors, we waited for rescue. I read in the paper that crews from as far away as Ohio and Florida were coming into the region, arriving like an army, some 500 trucks in all, here or on their way to help. Power in some of the towns around us had been restored but for us, they said it was simply "unknown" when we could expect to return to normal. All my basic needs were met and yet I was falling into a pit of despondence. I felt that unreasonable fear that life as I had known it might never return.

Routinely, I get up at 5 in the morning and start to write or read. It's the way I live. Five o'clock in the morning is as dark as midnight at that time of year so, during the outage, I would get up, light candles and resume the vigil of the night before. The wait seemed endless. I pride myself in being self-sufficient, well-prepared for storms and emergencies. I was stunned at how this outage had crippled me. In all the years I have lived alone, I never felt so isolated as I did during this time, deprived as I was of my phone, e-mail and the internet, all of which I use to stay in touch, 24/7, with that huge world outside my small, purposely remote life. I felt like a junkie, communication my drug.

Then one day, I was coming out of my neighbor's driveway, after a visit. It was the tenth day of life without electricity. I looked down the long downhill stretch of my road. In a blur of whirling orange and blue lights, a literal armada of trucks was parading up the road toward me. I thought I was seeing a mirage. The town's cruiser was in the lead — a police escort. It turned out that there were some thirty-five trucks in this rescuing army, all of them from Hydro Quebec. Apparently the high tension wires that run behind my house held the key to much of the outage in our area, as two of the towers had toppled over in the ice. I had seen helicopters buzzing around back there but had not realized they were lowering men and equipment to the affected areas, otherwise inaccessible from the road. In addition a fleet of smaller vehicles, carrying men who were organizing and directing this operation, buzzed around these big lumbering trucks like agile animals. In the history of this road, which dates back to the 1700s and which even today experiences only the occasional car, I can safely say there have never been so many vehicles on this road at one time.

They were here for two days, working from dawn to dusk. These men from Montreal, as I came to call them, did not speak English and worked with a translator. It was just days before Christmas and they, along with hundreds of other linemen from all over, had come such a distance to help us. I waved, clapped my hands and blew kisses at them to express my profound gratitude. In town, someone hand-painted a big sheet of plywood that read, simply, *Merci*! and leaned it against a tree. I was happy to see them and watch them work but all this excitement had not, yet, restored my power. They declined my offer of meals or warm refuge — they were here to work, they said. The damage was so complete they had to rebuild the entire grid from the ground up. They ran out of telephone poles, they ran out of wire, they ran out of transformers. Rumors flew. When a tractor trailer loaded with transformers was seen rolling through town, a cheer went up. I was told only: *Soon*!

On the twelfth day of life without power, I went out to buy more candles. Coming home, turning into my driveway, I saw a light on in my house. I wept at the sight. Inside, the house had come back to life without so much as a burp. Water ran from the tap, the oil burner rumbled on as if it had missed only one interim, rooms were illuminated with the flick of a switch, toilets flushed, my cell-phone could finally be recharged. When my phone rang the first time, I was startled.

In the days that followed, I cautiously put away the lanterns and water jugs and cleaned out my refrigerator, humming again at last, and brought the cold food up from the basement, which had served as my makeshift refrigerator throughout the outage. Two days later, I went to Vermont to celebrate Christmas with friends and on the way home, I saw Christmas lights and decorations for the first time and realized that our dark December had shuttered Christmas as well.

By February, enough snow had fallen to cover the massive array of fallen trees and branches that littered the lawn and fields all around my house and along the roadsides, everywhere in this region. When the snow melted in the spring, we were faced again with the memory of the time most of us would rather forget. We were fortunate: no one was injured, no one lost their home. But for months afterward, many people shared how long it had taken to recover from the experience of the ice. We were somehow changed.

It would be nice to think that there were lessons to be learned from all this. I think back on the isolation but I also think back on the lively and spontaneous community supper that gave everyone a hot meal and lifted our spirits. I think back on choir rehearsal at the elementary school, we, wrapped in our heavy coats, our scores illuminated by our headlamps. And on the evening I spent playing Scrabble with friends, something none of us had done in a long time. I think back on the afternoon I spent with two friends, an older couple who chose to stay in their house, even though their generator had failed them. The house was chilled, into the 40s, but we sat together in their upstairs parlor, a cheery hearthfire their only source of heat. A table of Christmas gifts and colorful wrap sat in the corner — no matter what, their grandchildren were getting their gifts! We pulled our chairs closer to the fire and threw logs on the flames. Ancestral portraits looked down on us from the walls and the candlesticks stood ready to be lit as the afternoon waned. Outside the window, snow sifted down, covering the tiresome glare of ice. We talked and told stories. We laughed. As darkness set in, I made my way home, past the fire station where the good men and women of our town were standing by. They waved as I passed by. My house was cold from my absence. I fed the woodstoves, lit the lamps and cranked up the radio one more time. I would never want to live through that again, and yet, when it was all over, it was all of this that I missed, that cozy feeling that we were all in this together — the candlelit community supper, playing Scrabble with friends, seeing our volunteers waving from the fire station — that part I would love to have back, all over again.

NOVEMBER 2009

With Lots of Love

M Y MOTHER'S FAVORITE part of the Christmas season was the exchange of cards. "It's the one time of year I get to hear the news," she would explain. She did not live far from where she was born and raised but many of her friends, following the end of World War II, had settled in faraway places.

Sometime in November, she would set up the card table in her bedroom, organize the cards and envelopes around her and begin. Like a scholar bent over an important work, she spent days crafting her cards, writing each one individually. In her round, open script, she shared what mattered to each of these farflung friends. A small tower of plump, sealed envelopes rose beside her. Once, in the 1950s, a cousin of hers began the tradition of sending out typed newsletters, not even signed personally. My mother felt cheated by this mass production of the yearly greeting.

She always tried to get her cards into the mail by the first week of December. She sent them off as if on the wings of carrier pigeons. She expected something in return.

And her wish was always granted. Waiting for the mail truck to ease away from the mailbox, she pulled on her coat, wrapped her head in woolen scarf, and tucked her feet into her fleece-lined boots for the walk up the driveway, often through new-fallen snow. She returned, clutching the thick, square envelopes, sometimes red or green, like prizes. "There's one from Claire!" she would exclaim. Claire, her next-door neighbor growing up, was by then living in Florida, the wife of an Army captain, and she always wrote the long messages for which my mother hungered. And there was June, who lived in Massachusetts. And Marguerite who haled from Georgia but who now lived in England with her husband, a teacher, and her children. My mother served in the Marines with Marguerite, a fact which both of them found amusing and perhaps the highlight of their lives. Neither of them were over five feet tall or 100 pounds and they both loved to laugh, which perhaps kept them on an even keel throughout the war. My father, too, received cards with long messages from his old friends who served with him in the African desert and on the island of Corsica. I believe it was through these Christmas cards, with their unmistakable warmth, that I discovered much about my parents' past.

She didn't open the cards right away but left them unopened on the hall table. When my father came home from work, they opened them together and sometimes read them out loud. My sister and I sat with them and heard about friends like Claire, whom we had never met, but about whom we knew a great deal.

Some of my friends have abandoned sending cards. Too expensive, they explain. Too time consuming. But, like my mother, I never want to lose touch. Without Christmas cards, I would never know that the little boys I once babysat for are now men, with interesting jobs and children about to go away to college. How can it be, I wonder to myself. Another friend is in remission from her cancer. Another is getting divorced, yet another married. All that life has to offer seems to unfold on this little Christmas stage, which, for my mother, began at a card table.

And so, beginning in November, I settle at the kitchen table and begin to write. My mother would be disheartened to know that most of us, by now, have adopted the method of her forward-thinking cousin, recounting the major events of our year in newsletter style. For the rest, the part that counts, I sometimes stay up till midnight, scribbling personal notes, watching snow fall, and, in the morning, mail them off with lots of love and the strong hope of a return.

DECEMBER 2006

Winter's Surprise

THERE'S A QUESTION that people who spend time here in the summer often ask me: What is it like in the winter? I don't know if they ask out of idle curiosity or if it's the question of someone who is thinking about giving it a try. My answer is never very long: I love it! I don't know if I've lived up here too long or why it is that I love the winters so much but there is no reason why I live here except for the fact that I love it, summer and winter. I'm like a dyed-in-the-wool sports fan: this is my team. If they lose continuously, I'm not happy but I don't give up on them. If they goof up, I still love them. And, you know, if they're on a winning streak, what more can I say? I'm on cloud nine. Besides, if I only stick around for the good times, what kind of friend am I?

Last winter, to be sure, was a great one for the winter lovers among us. The storms were reasonably spaced, beautiful to observe, and not terribly unmanageable. Just right. Enough so the ground and the roads stayed a lovely bright white all through the season. If I'd had a horse and sleigh, we would have been mobile from December through April. I took more photos last winter than I have in years. As well, we didn't have a single ice storm nor a single power outage. And the temperatures only dropped well below zero once, that I can recall. And the spring came soon enough, a welcome renaissance. I like these changes that come round to remind us of the wheel of life. If there is such a thing as a perfect winter we had it last winter, a time that would answer all the worries of any would-be year-rounder.

It does help to be a writer as the winter lends itself to working at the desk. One January, I sat down at my computer and started writing a book. By February 29, I had a full length manuscript (plus a tired rear end). (The book was later published as *Saturday Beans and Sunday Suppers: Kitchen Stories from Mary's Farm*). I seriously doubt I could have done that during the hot and busy months of July and August. After Christmas ends, the gestation period begins. Cocooning sets in — even the mention of the word gets me in the mood.

I do think it would be hard to live up here through a winter if you didn't have friends, good friends whose company you enjoy. And I think it's important to have an occupation, paid or unpaid. You have to stay busy. There are all kinds of things to keep us going here. The Christmas season, with its parties, festivals, and musical events, is so busy most of us sink into blessed relief once it's over. The midwinter is the toughest part for those who dread the winter. Last winter we put on concerts and art shows at the church and held a dramatic reading, all as fund-raisers. It was wonderful fun to plan and then put it all into motion, rejoice in the money we raised for the church. These things do keep the days moving swiftly. Soon enough, the sap is flowing, in the trees as well as elsewhere.

If you doubt the winter, I say, give it a try. You might surprise yourself.

BLOG ENTRY

February Secrets

FOR SOME UNKNOWABLE reason, nineteen of my good friends have birthdays in February — if you count my old dog, Mayday, who was born on February 20, that would be twenty. I can hardly keep up. And so I have solved this problem by throwing what I called my February birthday party, inviting all my friends who were born in February. That way, I can celebrate all of them at once, with one helluva meal and one single cake for all of them, thus eliminating the almost daily need to send out a card or some other signal of my love for them. This idea has evolved into a joyous nearly annual event that we all look forward to, not the least because of the bleak reality that is February. Everyone is itching for a party at that time, especially my friend and neighbor, Annie, who lived down the road and relished a celebration or "festa" as she always called them. Her birthday was in the middle of the month, which was usually when I scheduled it, for balance. Sometimes the party fell on her actual birth date, which tickled her. Annie never revealed her age but she appeared youthful, perhaps because of her *joie de vivre*.

Last year, I turned sixty. In December. My mother, like Annie, concealed her age, turned fey when the question came up. I don't remember when she reached sixty because she did not allow it to be known. To be fair, she looked a lot younger than she was. No matter, every year I accumulate, I remember that my husband, Paul, who was 39 when he died twenty years ago, had many fewer. And so, the advancement of age does not seem to me to be something to hide or bemoan, but instead something to celebrate and a fact for which to be grateful.

And so I chose December 13 for the date of a big bash and invited all my friends, old and new. I thought it would be significant if I could have sixty friends present for my birthday bash. To my amazement, almost everyone could come! I could hardly wait. But the universe delayed my pleasure: the party was pre-empted by a horrific ice storm which knocked out power and phones. With no communication, fourteen of the sixty turned up for a modest celebration, which took place by candlelight, many of the celebrants wearing headlamps. So it wasn't until almost February that the rescheduled gala took place. Most (but not all) of the original 60 joined in and it was momentous, indeed. I could always count on Annie to bring a special touch to any festive event and she arrived with a crown for me and a hat for Mayday. Many among us had also turned sixty that year and so we all wore birthday hats, blatted into noisemakers, and blew bubbles into the woodheated air. There was a feast to make the gods faint. Three cakes, all decorated, sat in waiting while we worked our way to that end of the evening. Love filled the rooms.

A couple of weeks later, I called Annie to wish her a happy birthday but she told me she was not feeling well. To my astonishment, she died suddenly the next day. I'm still wondering how it could be. The write-up in the paper revealed that she was 78, much older than I had thought. I readjusted my thinking. She kept her secret well and I'm glad of it, admire her skill. As a result of all of this, no February birthdays were celebrated last year. This year, though, for sure.

JANUARY 2010

In the Middle of the Night

A FEW YEARS AGO, I advised a woman on writing her memoir. I had known Mary Liz for a few years before that and once, she showed me an essay she had written about a plant she had been coddling for the past fifty years. The plant was a Night Blooming Cereus, a gangly, cactus-like plant that is quite drab and ordinary most of the time. A few times a year, the Night Bloomer develops buds on its spindly branches and, somewhat unpredictably, the buds burst into bloom — but only in the middle of the night. By morning, they are like broken party balloons hanging limp from their branches. They leave behind a powerfully sweet, haunting fragrance that lingers into the daylight.

Hers since the 1960s when she rescued it from a friend's garbage, the Night Bloomer has taken Mary Liz through the many phases of her life. In her heyday, she and her husband and friends often sat through the night to observe and celebrate the magnificent reveal of the mysterious flower. Corks popped as the astonishing, starburst of a pure white bloom slowly unfurled. Eventually, Mary Liz and her husband moved to a retirement community. Fortunately, the facility had a greenhouse, where Mary Liz installed the favored plant. They no longer stayed up till 2 or 3 in the morning but instead, on the night of the bloom, other residents came to the greenhouse in robes and slippers to watch the show, toasting paper cups of champagne (or perhaps ginger ale) to the showy, explosive white blooms, before retiring to their apartments down the hall.

Soon after they moved to the retirement home, Mary Liz's beloved husband, Bruce, died. They had been sweethearts since 7th grade. After some time had passed, Mary Liz started sending a weekly email to her friends and family, just to let them know how she was doing. I was one of the lucky recipients. She was, as she put it, "in my end game, the last stop on my life's journey" yet she clearly did not want to be the grieving widow. These messages accumulated, full of fond memories, upbeat reports, serendipitous encounters, and, of course, updates on the Night Bloomer. I was impressed by her candor and fearless approach to this "end game." As well, this plant seemed like a great metaphor for her discreet, concealed life of joy. I suggested to Mary Liz that, together, we could use these emails to create a memoir and track the progress of her loss. We met weekly, which meant, for me, a weekly immersion in Mary Liz's life and the lives of her children. We spent probably a year on this project, excerpting from the emails and knitting them together and then Mary Liz filled in gaps that required her to feel the loss all over again. It was hard work but Mary Liz put her shoulder to the wheel and proved herself a fine assignment writer.

Mary Liz titled her memoir: *Night Bloomer: Reflections on Good Grief.* At the end, the ninety-year-old Mary Liz wrote this: "I am blooming, perhaps not as exotically as my Night Bloomer, but day by day, week by week, flourishing, moving into a letting go of my own."

Mary Liz rewarded me with a cutting from her old Night Bloomer. It looked precarious but I knew what lurked within. I repotted it and set it in a sunny window in my dining room. One day I smelled this amazing perfume. *Whose was that?* I wondered. I went into the dining room and saw the bedraggled bloom. I had missed the show. For the Night Bloomer, vigilance is essential and the search for meaning lasts longer than a midnight toast. Like life, I never know when the bloom is coming.

MARCH 2015

The Winter of a Thousand Springs

WINTER BRINGS with it an apprehension, a raised expectation. We consult the almanacs and listen to the prognosticators. Never mind that they are often wrong. We always want to know what to expect, hope we are ready. In general, we expect snow. And plenty of it.

Preparations begin in late fall. The screens are removed from the porch and the summer furniture stashed in the horse barn. In its place, three cords of wood are stacked. Onions, potatoes, squash, cabbages and apples are stowed in the cellar. The snow shovel rests beside the woodpile on the porch. The table thus set, we await the banquet.

I have a new neighbor, Anne, who is not a new neighbor at all. She has been here far longer than I, but always in the summer, never in the winter. Two years ago, she retired, prepared for herself a new home that would embrace her through the winter months, and moved up from the city. I worried that the long winters would be difficult for her. We have had some winters in the recent past that have been brutal. But last winter was mild and easy, a frustrating succession of calm days carrying balmy temperatures. At least twice, the hayfields turned green, this in January and in February. Lilies and bulbs poked up through the soft earth as the sun beat down. Roads remained clear and we drove here and there without regard for the forecast. Weathermen stumbled in their explanations, but these storms that I wait for never came.

Instead of snow, came wind. Up here on the hill, winds can reach the rate of a speeding car, tossing small objects into the air, toppling trees and pushing snow into massive drifts. But, because we who live here on this hill in the winter are not exactly a population center (pop. 3, up from 2), no notice of these storms are made, nothing recorded, only our memories of "the time when the lights went out." And so they did, one cold day in February as the door of my car was nearly torn from my hand when I tried to make a quick exit that afternoon. By evening, the electricity was off at my house. I called Anne to see if she needed anything and found that she was perfectly fine. "I have a generator," she said. "Would you like to come for dinner?" I accepted. Soon after that, several other nearby friends called to see if my lights were off and reported that theirs were, too. Apparently it was an area-wide outage. We all ended up at Anne's new house, a glowing oasis in the storm, traveling up her long driveway, bearing contributions from our dark refrigerators. It was an unusual evening, wherein lamps seemed ingenious, as did the automatic heat. Good conversation flowed like the blessed water from the tap.

Soon enough our power was restored and then the weather turned mild again. That evening remained our single winter adventure. Plenty of wood was left on the porch and the snow shovel had hardly budged from its lean beside the door. I called it "the winter of a thousand springs." The disappointing months turned to an imperceptible spring, leaving me hungry, a bit grumpy, as if that fine meal I'd been promised was never served.

JANUARY 2007

Peace Log

LIVING IN THIS quiet place, I have rarely had the opportunity to call the police. Once, I called about someone hunting out of season, once about a possibly rabid fox and another time I reported young men dancing naked in the middle of the road at midnight (my parents were visiting at the time and were shocked and frightened by the spectacle. Otherwise, I would not have called.) But, according to the "police log" which appears in our weekly paper, my fellow residents have many reasons to call for help. Or assurance.

The police log is the section of the paper to which I turn first. The entries are brief, five or six lines at most, in small type, cryptic renditions of fender benders or lost wallets, a weekly sketch of law and order in our area. A longtime favorite, posted some time back, cited a car parked at the shopping center with a goat inside, the windows rolled up. It was a hot day. An officer was dispatched but by the time he arrived, the car was gone. Did the goat live or die? We will never know.

Another of my favorites was the item about a landlord who called in to ask that the police evict his tenant. The police asked the reason for the request and the man replied, "Because he's a snot." The police informed him that there are no laws against being a snot.

We are often treated to the exact quotes, as the one above. Without that quote, we would have missed the salient detail, tenant as *snot*. In that report resides a short story, maybe even a novel.

Others simply enlarge my impression that it is almost absurdly safe here, maybe even comically so.

This one was listed under the heading "Road Hazard": *At 1:07 a.m. (police) found a fully intact toilet on the center line of Peterborough Street. According to police, the lid was up.*

That was it, in its entirety. No explanation or resolution to that whodunit. (But I liked knowing the toilet was "fully intact" and that the lid was up.)

Sometimes we are left to wonder whether it's the person being reported or the person reporting who is out of touch with reality.

At 9:40 p.m., police responded to the shopping plaza for a report of a man walking with a light on his head. Police located the man and determined nothing was wrong.

A more recent entry recounted that a "large bong" had been found in the parking lot of a local supermarket. (For those in the dark about such things, a "bong" is a somewhat exotic pipe through which marijuana and other illegal substances are smoked.) The report included the information that the bong had a "heavy residue" and ended by saying that the police were holding the lost item at the station and the owner could come and claim it. Either the police have a sense of humor or they are clumsy detectives.

Here is one from a couple of years ago: *At 4 a.m., police responded to a burglar alarm at the Bank of New Hampshire. A snowflake decoration had fallen from the ceiling and set off the motion detector alarm.*

We do have robberies and we even have had a murder or two over the years. But most of what happens here is like that. May it ever be so.

MARCH 2007

Holy Rummage

OUR CHURCH HAS a rummage sale, spring and fall. I've come to think of it as my savior. It starts with the horse sheds. Townspeople know that, throughout the year, they can leave off unwanted items in one of the bays of the old horse sheds beside the church. I can't always manage to synchronize my need to unload with the proximity of the sale but the horse sheds, high and dry, safekeep the donations for months until the next sale. Lift the door and unburden yourself, a truly welcome invitation on any level.

The church accepts all kinds of things, clothes, linens, dishes, skis, household items, even couches and small furniture. Items donated need to be clean and useful. No broken appliances. No clothes that need mending. No gravy-stained tablecloths, please. The week before each sale, April and October, a rugged corps of ladies (and a few men) come together. It is a full week of work for these volunteers, 9 to 5 each day. They sort, mostly the clothes — jeans and t-shirts, jackets (and a few ties), sweaters and children's clothes. Shoes of all sizes and styles. Such mountains of apparel pile up, one might think there would be no clothes left to be worn in the entire town. Irons, toasters and telephones are dusted, plugged in and tested. Small crystal treasures are appraised and priced, as are dishes and glasses, skis and skates, jewelry and oddments.

I take advantage of the opportunity the rummage provides all year long as I occasionally have the need to pick through my closet or re-organize my dishes. I use the tried and true rule: if I haven't worn something in two years, out it goes. Similarly redundant appliances or mistakes *(why did I buy these shoes? They hurt me every time I wear them!)* go into the bag. In the end, I've made more space in my cupboards and have packed a shopping bag full of things maybe someone else can use. Off to the horse sheds it goes.

The ladies who sort hold high standards. They grumble through the week, as they pull out items that don't meet the criteria. *"This should have been taken to the dump!"* they exclaim indignantly, item after item. Such things are set aside and donated to a charity that happily comes to take away the rummage's cast-offs. *"When are people going to learn to just throw things out!"* I hear this quite often as the tired ladies rest up after their usually very successful sale. When I hear them say it, I cringe a little as I know I'm guilty of this sin. I have trouble throwing something away and somehow it feels better to give it to the church than to the dump. It's hard for us to believe things can't be reused, somehow. *Use it up, wear it out, make do or do without*, my father used to chant. So where, exactly, does the wisdom of that stop? We struggle with this commandment up here in the north country.

The sale itself goes onto my calendar. I never miss it. There is always something that catches my eye — over the years, I've found perfect sets of sheets, favorite t-shirts (do I love them more because they only cost a dime?), a fabulous set of wine glasses and a perfect down parka. You never know what will be there. I have a friend who still boasts that he bought the like-new Armani suit he wore to his wedding from the rummage. Five dollars. I know that slightly redemptive feeling, as if we've beat the system but in a noble way. We exit the church, grinning, gripping our treasures, having managed to obey several commandments at once.

MARCH 2008

From the Ashes

Many years ago, my mother was in love with a soldier who went to war. He was shot down on his first mission in the South Pacific, leaving a huge sadness in our family. In his will, he left all his belongings to my mother. Mostly, that amounted to a 1937 Ford, gray with a tan convertible top. My mother's emotions around that car were perhaps too strong for her to ever drive it. Instead, not knowing what else to do with her grief, she joined the Marines, and while she was gone to war, she lent the car to her sister. Eventually the loan became permanent. We came to call it the Old Gray Ford (later, just OGF), such an integral part of our extended family, so much a part of our present that we almost forgot its past.

We all loved the car as it grew into antiquity, showing bits of rust and enduring frequent breakdowns. Frequently, my aunt drove us to Singing Beach with all of us in the back seat. We all knew exactly where to sit on those leather seats to avoid the springs that had popped up from beneath. When I came of age, my older cousin Mac taught me to drive stick shift on this car and also how to work the choke — tricky business. Mac used the car all through his college years and used it as the "getaway" car for his wedding and carried it onward into his life.

Eventually, the car went into storage, which is a polite way of saying it somehow disintegrated into pieces in a pile in Mac's barn. The years passed. We all felt heartsick to see such a sad sight.

We not only forgot where it came from, we almost forgot it was there. But somehow Mac's daughter, Hayden, did not forget the OGF, though it's a mystery to me how she remembered it, since she was not alive ever to have known it as a living, driving, moving being. Still, she was planning her wedding and said to her father one day, I would love to be able to drive away from my wedding in the OGF!

And so it was last May that I accompanied Mac to a place called RMR Restorations in Hollis, New Hampshire, not so far from my home, where men who know about such things indulge in the act of resurrection. Daily. Buckets of rusted parts were wheeled in. From its long storage, the chassis and a couple of doors were brought up on a flatbed truck. I entered the operating room with trepidation. In the OGF resided a deep well of emotion I hadn't visited in many years. Of all the rusty pieces before me, I could identify only the steering wheel and the hubcaps. We told the mechanics the story of the car's life in our family. Standing in a quiet semicircle, the men listened respectfully. Then we left them to their magic, which they performed over the next six months.

In October, on the beautiful blue-sky day of Hayden's wedding, a shining OGF sat beside a house by the sea. The gray paint gleamed like polished enamel. A thin, red pinstripe ran the length to the rear fender. Hubcaps were like mirrors. We all hovered around it, feeling a bit like we were seeing a ghost, touching the imagined. Suddenly, we were afraid of leaving fingerprints on a car we used to treat like a comfortable old shoe. I climbed into the passenger seat. The car smelled of leather and hot sun. Mac performed the ritual of working the choke and pumping the accelerator. The engine burst to life, a sound familiar as a friend's voice. He pressed the gearshift into first and we rolled out onto the road. Thinking about a young soldier who went to war and never came back, about my mother, who couldn't bring herself to drive this car, about the years and the sheer will that have kept the OGF alive — or on life support — that well of emotion overflowed. The wedding was picture-perfect. Of course. The Old Gray Ford was with us.

MAY 2011

The Things We Keep

AST YEAR, I accomplished something I didn't think possible: I cleaned out my barn. Rolling open the big doors revealed a great hodgepodge of objects from the past, files from stories I have written over the years, family papers, and things I think I might need or might fix someday. Lacking a compelling reason, one can let all this lie, like the sleeping dog. However, there was a party coming up and the barn had to be used. I kept putting off the great purge until one soft, warm June morning, I put on an old sweatshirt, rugged shoes, and gloves and rolled open those forbidding doors. I had asked John, who had done some good work for me in the past, to help in this process. He actually looked delighted.

I began with the boxes filled with papers. I sat on a milk crate in the light of the barn's one south window, sunlight illuminating the pages before me. Each box sent me into reverie. So many other times, so many other places. Could I really have lived this long? As I opened the cartons at random, it was like watching my life pass before me. Photos of my parents holding my little hand at the beach. Photos of me and my college roommates lounging in our eclectically furnished, flower-child dorm room. Letters from old boyfriends. I found diplomas with the corners chewed by mice. Why do I need these at this point in my life? Photos of me and my first husband building our first house. A filed marked "divorce papers." I didn't think I still had them. Boxes and boxes of files from stories I have written over the years. Spiral notebooks filled with notes, phone numbers, names now forgotten. Trunks of old clothes. I sorted and sorted.

This wasn't so much a physical task, though it required some muscle, but instead, a work of the heart. To be kept was the three-piece bobsled, who knows how old, which my father cleaned up and painted red and gave to me the year I moved to New Hampshire; my grandfather's surfboard, procured on a trip to Hawaii in the 1930s; and the Singer treadle sewing machine in good running condition (always living with one eye on the apocalypse). But then there were those pink monogrammed towels my mother bought for me, which I never used. The sweater my long-gone grandmother knit for me but which never fit. This kind of gift causes paralysis in me. I can't give it away or send it to the rummage, or heavens, throw it away. Something in me won't allow that. And so it all piles up, things I don't want or need but things that, nevertheless, carry with them an ocean of memories. Perhaps what I'm trying to keep is the memory of the love and generosity these people brought me when they were alive.

It seemed an impossible task. But not for John. "What are you going to do with *this*?" he would ask, holding up some clearly dilapidated item. I began to see through his eyes.

There was a lot of carnage and many trips to the dumps or to the church rummage but in the end, I saw the walls and floor of the barn for the first time since I've lived here. At the end, John looked around and asked me, "So what are you going to *do* with this now?" he asked, as if we had actually created something new. I'm sure he didn't want to hear my answer which was, "Probably start filling it up again."

MAY 2013

Graduation Day

The older I get, the more I crave good strong help. In this quest, I've encountered some frustrations. I once hired a young man to help in the garden and after an hour or so, I looked out the window and saw him sprawled on the ground. Thinking he had hurt himself or passed out, I rushed to the scene whereupon he rose up, explaining that he was "just resting." But that was rare. In my life since my husband's passing, it's been my privilege to get to know a number of wonderful young people. They come to do chores and I watch them grow up. And move on.

A few years ago, my friend Mel struck a deal with me: he would come with his son, Josh, and the two of them would work together, do whatever I needed done. In return, I would put money into Josh's college fund. I can't imagine turning down such a deal. And so they began to come, mostly after Mel got off work. I had my list. Wallpaper in the back bedroom needed to be scraped off. The rowboat, which was resting in the weeds beside the hayfield, needed a coat of paint. Pruning, weeding and hacking back the bittersweet are perennials on the list.

Josh was fourteen when he first started coming to work here, even then a tall, amiable fellow, always with a smile and a certain quiet enthusiasm. Early on, another quality emerged. I felt the big rock behind the house should be surrounded by blooms rather than weeds. So I set them to digging a lily bed. As is not unusual in this terrain, they soon hit upon a rock but the more they dug, the bigger the stone became. I told them to leave it alone but Josh wanted to finish the job and so in the darkening of that spring afternoon, we left one shovel handle behind and started on another. We brought out crowbars and chocks, working like slaves on the pyramids. Finally, the grip of the earth let go and the giant heaved up, big as a car engine, and Josh rolled it triumphantly into the woods. That was a good introduction to Josh, tenacious and patient in his work.

Each year, Josh grew taller and more interesting to talk with. On their first day here last spring, we walked down to the raspberry patch which is in a particularly soggy area. High school graduation was soon and in the fall he would be heading off to the college of his choice. And so there was a certain amount of levity between us and, on my part, a touch of sadness as I knew these times would soon end. Josh set to the chore with his usual zest. I identified the raspberry plants for him, as some of them were completely obscured by weeds. With his gloved hands, he set aside the canes and pulled out the mats of thatch and pigweed, which clung to dense soil. We tilled in peat moss and loam and, as the sun began to set, tucked the canes back into their (temporarily) weed-free bed. I can't think of too many things that are more satisfying than a freshly turned garden bed, and this particular chore gave that good feeling of new potential. Like a young man with his whole life ahead of him.

MAY 2007

🏵 Sneak Attack

O NE NIGHT LAST SUMMER, I was lying in bed, reading, my dog asleep against my side. The comfortable silence of the late hour enveloped us as the slight breezes of the midnight hour moved through the curtains. Of a sudden, an intruder cruised into the room on silent wings. I jerked the covers up over everything but my eyes and watched in horror as this creature took possession of my room. The bat itself was not that big but its shadow, cast from the light of my bedside lamp, created an image something like a stealth bomber, circling to land. In frantic, jerky circles, the shadow orbited erratically, the perfect prelude to an Alfred Hitchcock film. And then, as silently and suddenly as he'd arrived, he exited.

I lay there for a minute, wondering where he might have gone. Mayday snored on. I slunk out of bed and, on hands and knees, made my way out to the hallway. I turned on the light. My brain was mud. My heart was panicked. I recalled with intense nostalgia the night my late husband herded a bat out of the house with the kitchen broom while I crouched mortified in the corner. I couldn't even think where the broom was. I was trying to remember if bats were drawn to light, or if they were repelled by it. Judging by the fact that he had come into my lighted room from the darkened house, I decided they were drawn to it. At that moment, the bat swooped into the hallway from the kitchen, grazing my head. I hit the carpet and lay there, flattened, until the raid had passed. At which point I resumed my crawl to the living room.

I turned on the light to the porch and opened the door. Hoping he would fly toward the light on the porch, I hunkered down into a chair in the dark living room and waited. Hours passed. No sign of the bat. At last, he zipped by me out to the porch. I leapt up but before I could close the door, he zipped back inside. By dawn, I was not only exhausted but clueless. Where had he gone? Where was he hiding? Perhaps I had dozed off and missed his latest move?

As soon as the hour was decent, I began to call friends for helpful suggestions. One of my friends told me to wait for dark, leave all the lights on in the house and the door open. "He'll leave," he said. Another went into great detail about where the bats will hide. "My father always found them behind the chiffoniere," he said. "He had the knack of being able to nudge them into a paper bag and carry them outdoors." The implication was that there were lots of bats, hiding in lots of tiny slots around the house. I didn't want to follow that thought. Another friend suggested a butterfly net. I pictured myself capturing the little Dracula in my net. I called yet another friend and asked to borrow his fish net. By noon, I had the net at the ready beside the back door.

When darkness fell, I was watchful, primed for action. I allowed him the run of the house but slept with my bedroom door shut, lest he decide to make another reconnaissance mission. The night passed without incident. And another. Cautiously, I left my door open. A week passed and then another.

I never saw the bat again. I don't know how long they can live behind the furniture or under the windowsill. I have invested in a fish net of my own and I am still waiting.

SEPTEMBER 2007

🌀 Dark Waters

HOT SUMMER NIGHTS make the young restless and now that I'm older, I wonder why. I was once guilty of pumpkin smashing and a few pranks worse than that so it's not that I don't understand but when I think back to such a time, I truly can hardly believe that I did those things, that I am that same person. I guess that is what is meant by growing up or maybe even redemption.

One of my favorite stories of life in these parts happened when my husband and my parents were all still alive and we were together, my elderly parents here on a visit from New Jersey. It was June but it was hot and we all decided to go out to eat rather than heat up the little house by cooking.

We were on our way home, late in the evening. As we were passing by the pond, which was a short distance from our house, suddenly several young men leapt in front of the car, causing us to come to a complete stop. Naked, they danced exotically in the glare of our headlights. Later, I realized the genius of their exhibition: the headlights, at their low level, revealed nothing but the boys' privates. The rest, especially their faces, remained in the dark. The four of us sat in the car, stunned speechless except for my mother's initial shriek. At last, the giggling young men ran off into the darkness and we proceeded home.

I would not have done so but my parents insisted I call the police. Back then, and even now, our police force consisted of one man, who sometimes wore a uniform and sometimes showed up in his farmer's jeans. I called him, a little embarrassed, and dutifully reported the incident.

"Yup," he said. "I'll check it out."

We heard nothing further. My parents returned home, somewhat worried that the area in which we lived, which was mostly woods and water, was not as safe as they'd imagined.

A few weeks later, Paul and I were out for a walk along that same stretch of dirt road and the constable came along in his cruiser, which was not the newest model but it was reasonably equipped. Suitable.

After some initial chatter, I asked him, "So, did you ever find those naked boys that night?"

"Oh, yes," he said, with a slight chuckle. "I came right down after you called. I slowed down when I got to the pond and, darned if they didn't hop right out in front of me, just like you said! I let them dance a bit," he said, and paused a little before he went on: *"And then I flipped on the blues!* You never saw barefoot boys move so fast. They dove right into the water. I went down there and tried to wait them out, spent about an hour there, but they outlasted me. I never found them."

We knew that pond, haven to snapping turtles and water snakes. I wondered which was worse, a prolonged immersion in those black waters, standing stock still, or being taken in for exotic dancing on a dirt road.

That was probably twenty years ago now and those boys are men, probably fathers. I wonder if they ever think back on that night of revelry and tell their story, as I do, or if they blush at their imprudence and ask for forgiveness.

SEPTEMBER 2008

🐝 Queen Bee

L AST FALL, A YOUNG MAN who lives nearby knocked on my door. He wanted to know if he could keep his hives in my field. He explained that his bees, living on the side lawn of his house, near the woods, had died. He didn't know why. He thought they might do better in my open fields. I had read that bees are not doing well, anywhere. Whole hives were dying. Mystery surrounded the subject. Pretty soon, there were two white boxes of bees sitting silently at the edge of my east meadow, an air of expectation surrounding them.

Once, years ago, I rode to Maine in the middle of a June night with a man named Floyd Smith who kept his bees in the Maine wilderness throughout the summer. He called his honey Wilderness Honey and he had customers who waited for the sweet jars he provided in the fall. We left New Hampshire at dusk and drove through the night. Every once in a while, he would pull off to the side of the road and, in the silence of that dark night, he would get out and walk around the fenced trailer which carried more than a dozen hives, checking on his bees. They were asleep, which is why we were driving in the middle of the night, so the bees wouldn't know they were being taken hundreds of miles from where they had slumbered through the winter.

He taught me a lot about bees on that trip, about the queen and her life inside the dark hive, about the worker bees who come and willingly serve her, making millions of trips to gather the nectar, carrying it to the hive before they die an early death, usually within weeks. The queen lives on. The bees inside their hives are the epitome of community, all love and cooperation. Servitude as well. We arrived at his paradise beside the West Branch of the Penobscot in time for breakfast — eggs and bacon, toast and honey — which he rustled up on the wood cookstove inside the cabin. And then he set the bees loose into the cool wilderness where life was just emerging. All summer, they worked the pollen loose from the tiny wildflowers of the deep woods.

The bees in my meadow had an easier time. As the spring grew into summer, the moisture from the meadow rising, I saw them working the lilacs and the bleeding heart. Full summer, hot as a griddle, I found them suspended in the blueberries and hanging like small jewels from the frilled clover blossoms. When I was in my garden near the hives, I could see the bees exiting and entering, exiting and entering, a little industry in my meadow. Once in a while, the young man would come, park his truck near the hives, get out and pull on his bee suit and hood, protective gloves. Like a moonwalker, he would plod to the hives, anesthetize his friends with his smoker and work the trays. It was a dreamy pageant, the bees in their boxes, the man who came and went, keeping them happy, the meadow alive with their tiny beating wings.

One day I came home from work to find a plump jar on the table on my porch. The setting sun lit up the contents, creating a little sun of its own. I took the honey inside, suddenly feeling like a queen.

MAY 2008

✿ My Bohemian Paradise

I N THE EARLY PART of last winter, I stacked wood in my shirt-sleeves, mowed the lawn and fretted that no ice had yet come to the lakes. Even the birds were confused. For quite some time during January and February, I enjoyed watching a pair of bluebirds cavort in the brambles across the road and dart back to my porch, where they pecked away at a Christmas display of greens and red winter-berries. This was the third of our disappointing winters. Boots, hats and scarves stayed in the closet all the way till February. Many here rejoiced in how easy it was, no snow to shovel, no slippery roads, no bone-chilling winds. But I, perhaps too much a contrarian, craved a good snowstorm and the creaking, squeezing noises inside this old house, provoked by a night below zero.

Perhaps I long for those sounds because it's been otherwise so quiet here. In the past year, no walls were moved, no foundations poured, no floors sanded or walls painted. The only change was the replacement of several windows in the el, which has made a big difference. Curtains no longer puff out during northeasters. I didn't realize that living with those old, thin windows, I could hear almost everything: the occasional car that passed by, the long approach of the snowplow, the crack of a hunting rifle. It was a bit like living in a tent. Now, with the new windows, the silence, always notable, is almost complete. I may not miss the cold winds that blew through the room but I do miss that closeness to the outdoors, summer and winter. Now, I actually have to *go* outdoors to *be* outdoors. In the ten years I've been here, the house has transformed from an ancient, drafty, seven-bedroom farmhouse to a snug one-bedroom home, flooded with sunlight.

I have one last bastion of unfinished territory, a roomy attic space under the eaves, with new light brought in by a big, south-facing dormer and a skylight. Fresh out of funds but not out of need, I determined to make this a place for family and friends to stay when they came to visit. I moved beds up there and put thick rugs on the floor. Bedsheets, pulled tight and stapled to the rafters and knee-walls, give the appearance of painted walls. A bookcase holds a raft of worn paperbacks, including *A Prayer for Owen Meany, Crossing to Safety,* and everything Farley Mowett ever wrote. I tacked the many Bread and Puppet posters I've accumulated over the years to the roof boards between the giant timbers of the old frame. Heat drifts up from a register over the cookstove so the warmest place is right next to the bed, an old cannonball four-poster my father rescued from a junk shop back in the 1940s, in anticipation of marrying my mother.

I call this my "bohemian paradise," a place where you can still smell the old wood and see the open history of the house, including the charred beams from a house fire that was quenched before it took the house and the huge opening for the original center chimney, long since removed and boarded over.

I will have to finish this room someday, add insulation and sheetrock, make it really nice, but, no hurry. It's a bit like the weather and my contrary nature: don't make things too comfortable. It makes me uncomfortable.

JANUARY 2008

❧ Keeping Watch

ALMOST RAN OUT of wood last year. In the middle of winter I had to scramble and find some good dry wood, just about as easy as finding ripe peaches at that time of year. I sometimes think that the best way to save on heat might be to just go to Florida. I have an aunt who lives on the ocean side. She sends me photos of her balcony overlooking the turquoise ocean and a clipping on cheap air fares. It sounds nice. Another friend teaches in Miami and urges me to come. I don't know about Miami. I worry about things such as getting lost and where would I park my car?

My mother hated winter and loved Florida, so every year during the late 1950s and early 1960s, we would pack up the Ford station wagon, strap our bikes to the roof, and drive down to Florida. The bitter cold slowly receded, replaced by the humid heat of the south, which blew in through our rolled-down windows. The three-day journey took us past cotton fields, sharecropper's shacks, and Burma Shave signs. The heavy fragrance of orange blossoms signaled that we were almost there. Our destination was Delray Beach where we had an apartment on the second floor of an old wooden build-ing surrounded by coconut trees and a rugged kind of grass that was hard on tender bare feet. The apartment was small with a big screened porch. My sister and I slept on the porch as it was cooler there and also interesting. The lady next door played cards with her friends till all hours and we enjoyed watching them trade cards and refill their glasses as the night wore on. Their talk and laughter, the clink of the ice cubes in their glasses, along with the stirring of the fronds against the screens, lulled us to sleep.

We could ride our bikes to the beach, which was a great expanse of white sand edged by the unbelievably clear ocean. On the beach, we lay on bright beach towels in our new bathing suits, dove into gently curling waves and walked the length to find shells and other treasures. At night we would find little restaurants that were not too expensive and on rainy days we strolled the village and poked around in the shops. Occasionally, on particularly warm and indolent nights, we set forth for Palm Beach to see the mansions there, imagining the opulent lives within. If I could go back to that time and have my father drive us all down to that same place of my mind's eye, I would leave my woodstove in a minute for the pleasure that journey might bring.

But, alas, such a place no longer exists. And I've become joined with winter. Like a night watchman, I no longer trust that winter can pass safely without my vigilance. Moose tracks crossing the field, the embracing warmth of the stove as I come in from the cold, the way the snow outlines every board on the barn after a night of driving snow, the steady song of the wind, these are the treasures that I guard. If I let the stoves go cold and abandon my post by the window, I would feel I had turned my back on a friend in a time of need. Resolute, I stay on. But this year, I've added an extra cord to the pile.

JANUARY 2009

❧ Stillpoint in the Whirling World

WHEN I FIRST CAME here to Mary's farm, I named the place Stillpoint because it was so quiet here and because it was the stillpoint in my turning world, and it still is that, even as the world turns ever faster. The stillness in the early spring is especially profound, with the fields still deep in snow and the animals, for the most part, still sleeping.

Last year, my aunt died. She was the last of my parents' generation in our family to pass away and her passing prompted a great gathering of cousins in New Jersey, where most of us grew up. Only my cousin Carol still lives there. It was her mother whom we had lost. The service was planned for early April. As close to a reunion as we have ever had took shape as cousins we had not seen in decades flew in from London and Oregon, the rest of us drove down from New England and came up from D.C. So there was a lot of excitement about seeing each other, in spite of the sad occasion.

Driving down was like watching a film about changing seasons in fast motion. By the time we hit Massachusetts, the snow had vanished. In Connecticut, the grass was greening and in New Jersey, forsythia blazed and daffodils bloomed. When we arrived and opened the car doors, mild, soft air greeted us. No trip to Florida could have given such pleasure. I would prescribe such a trip any day for treatment of the winter blahs.

One of my cousins had a surprise for us. Somehow she knew who was living in our grandparents' house, a big old house with all kinds of secret places and wonderful memories, a place where we were all spoiled beyond words. And so she arranged that we should go there for a visit. En masse. The current owners were amazingly accommodating of our nostalgic mission.

The day after the funeral, we caravanned to the old stucco manse, two towns away. It looked very much the same, except the new owners had done some appropriate updating. They welcomed us and took us on a tour of the house. They lived in 21st century comfort but every floorboard, every outlook from every window, even the overhead of the old garage, brought back distant but clear memories. It seemed like an extraordinary privilege to be able to walk through one's past, in the present. They took us to the basement, which is now a comfortable game room. I recall it as a dark place where the coal was delivered down a chute and where my grandfather went each morning to shake the cinders down. The kitchen, where my grandmother left oatmeal to cook on the stove overnight, was radically changed. But some of the old cupboards had been saved. And they took us up to the attic where my grandfather would go on Christmas Eve to stomp around as if he were Santa coming down the chimney and we all believed it. Outside, the trees and the lawn were exactly the same. How could that be possible, I wondered? Except the new owners had planted dozens of daffodils that were, on that day in April, in full bloom. I was grateful for those flowers and for that house, a surprising stillpoint in the whirling world of New Jersey.

MARCH 2009

❦ Under the Exploding Sky

I
N THE NEXT TOWN to ours is a company that manufactures some
of the best fireworks in the country. As a result, most towns around
here hold extravagant fireworks shows on the Fourth. One of my
favorites is in a nearby town, where the show is hosted and paid for
by a private lake club. Over the years, they have perfected a system
that involves a raft with remote control ignition. I believe they lost
the float one year to disastrous results, but without injury, thank
goodness. I once saw a list of the 50 different firings, with names
such as Golden Rain, Spring All Year (50 shots), Double Willow,
Chrysanthemum, and Milky Way. (I especially liked the "Titanium
Salute," in this modern age of hip and knee replacements.) Just reading those names fills my skies with a shower of colorful sparks. It's
a private club but if I want, I can row my boat out onto the lake, lie
back and watch the show of light and color explode overhead.

Otherwise, the best seats for this display are in the cemetery,
just across the road from the club. Last year, friends and their children came for dinner which we grilled outside, listening to the pre-
liminary pops of home fireworks as the sky grew dark. It was a hot
night with clear skies, perfect for the celestial show. Around 8:30 we
drove down the road and parked near the cemetery where our ances-
tors have always enjoyed the best view of the lake and the mountain.
Carrying folding chairs and blankets, we walked the rest of the way
into the graveyard where many townspeople had already staked their
claim to a good seat. It is an old cemetery with faded slate stones
dating back before the Revolution. Next to a large Celtic cross, we

set up our chairs and spread blankets for the younger members of our party. Comfortable, we sat and talked, waiting for the initial flare. Around us, the entire cemetery had suddenly come to life with excited families exchanging news, sitting between headstones and under the beautiful spreading trees that overlook the lake. The noise resembled any theater awaiting the show.

As we chattered away, darkness descended. The first salvo, a line of white that shot straight up and blossomed high in the sky, silenced us all. Over the next half hour, we were treated to repeated explosions of golden rain, curlicues of color, and resounding booms that shook the earth (and undoubtedly a few bones) beneath us. When the finale came, we were not disappointed by the expected cacophony of explosions, whistles, retorts and bombs bursting in air. We screamed, whooped, laughed, shouted our approval and generally acted like ten-year-olds in our unbridled enthusiasm.

We have come to equate these warlike sounds with the end of a war and the birth of our nation. Beneath us there in that cemetery were some of our own war dead, who perished in one of the many wars this nation has fought. Likely the last sounds some of them heard were the very sounds that were delighting us that night. Even now, these sounds are ringing out in neighborhoods in Baghdad and in Afghanistan. Sitting in that profound place that bridges history and the present, joy and sorrow, I felt the weary irony that teeters between the fearsome face of war and the exhilaration of our freedoms. May we always strive to know the difference.

JULY 2009

⬡ Answering Back

THE RISE OF the soft curves of the fields, the seasons of the hay, the broad reach of the old apple trees, the long-blooming rose bush on the split rail fence, the in-your-face view of Monadnock, the brilliance of the night sky, these are just some of the aspects of the beauty that brought me here. It was never the house. In fact, early on, I was heard often to say that if the house were in better shape, I never would have had the opportunity to buy this property. But, as it was, I joined in with my neighbor, Anne, to save this pre-Revolutionary farm from development. She bought most of the land and put it into conservation and I bought the old house and the hayfields that surround it. A done deal, long enough ago now for an infant to have grown to gain the right to vote. The house, they told me, had been built in 1762 and the long, if incomplete, history of this farm was used to help fight a major highway from being built on its fields. Peeling away layer after layer of building materials gave us information and finally the glorious sight of its frame, its skeleton, its bones — the splinters of its timbers, protected as they were by the covers all these years, were almost as if fresh from the adze. For more than twelve years, the house underwent a gradual transformation to the place I now call home.

I was so intent on where I was going, I forgot to notice that this house was originally the work of one man. At first I didn't know. About six years into the job, I learned his name: Benjamin Mason. I felt then that it was nice to know his name and often thought about him and his family, living here under what must have been sometimes severe circumstances, no roads, no neighbors, no town. So, on I went with that morsel of information, still more interested in where I was going than where the house had been. But after the job was more or less complete (it's never over), I did a bit of arithmetic and realized that pretty soon, the house would turn 250 years old, quite an achievement for a house. Many early houses burned down or were abandoned and fell into their foundations. As well, when I first bought the house, it needed so much work, many people, including two architects, advised me to tear it down and start fresh. I know this is the fate of many old houses. So the fact that the house is still standing seemed well worth celebration. And, further celebration for the changes that have been made. Certainly still not the same axe but nonetheless and even because of all the changes, the house was ready for one heck of a bash.

When my neighbor Anne heard of my plans to celebrate the house's anniversary, she joined me and offered to help with the costs. As the year approached, I began digging in the archives to find what I could about Benjamin Mason, who came up here from Sherborn, Massachusetts, to what is now Dublin when he was 45, bringing with him his wife and his five children. In all, I discovered a man I wish I had known.

I already knew from doing the work on the house that Benjamin Mason was a master carpenter and timber framer but I discovered that he was also the framer of most of the houses in this neighborhood (none remain standing) and of the old Dublin town meetinghouse (a rock marks its place), Dublin's first selectman (the house was built before the town was formed), a fifer in the Revolution, a builder of roads (including the one that he lived on, the same road I now call the road home), leader of the Dublin church choir, and, finally, I learned that he was an acrobat. But I had more to learn. Dublin's town history said of Benjamin Mason that he was distinguished for his "agility, fearlessness and self possession." But reading in the Mason Family Register, I found this: "He was a man of uncommon agility and once, having raised the frame for a barn of ordinary size, he walked the whole length of the ridge-pole *upon his hands*, having no other support, his feet in the meantime upended in the air." I tried to imagine such a thing, hoping as well that it was the barn here where he performed such a stunt. History being what it is, I am free to believe that.

I was well aware that I hadn't rescued this house all by myself. There were a lot of people to whom I owed a debt of gratitude. Michael, Henri, Dan, Glenn, Brian, Harvey, oh so many, jobs big and small. So Anne and I carefully crafted our guest list, selected the appropriate size tent (let's just say Barnum and Bailey would have found it adequate) and asked the Dublin General Store to bring us some good luncheon food — I would augment the feast with baked beans, a few salads, and cousin Susan made up a huge batch of the famous family iced tea. In the archives, I had found a recipe for ketchup from one of the early Mason residents. I had a lot of big ideas to make this a memorable event. I was even thinking about fireworks.

Our plan was to attach the tent to my barn, which would provide good shelter in case of bad weather. This meant the barn had to be cleaned out. That occasionally brutal task took almost two months. Having a barn can be something of a liability: you end up keeping things just because you can. And I have taken full advantage of that opening. So there was a lot of carnage and many trips to the recycle center and the church rummage but in the end, I saw the walls and floor of the barn for the first time since I've lived there.

My sister flew in from Washington State to join not only the celebration but to help get ready. As well, my six cousins planned to come from all points. It was suddenly dawning on me that having more than one hundred people for lunch on my lawn was no small endeavor.

To celebrate the farm, I wanted to share the history with my guests. I thought a self-guided tour would be the best way so I mapped out the high points of its history all around its many acres. The original site of the house, the site of the pre-revolutionary English barn (which I sadly had to have taken down), the brickyard across the road where bricks were fired and used, in some measure, to build the brick mill village just a mile down the road. Inside the house, I printed out narratives in each room, explaining how the house had evolved: where once was a living room, now was a kitchen (which before that was probably the original kitchen); where now there is a dining room, once were two bedrooms; where once the two sisters lived almost exclusively, now was a separate apartment for seasonal rental. On and on, the evolution of a house of this age is far more than a short story. I made signs and stapled them to wooden stakes. With my lawn mower, I cut paths to each site and pounded the signs into the ground wherein the significance of that piece of ground came alive, just for that day.

On a special table in the barn, next to the serving tables, I arranged the square-cut nails, the pottery shards, the two old spoons, a broken brick I pried out of the ground down at the now-barely-visible brickyard, all the little archeological bits and pieces that I have collected over the years, and made small labels for each token. In essence I was creating a small, one-day museum. In the scope of the history of this country, this is not a significant place, this is no Sturbridge, no Deerfield, nothing terribly dramatic ever happened here. The house, a typical big-house-little house-backhouse-barn, is quite ordinary and without flourish. My digging found no diaries to explore or other caches of historical pizzazz. Plus, I have changed the house so much, it is not historically recognizable. There were only two old photos to be found in the archives, both taken in 1946, so we were lacking in graphics and visuals. Imagination was all we had to work with. But this place represents the extreme efforts of one man, one continuous family, the fortunes of time and the elements, and the determination of an aging woman who wanted to leave it better than she found it. It was all worth one glorious day of celebration.

The day before the party, my sister and I were busy in the kitchen, preparing food and drink. The list of things to do was very long and my brain was scrambled. How could it all possibly get done before noon the next day, when guests would begin to arrive. Around 4:30, we sat down on the lawn out front to watch the oncoming storm. Thick and powerful lightning bolts shot into the trees across the field. We took shelter inside and resumed watching the storm march down the mountain toward us. When it finally arrived, the rain was torrential. We couldn't see anything except a gray wall of water. The electricity flickered and then went out. Late in the evening, my cousins arrived and once they had all piled into the house, soaking wet, we all gathered for dinner by candlelight and exchanged stories of our adventures. So far. After dinner, I put the beans to bake in the gas oven overnight. And then slept soundly for an early rise.

The day of the party dawned as if a stage set. The tent was standing ready. The power was back on. The smell of baked beans filled the house. My sister and I set about to decorate the tables beneath the tent with Mason jars filled with JoePie weed, golden rod, Queen Anne's lace, black-eyed Susans all cut from the road-sides. In the cool, dry blue-sky morning, we transported all the platters and many drinks and jugs of iced tea to the tent. Friend Jonathan set up a sound system, hanging the speakers from the apple tree, which provided music and also a microphone so that I could say a few things once everyone had helped themselves to the buffet. I wanted to thank so many people who had helped me all along and I wanted to raise a toast to Benjamin Mason, and let us all stop to think for a moment what he had started here so long ago. I wanted to invite everyone to walk the trails I had mapped out to the signif-icant historic spots on the farm.

A stream of guests arrived, happy in the warm August sunshine. Under shelter of my clean and newly resurrected barn, the food was arranged on several tables, drinks as well. I felt a very happy, festive mood all around me. After everyone had enjoyed a good meal, I got up to take the microphone, but as I did so, my friend David came over to me and showed me the weather map on his smartphone. He said, "I don't mean to alarm you but you might warn people that they have about an hour before this hits." I didn't need to look hard to see that there was a huge storm headed right at us. So I didn't get to say all that I wanted to say. I said a few things, most especially the expressions of gratitude I wanted to make and then I told everyone to hurry and take their tours of the house and the grounds. Because there was a big storm coming. The clear blue skies above us betrayed what was on its way.

Everyone fanned out to the various highlights of the old farm. The hour passed swiftly. Even with our warning, the skies turned black and the thunder rolled in with such swiftness, it still seemed like a surprise when the storm arrived, something of a clone of the storm of the day before. Bucketing rains, lightning, thunder. I watched as my guests headed for their cars and hoped everyone was safe. The power went out again, which made clean-up challenging. I kept thinking what it would have been like if that storm had arrived even one hour earlier, while we were serving lunch. And what it would have been like if we had not had that warning from the device I sometimes think is all-too present in our lives.

The next day, a friend called to tell me something else. She and her husband had fled in the storm, perhaps a bit ahead of the others. They drove through the downpour a very short distance down my road, a road, that, incidentally, Benjamin Mason had originally built, when there on the side of the road, a tree was on fire, a brilliant fire. While they watched the fire in the blazing tree spread to the next tree, in spite of the buckets of rain, they called 911. The wire dropped into the road. Then, in one single moment, a huge billowing cloud of steam burst upwards as the pouring rain finally extinguished the blaze at once. "That was a supernatural ending to your party," my friend told me.

I wish I had seen this brilliant flame turn to steam in the driving rain. It made me think about the order of things, how there had been so many obstacles to pulling this party off, how we had somehow managed to schedule it for the weekend when we experienced two of the most intense storms of the summer. I was especially intrigued with the loss of electricity two days in a row, two very important days in the life of this house that Benjamin Mason built. We don't lose power very often in the summer. But as we lit the candles for our meal the night before, I was reminded that Benjamin Mason never had any power to lose.

In so many ways, we had summoned Ben Mason into our present, into our 21st century reality, maybe he was answering back, maybe throwing a lightning bolt down into the trees to give us the fireworks we lacked, maybe doing some handstands up in heaven.

It may have been the beauty of this land and its dramatic sky that brought me here but the house, its history, its voices, the thought of the many feet that have touched its floors, this is what is so meaningful to me now. I'm only here to make it better, to make it last.

APRIL 2013

About the Author

WRITER, editor, journalist, essayist, and lecturer, Edie Clark has written extensively about New England in award-winning feature stories for more than thirty years. She has been a Fellow at The MacDowell Colony, Hedgebrook Writer's Colony, and a Visiting Writer at Northern Michigan University. She teaches writing and journalism at the graduate and undergraduate level and is a frequent lecturer on many topics. She lives and works at her home in Harrisville, New Hampshire. For further information, go to www.edieclark.com